This is the first book to discuss in detail how rap music is put together musically and how it contributes to the formation of cultural identities for both artists and audiences. It also argues that current skeptical attitudes toward music analysis in popular music studies are misplaced and need to be reconsidered if cultural studies are to treat seriously the social force of rap music, popular musics, and music in general. Drawing extensively on recent scholarship in popular music studies, cultural theory, communications, critical theory, and musicology, Krims redefines "music theory" as meaning simply "theory about music," in which musical poetics (the study of how musical sound is deployed) may play a crucial role when its claims are contextualized and demystified. Theorizing local and global geographies of rap, Krims discusses at length the music of Ice Cube, the Goodie MoB, KRS-One, Dutch group the Spookrijders, and Canadian Cree rapper Bannock.

**New perspectives in music history
and criticism**

Rap Music and the Poetics of Identity

New perspectives in music history and criticism

GENERAL EDITORS
JEFFREY KALLBERG, ANTHONY NEWCOMB, AND
RUTH SOLIE

This series explores the conceptual frameworks that shape or have shaped the ways in which we understand music and its history, and seeks to elaborate structures of explanation, interpretation, commentary, and criticism which make music intelligible and which provide a basis for argument about judgments of value. The intellectual scope of the series will be broad. Some investigations will treat, for example, historiographical topics – ideas of music history, the nature of historical change, or problems of periodization. Others will apply cross-disciplinary methods to the criticism of music, such as those involving literature, history, anthropology, linguistics, philosophy, psychoanalysis, or gender studies. There will also be studies which consider music in its relation to society, culture, and politics. Overall, the series hopes to create a greater presence of music in the ongoing discourse among the human sciences.

ALREADY PUBLISHED
Leslie C. Dunn and Nancy A. Jones (eds.), *Embodied Voices: Representing Female Vocality in Western Culture* 0 521 58583 X
Downing A. Thomas, *Music and the Origins of Language: Theories from the French Enlightenment* 0 521 47307 1
Thomas S. Grey, *Wagner's Musical Prose: Texts and Contexts* 0 521 41738 4
Daniel Chua, *Absolute Music and the Construction of Meaning* 0 521 63181 5

Rap Music and the Poetics of Identity

ADAM KRIMS

PUBLISHED BY THE PRESS SYNDICATE OF THE UNIVERSITY OF CAMBRIDGE
The Pitt Building, Trumpington Street, Cambridge, United Kingdom

CAMBRIDGE UNIVERSITY PRESS
The Edinburgh Building, Cambridge CB2 2RU, UK   http://www.cup.cam.ac.uk
40 West 20th Street, New York, NY 10011–4211, USA   http://www.cup.org
10 Stamford Road, Oakleigh, Melbourne 3166, Australia

First published 2000

Printed in the United Kingdom at the University Press, Cambridge

Typeset in Palatino 10/12pt [CE]

A catalogue record for this book is available from the British Library

Library of Congress cataloguing in publication data

Krims, Adam
Rap music and the poetics of identity/Adam Krims.
    p.   cm. – (New perspectives in music history and criticism)
Includes bibliographical references, discography, and index.
ISBN 0 521 63268 4 (hardback)   ISBN 0 521 63447 4 (paperback)
1. Rap (Music) – History and criticism.   I. Title.   II. Series.
ML3531.K75 2000
782.421649–dc21   99-36013 CIP

ISBN 0 521 63268 4 hardback
ISBN 0 521 63447 4 paperback

for Natalie and Stéphane

Contents

Acknowledgments

This book could never have come into existence without the help and support of a great number of people, to whom thanks are simply not sufficient; their traces are everywhere in the book, and it is only fitting to acknowledge them here. Much gratitude is owed to Jeffrey Kallberg, whose advice in the face of my blunders was patient, wise, and kind. Likewise, Ruth Solie's and Anthony Newcomb's suggestions and helpful critiques have made this a much better book than it would otherwise have been. A special thanks also to Penny Souster of Cambridge University Press, whose patience through a number of my missteps and laggings was remarkable. Thanks are also due to Darren Tootoosis, who opened up a world previously unknown to me and treated the project of this book at least as lovingly as I have. Natalie Chute deserves real gratitude for the patience and humor with which she endured the maddening process of negotiation with record companies and publishers. Important aspects of this book would also not have been possible without an H-FAR grant from the University of Alberta, which permitted crucial research. Similarly, I am indebted to a number of people in Holland, whose generosity always astounded me: Helen Westerik of the Nationaal Popmuziek Institut (NPI) laid out foundations for me and saved my research, at one point, from sheer collapse; and both Gert Verbeek and Jaap van Beusekoom of the NPI have likewise provided invaluable assistance for me. In the NPI, the Netherlands has an institution in which it should have great pride, with a wonderful staff and facilities. Mir Wermuth's generosity with her time and materials made an otherwise daunting project possible and infinitely richer. Saskia Slegers's time, and her material and logistical support were all much needed and much appreciated; the Spookrijders are also to be thanked for their assistance and encouragement. Great thanks go to Laurens van der Heijden for his years of friendship, and for allowing me a unique glimpse of the Dutch music business; Nana Jongerden also merits warm thanks for her help, friendship, and hospitality during my research in Holland.

Very special thanks go out to those who have responded helpfully to sections of the book: David Cohen, Robert Kelly, Robert Kendrick, Henry Klumpenhouwer, and David Lewin. Likewise, the members of the Institute for Popular Music at the University of Alberta have provided both a base of professional support and constant intellectual stimulation; thanks to them all, and especially Henry Klumpenhouwer for holding me to the highest intellectual standards. Thanks are also due to Warner Chappell, Jive Records, Zomba Music Publishing, and Windswept Pacific Entertainment for their permission to reprint lyrics and details of songs.

Special mention must go to my late mother Edna Krims, for nurturing my early interest in music, and to my father Marvin Krims, an inspiration academically and personally and someone whose unflagging championing of education I hope to pass on to my own family. Jonathan Bernard, Robert Morgan, and David Lewin deserve thanks for early support and encouragement. The most profound gratitude of all must be extended to my wife Natalie Boisvert, who had to live with me while I became "Book-Writing Boy," and who tolerated me with humor and supported me with love; and to my son Stéphane Krims, whose gentleness and undying love were always my greatest source of joy when I felt unable to write another word. It is to Natalie and Stéphane that this book is gratefully and lovingly dedicated.

Introduction: music theory, musical poetics, rap music

This book is about commercial recorded rap music. It is thus not a book principally about hip-hop culture, about underground, more "authentic" or "resistant" scenes, or about Afrodiasporic music or culture – although it must be understood that all of the above (and a good deal more) are crucial to an understanding of commercial rap music and will often form crucial points of reference. Instead of projecting rap music as resistance, I emphasize the cultural and, for that matter, economic dominance of the rap music *industry* worldwide and its multiple cultural and political effects. Such is the form in which a great many people know it and make it part of their lives: as recorded (and only occasionally live), mass produced and distributed popular culture.[1] Such an approach is not necessarily amenable to those uses of popular music that validate the latter as an upsetter of consensus and challenge to oppressive (usually discursive) hierarchies. But it is less a purpose of this book to paint rap music as cultural resistance than to outline the poetics of its functioning in the formation of ethnic and geographic identities. Whether those identities should be labeled "resistant" or not is most certainly a crucial question, but one whose consideration is worth, at a minimum, a separate monograph. I will, at this point, only remark that I think a healthy skepticism is in order regarding what one might deem the "cultural resistance industry." A careful reading of the rap industry might suggest the pliability of capital and the extent to which a politically engaged culture such as hip-hop can most easily be put to the service of dominant ideologies. In the meantime, whatever even symbolic challenges rap music might hold for capital do not seem to be perceived by the broader culture as seriously threatening, unless one counts the moral panics about so-called "gangsta rap" and related cynical efforts by political figures such as C. Dolores Tucker and William Bennett. Whether, on the other hand, rap music might sometimes be "resistant" in the sense of carving out spaces of freedom and

---

[1] My discussion also does not focus on hip-hop DJing culture, a fascinating topic (and fascinating music) deserving much more academic discussion.

1

pleasure is another matter. Such a notion could be true while none-theless consistent with the workings of capital.[2] But the question of "resistance," and the related workings of aesthetic/political valida-tion, as widely and legitimately discussed as they are, will take a back seat to the principal argument to be made here. Instead, I will advance an argument that the sonic organization of rap music – both the rapping itself and the musical tracks that accompany it – is directly and profoundly implicated in rap's cultural workings (resistant or otherwise), especially in the formation of identities.

This book differs from, and may supplement from a different perspective, examinations of hip-hop culture that theorize its embeddedness or expressive value within African-American traditions. A full-length study of that topic would be eminently worth while, a needed addition to the literature on hip-hop culture and rap music.[3] Similarly, ethnographic studies of the ways in which different audiences redeploy rap music in their social interactions – differentiated by age, race, gender, class, and other significant categories – should illuminate dimensions of its effects that can only be seen by detailed involvement in the music's localized contexts. Significantly, none of the fine book-length published ethnographic studies I have encountered of popular music's social workings – such as Cohen (1991) and Finnegan (1989), though the latter's generic scope is wider than what is normally called "popular music" – deal at length with rap music.

This book does not attempt to fill that gap. Instead, it deals with rap music as it has been transformed, commodified, and globalized by the music industry; in other words, it addresses rap music as media content. The "rap music" projected in that context is, of course, a profoundly impure product, one that has by no means lost its origins as an African-American vernacular practice, but in which, nevertheless, that origin survives in transformed resonances, gestures, and counter-gestures, and in newly re-localized cultural inflections. Nevertheless, the intention here is not to validate rap as a hybrid or syncretic form, an assertion that is perfectly true but risks losing the concrete social contexts in which it becomes imaginatively revalidated as something "real," something which, to adopt the intransitive usage endemic to hip-hop culture, "represents."

---

[2] This second sense of resistance is more consistent with Lawrence Grossberg's (1992) idea of the role that rock music has played in everyday lives.

[3] Keyes (1996) provides a glimpse of how such a study might proceed and Rose (1994) indicates the embeddedness of rap music in African-American traditions. But a more consistently ethnographic study is, in my view, much needed, as well as one that extends the topic into earlier African-American expressive culture (examining at length, for example, toasts, oral musical traditions, and so on).

I focus on what seems to me a relatively neglected but crucial aspect of rap music's cultural force: namely, the particularity of its sounds. The central thesis offered in this book – that what I call the "musical poetics" of rap music must be taken seriously, because they are taken seriously by many people in the course of its production and consumption – is meant partially as a corrective to the vast majority of rap and hip-hop scholarship which takes the music seriously but gives little, if any, attention to its musical organization. Such approaches, I will argue, miss some of its cultural workings. That so many studies of rap music should do this is certainly understandable, given the rather mixed reputation that so-called "musicological" approaches have gained in the world of popular music scholarship. Indeed, as Chapter 1 will make clear, I agree with many of the reasons that scholars tend to avoid detailed musical analysis of popular musics and tend even to regard such approaches with a measure of suspicion. However, I want to argue, among other things, that both the production and the consumption of rap music implicate inextricably how the music sounds, and that furthermore, the cultural engagement of both producers and consumers of rap music is partially contingent on their understanding of rap's musical organization. Hence, the title of this book is meant to indicate that identity in rap music indeed has its poetics, and that the poetics is partially – and crucially – a poetics of musical organization. Whether such a claim could then be extended to all music is both an engaging possibility and perhaps an oversimplified question. My personal belief, for which I could only provide anecdotal evidence, is that rap music culture, as a fan culture at any rate, may embed its identity formation more deeply in the sound of the music than do many other rock-related fan cultures. The degree to which a rap (or more generally: hip-hop) fan will defend the authenticity, originality, and sophistication of her/his favorite rap style/genre/ artist/album/song is virtually unparalleled in my experience (perhaps almost matched by some jazz fan cultures). On the other hand, quite a few musical fan cultures focus quite intently on artists' musical styles and even particular songs and albums (for which see, for example, responses to Tori Amos's 1998 album *From the Choirgirl Hotel*). It may well be that the degree to which consumers, at least, and perhaps even producers as well, engage musical poetics in forming their identities depends very much on the genre involved, or perhaps even individual artists (not to mention individual consumers and/or subcultural groups). What follows focuses on the very particular world of rap music; if I can make the case there for considering musical poetics as a subset of cultural theory, then this book will have achieved its principal goal. In the meantime, Chapter 1 will make a more generalized plea for the relevance of musical poetics for cultural studies.

The book delineates several trajectories at once, trajectories for which I will try to indicate some kind of interweaving, if not quite a unity. It is intended both to be a work of "music theory" and to help broaden the scope of that phrase. It is intended also to be a work of "musicology" and to reinforce the already-present tendency to broaden the scope of that term, as well.[4] At the same time, this study is meant to subsume both music theory and musicology under the rubric of cultural studies, and to argue that the first two need to be conceived merely as specialized fields of the latter. But if the concerns just described seem remarkably oriented toward the defining of disciplines, then at the same time it is crucial to keep in mind that the more "concrete" topics of the book – rap music, musical poetics, and the formation of cultural identities – are the material and unique social practices that invite such disciplinary shifts. Another way of saying this is to assert that the advent of hip-hop culture (including rap music) and the disciplinary crises of musical academia are not unrelated, but rather may be responses, in very different registers, to surprisingly similar social situations (which, nevertheless, are far from affecting all those involved to equal extents).

So an investigation into rap music and cultural identity, from the standpoint of a music scholar oriented toward cultural studies, is, so to speak, a different face of an investigation of musical disciplines and, inevitably, of cultural studies as well. To recognize that the organization of middle-class scholars' activities and the trajectory of a music readily identified with the United States' underclass might somehow crystallize around the same issues is not necessarily to efface the gap between bourgeois and proletariat, or between dominant and dominated. Rather, it is to recognize the extension of the mechanisms of capital, and also of ideologies, into far-flung domains that may sometimes converge in surprising ways. But which social groups find themselves somehow intertwined in academic studies of rap music? Certainly not just middle-class academics (of whatever ethnicity or "race") and an African-American working class, for quite a few reasons. For one thing, the single largest purchasing group of rap music may well be middle-class, white teenagers;[5] The

[4] The work of such figures as Susan McClary, Lawrence Kramer, Gary Tomlinson, Jeffrey Kallberg, Suzanne Cusick, Robert Fink, Mitchell Morris, Philip Brett, and quite a few other musicologists, all shows that musicology has, over the past decade or more, been engaging cultural studies in a more thoroughgoing way than had often previously been the case. It is hoped that this book can both partake of that trend and advance it in some new directions.
[5] Rose (1994) correctly points out that no official statistics seem to prove this widespread contention. However, a survey has shown that 74 percent of rap recordings sold in the first six months of 1992 were purchased by whites (cited in Lusane 1993). Still, such figures never tell the whole story, and that is especially true in the case of rap, where,

RIAA announcement that in 1998, for the first time, rap was the best-selling musical genre in the United States certainly suggests a broad base of consumption. Like rock 'n' roll before it, rap attained a high degree of commercial success only after gaining appreciation from the most powerful record-buying audiences. (Of course, in other respects, the trajectories of the two musics may differ greatly.) But not just North American middle-class teenagers are implicated: for rap music has become truly global. There is now scarcely a country in the world that does not feature some form or mutation of rap music, from the venerable and sophisticated hip-hop and rap scenes of France, to the "swa-rap" of Tanzania and Surinamese rap of Holland. And although it is safe to say that many principal trends and styles of global hip-hop culture still tend to emanate from the United States, rap music changes faces in different societies. At the same time, it always maintains links to global (or globalized American) developments. Thus, rap music outside the United States may always be said to respond to both local forces and global forces (especially, of course, those of the United States itself). One of the principal tasks of the latter part of this book will be to trace both the local and the global forces by which rap helps to form imagined identities in non American contexts. The effects of global rap music are by no means one-way from the United States outward; in addition to the well-known formative (and ever-renewing) role of Jamaican music in rap, hip-hop culture and rap music continue to respond to forces outside the United States, as one might witness in the relatively recent revival of popular interest in DJing, spurred in part by forces in Japanese and European hip-hop culture.[6] Still, scholarship on rap music tends to focus, with very few exceptions, on the United States.[7] While this is

to a greater extent than most other musics in North America, a great amount of material is circulated in the form of bootlegs, local (i.e., non-commercial-label affiliated) cassettes, homemade mixtapes, and other formats not necessarily represented in surveys and statistics. And, of course, the unofficial formats are more likely to be consumed by less affluent audiences, so that published sales figures almost certainly exaggerate the predominance of moneyed listeners.

[6] The special 100th issue (January 1998) of *The Source*, the most widely circulated hip-hop magazine, contained small features on hip-hop scenes in London, Jamaica, Vancouver, Paris, Senegal, Italy, Japan, Holland, Spain, and Hawaii. (The mix of geographic scales in the list itself conveys, one could speculate, some information about the American popular imagination.) Figures such as DJ Honda of Japan, not to mention descendants of immigrants to the United States, such as the Filipino-American members of the Invizible Skratch Picklez, have greatly contributed to the revival of hip-hop DJing's popularity. It is also instructive to note how countries other than the United States sometimes police "true" hip-hop culture and history more self-consciously than many in the United States itself. This point will recur in Chapter 5.

[7] Rose (1994), for example, in her fine study, says very little about rap music outside the United States.

understandable, given the predominance of the United States (culturally, and still, to some extent commercially) in rap music, it also slights the vast majority of the world, in which locally inflected hip-hop scenes and rap music have sometimes been in place for well over a decade and continue to develop. This book cannot by itself rectify the relative slighting of non-United States rap music and hip-hop culture, but it can at least suggest one possible approach to the topic, informed, of course, by the broader concerns of the book.[8]

The foci on both recorded rap music and non-United States rap music might seem jointly to raise the spectre of what to some would be a politically frightening prospect, namely the erasure of the specifically African-American (or more broadly, as Gilroy 1993 argues, black Atlantic) origins and cultural embeddedness of rap. It may be true, to a certain extent, that widening out from rap music's specifically African-American context risks repeating the history of appropriation, and subsequent historical repression, that is so familiar in receptions of African-American culture, especially music. And indeed, discussions of African-American culture cannot be separated from any examination of rap music, as they are not here. What must be attempted, then, is the simultaneous retention of rap music as embedded culture and as mobile culture (which, then, re-embeds in new locations). Or, alternately, one might try to retain a picture of a vernacular culture and a mass culture. Such a thing is simultaneously impossible and necessary; impossible, because at any given moment any representation will emphasize one aspect over another, but necessary, because both are indispensable truths. This study, if it falls overly much into the mass culture part of that equation, should not be taken as negating the vernacular aspects of rap music (aspects better explored in Rose 1994, Potter 1995, and Keyes 1996). Being a white, middle-class academic exacerbates the tangle of objective situational impossibility. Examining vernacular culture, I risk appropriation of a culture that is in no way "mine," and many of whose participants pay a price I have never paid for partaking in that culture. Examining a mass culture derived from the commodification of that vernacular culture, I risk another form of appropriation, namely validating the increasing distancing of commodified forms from the underprivileged creators of those forms, and the continued profit of more privileged classes and ethnicities. In opting for the latter risk – a risk that seems greatly more desirable than declaring discussion of this important music out of bounds or greatly restricted – I can only encourage

---

[8] It is my understanding that there is a forthcoming volume, to be edited by Tony Mitchell, on global hip-hop. This is very much a welcome development. Here it should be noted that Jamaica is often considered by American hip-hop scholars as a factor – albeit formative rather than continuing – in the music's history.

readers to refuse, at least temporarily, moralizing discourses about that choice (which s/he can always restore). Instead, I would want to direct a focus to situations – global capital, racialized oppression, and the inevitable complicity of culture in both of them – that render either choice fraught with dangers and eminently unsatisfactory.

Any claim I could make to hip-hop authenticity would be preposterous. So I do not make it. My connection to rap music and hip-hop culture is that of an ardent fan, someone whose musical life has been saturated by rap music since (roughly) 1990, who is at times a rap performer (as instrumentalist and producer), who is both a producer and a consumer, but who is by no means close either to hip-hop's original cultural existence or to rap's current source of authenticity. To say that is not to dismiss people who demand authenticity, only to say that this book assumes some function for cultural studies, which is mainly practiced by middle-class academics. If my presence in the rest of the book can be charted, then I am assuming (indeed, not-so-secretly hoping) that it may be charted in the way that Žižek describes Lacan's view of the Subject – that the Subject is signaled by that which "perturbs the smooth engine of symbolization and throws it off balance ... an anamorphic entity that gains its consistency only in retrospect, viewed from within the symbolic horizon" (Žižek 1994, p. 31). My presence as a Subject, in other words, might be constructed in the places (or better: *as* the places) where my own attempts at smooth symbolic articulation break down, and where my own (contradictory) social situation can be posited, retrospectively, as a cause.

I do, however, wish to claim some proximity to rap *fan* culture, and indeed, much of the argument of this book (more explicitly laid out in Chapter 1) is that the ways in which consumers behave seem to be determined, in part, by the aspects of rap music I will discuss. Although at certain points, the ways in which I discuss rap music would be foreign to most of its audience (and such is often, of course, the situation of the cultural studies academic), I take extreme care to integrate to my account the reception of rap music by a broader audience. And I hope that the results of both my experience of hip-hop communities and any information about audiences that I have been able to integrate here will broaden a perspective that nevertheless will remain, of course, very much reflective of my own social situation.

Rap as postmodern, rap as aspect of identity

It has been well demonstrated to what extent rap music may model processes much sought after in postmodern social theory. Russell

Potter (1995), for example, argues persuasively for its status as a model resistance by the standards of (among other things) Bakhtin's dialogics and de Certeau's heterologies, arguing that African-American vernacular cultures have long been, and continue to be, sites of discursive challenge to dominant forces. From a different (but overlapping) perspective, Shusterman (1992) advances rap music as quintessential pragmatism, the latter term being defined (as it so often is in philosophy, for instance, by Richard Rorty) as a more philosophically elaborated (and more American) reworking of much postmodern theory. And Rose (1994) balances the widespread decrying of rap's gender politics (to which she is largely sympathetic) with a focus on women's discursive interventions. Indeed, all of these scholars make compelling cases for rap as postmodern practice (and in Rose's case, that would include rap-as-music-of-postmodernity, particularly the post-industrial city), or at least as a particularly appropriate object for theoretical description. It seems, at times, that rap music would have to have been invented by postmodern theory, had it not been there, poised to exact its tribute. Lest such a remark appear unseemingly cynical, let it be added immediately that there can be little doubt that rap is extremely appropriate music for modeling what it is that cultural theorists like about "resistant" culture. Were it not for the moral panics which have congregated around it since the early 1990s, one could well expect rap to have become one of the more canonical objects for discussions of postmodern culture.[9] But the discussions in this book – principally involving rap's musical organization and its involvement in various cultural processes in various places – while they do look toward identity formation, do not necessarily take the further step of locating social resistance in those identities. Instead, what Jody Berland (1998, p. 138) calls "the populist optimism of cultural studies" is withheld here, in favor of the more modest proposal that rap music participates in identity formation, whatever the role or effectiveness of the latter in challenging domination. Certainly, a strong case could be made that the history of hip-hop culture demonstrates precisely how marginalized cultural practices can be deployed to reinforce, at least as much as to challenge, dominant discourses (so-called "gangsta rap" being only the most famous example). Such an observation can be taken less as a restatement of mass culture theory than as a barometer of globalized capital and race relations.

---

[9] This is not to say that moral panics are the only obstacles to scholarly interest. Rose (1994) and Keyes (1996), for instance, both argue convincingly that scholarly judgments about music tend to miss or denigrate that which makes rap both comprehensible and African-American.

The focus on rap as a source of identity among its artists and audiences is not discontinuous with recent concerns in popular music studies.[10] And neither popular music studies nor partially-overlapping disciplines such as ethnomusicology have lost sight of music as a process of collective self-definition.[11] Indeed, the association of rap music with marginalized and aggrieved groups virtually guarantees that the carving out of discursive presence will take center stage in serious discussions. In addition, it is arguable that hip-hop culture, with its focus on "realness" and claims of cultural ownership, foregrounds identity with an explicitness well-nigh unprecedented even in the ethnically and gender-loaded world of popular musics. So, this book focuses to a great extent on rap music's role in forming cultural identity – among other things, in order to take seriously hip-hop culture's claims to popular cultural critique. While it might not automatically be assumed that rap's identities automatically challenge the most powerful forms of domination, it is most certainly assumed in this book that understanding how identities are formed – whatever they do to whomever – will remain a basic aspect of rap and hip-hop studies. What I hope will be at least one unique contribution of the book, the delineation of how rap's *sounds* figure in identities, may broaden notions of cultural formation to areas sometimes too broadly consigned to difficult (not to say unimportant) categories like pleasure or investment. In addition, some questions will be posed and explored here about the *geographies* of rap music and their relation, in turn, to sound and identity. In particular, I am interested in the music's particular playing-out of the dynamic, described in Lipsitz (1994), among others, in which culture is continually globalized and relocalized. While Gilroy (1993) describes a related process specific to the black Atlantic, and that process is of obvious significance to hip-hop culture, rap music has been globalized well beyond African communities and may, I think, be said to have passed into a number of both commercialized and hybrid social contexts. Or, at least, much of it has: there remain, to be sure, African-American communities (not to mention other Afrodiasporic, such as Jamaican, communities) in which rap and hip-hop culture survive as local traditions, more closely related to oral traditions and vernacular musico-linguistic practice. But the emergence of a whole problematic of music and place, represented by

---

[10] Lipsitz (1994) is a particularly good example. But the discussion and works cited in Chapter 4 of Negus (1996) suffice to show an intense focus on issues of identity in popular music studies, particularly among cultural-studies approaches.

[11] Stokes (1994) collects a number of essays that illustrate this concern in ethnomusicology. In popular music studies as a whole, identity is a central current issue (worked out in perhaps its most generalized fashion in Garofalo 1992).

collections such as Leyshon et al. (1998) and previous efforts by geographers, suggests that both concrete effects of global and local realities as well as poetic establishment of place and memory belong in the rap music equation to a much greater extent than current scholarship reflects. Three approaches to this very complex problematic appear in this book, one of them proceeding via media products exclusively, and the other two proceeding through a combination of media content and on-site study.

My uses of the terms "rap" and "hip-hop" need some explanation, since both terms (especially the latter) are the objects of some contestation, and fans of the music and the culture in question are often particularly fussy about their usage. One thing is certain: "rap" describes only a kind of music, whereas there is also hip-hop dancing (breakdancing), hip-hop visual art (graffiti), hip-hop clothing, and, depending on whom one asks, perhaps other hip-hop things as well (as when the magazine *The Source* refers to itself as "the magazine of hip-hop culture and politics"). But this is not the only possible distinction between the two terms. For one thing, there is music that is often labeled "hip-hop" that may not include rapping, such as some "trip-hop" (e.g., Tricky, Portishead, Goldie), and much "hip-hop" rhythm and blues and soul music (e.g., Mary J. Blige, Total, KC and Jo Jo). For another thing – and here things get both a little trickier and a little closer to the main themes of this book – there is some rap music that many consumers of the musics would deny the status of the term "hip-hop." When this is done, the distinction is usually intended to enforce a notion of authenticity, with "hip-hop" held out as a term of validation denied to more "commercial" products. One can see that dichotomy in operation when hip-hop artists or fans denigrate a certain performer or song as "rap" while holding out some contrasting music as true hip-hop. Puff Daddy, for example, might be said to be a commercial rapper, while the Beatnuts bring the *real* hip-hop. Sometimes the validatory status of the word "hip-hop" is elevated to something approaching reverence, as when KRS-One says that "rap is something you do, Hip-Hop is something you live."[12]

I may thus risk being misunderstood when I use the word "rap" in this book's title and frequently for music for which both I and many other die-hard hip-hop fans have the highest regard (e.g., the music of the Roots or the Goodie MoB). In doing so, I do not intend to invoke the dichotomy by which "true hip-hop" is often claimed by its own fans against an assumed background of more "commercial" music; and it will become clear in this book that my attitude toward "authenticity," and to the distinction often made between "true" art

[12] Quoted in Copeland (1995), p. 58.

10

and its degraded "commercial" double, is a critical one. Although it is most certainly a crucial distinction for understanding the cultural force of rap music, I maintain the more general tendency in popular music studies to regard it as a matter for discourse analysis. But that is not why I refer to most of the music discussed in this book as "rap." Rather, it is to narrow the focus of my study to that music in which rapping is a principal feature. In my view, studies of R&B hip-hop, hip-hop DJ art (or, to use the neologism, "turntablism"), and hip-hop culture overall are greatly needed (and ultimately, of course, form important contexts for rap music); but this book focuses more on rap music *per se*. Part of the reason for the narrowing of the focus is a major argument to be made in this book, namely that rap music has developed its own cultural and (inseparably) musico-poetic dynamics. Thus, widespread assertions about its inseparability from hip-hop culture may be true in some important respects, but it is also true that rap has developed its own relatively autonomous musical dynamics which merit examination.

The reader may assume for the purposes of this book that when I refer to music as "rap," rather than as "hip-hop," it is for that narrowing purpose, and not in order to withhold the validation that I believe the majority of the music I discuss may well deserve. If it seems that I fuss too much over this terminological binary, then I hope that an anecdote will show that even in academia, the binary holds some considerable force. Recently I attended a convention largely composed of popular music scholars. I had been invited to chair the session on African-American musics, arriving, in fact, to find that it was the *only* session on African-American musics. I was therefore relieved and delighted when a friend of mine introduced me to a colleague of hers who, my friend told me, also researched hip-hop. The colleague and I instantly paired off and began talking excitedly about our work. She told me of some courses she had given and a paper she had just written, which she was hoping to submit for publication. We talked about journals that might be interested, and I made some suggestions. She then asked me what work I had recently done, and I mentioned two papers I had then just finished. As soon as I named the artists concerned – Nas and the Wu-Tang Clan – her expression changed markedly, and she declared, not bothering to hide her disgust, "That's not hip-hop – that's rap!" The palpable offense that she took at my conferring the title "hip-hop" on what she clearly considered to be degraded music reminded me that the shifting, often mystified and emotionally charged meanings of "hip-hop" are fraught with dangers when one is simply discussing rap music. I do use the term "hip-hop" in most of my daily life, but for this book I have decided often to use the more restrictive term "rap," hoping that the reader will realize that I personally consider rap to be a form of hip-hop music. At the same time, in contexts where I do not believe confusion is likely, I sometimes use the phrase "hip-hop music"; when I do so, unless I specify otherwise, the reader may assume that the phrase leaves open a wider possible field than the phrase "rap music," and that I often say "hip-hop music" for the sake of indicating an opening up of rap music into the broader world of hip-hop culture.

Analyzing rap: an outline

By its social situation, rap music invites perspectives from Afro-American studies, communications, cultural studies, and media studies, to name just a few – in other words, the collage of back-grounds and approaches we may call "popular music studies." Part of the reason for its inherent interdisciplinarity is the situation of popular music in general, scattered among the above-mentioned fields and quite a few others, including, more recently, musicology and music theory. The scattered state of popular music studies may sometimes prove frustrating to parties who seem to be talking across vast divides; but at the same time, popular music's collage of disciplinary forces offers opportunities for new combinations and intersections. The project of this book is an attempt at just such a combination, stemming from some special issues in rap music.

The opportunity for the new combination to be attempted in the following pages stems from a traditional function of music analysis – aesthetic elaboration – and its odd points of contact with, and simultaneously suspect status in, popular music studies. It is both an oddity and an opportunity that in the academic world of popular music, the fact of examining a certain repertory often seems entwined with validating it. Although the coupling of examining and validating is not exclusive to popular music studies – it could be argued, for instance, that any time one analyzes something publicly, one implies its worthiness of study – scholars in the area do seem to assume something of a supplementary burden of proving their object's value. That extra burden may stem, in popular music studies, from the historically denigrated place of popular music in music studies overall and the particular tenacity of the high/low split in Western musical culture.

The precarious status of music analysis in popular music studies is thus (perhaps unfortunately) inseparable from the question of validation. One cannot avoid having one's discussion bound up with notions of aesthetic judgments and the political consequences both of such judgments and the music about which they are made. And, of

12

course, in the case of rap music, questions of aesthetic value and political benefits and dangers could not be more acute, or more publicly known. Rap finds itself, especially in the United States, in the midst of public political controversy perhaps unmatched since the advent of rock 'n' roll in the 1950s (and, I would argue with Houston Baker 1993, finds itself a nexus for a broader, racist moral panic about young black males in general). And in addition, rap (more under the term "hip-hop") finds itself the focus of a counterbalancing validation of African-American art and identity. Both Rose (1993) and Keyes (1996) are correct in pointing out that, among other things, public battles over rap music are to some extent driven by the cultural ignorance of those who villainize rap, particularly ignorance of African-American linguistic poetics and musical aesthetics. (There is, of course, much more involved as well, as both Rose and Keyes recognize.) Thus, the stakes of sorting out just how rap music works socially, what it is and what it does – the last two items being, of course, no more than two different ways of stating the same problematic – are unusually high for popular music studies. Such a project bears not only on the context of the United States, but more broadly, because of the ways in which racial dynamics are globalized, on varied contexts throughout the world.

In fact, even the somewhat narrower project of validating rap via expositions of some of its poetics, turns out to be a project of a surprisingly high percentage of scholarship, occurring far more frequently than in any other genre I know of. Perhaps symptomatically of rap's precarious cultural position, much of the scholarly work on the subject has been concerned to demonstrate that rap has its own logics that must be understood. Thus, studies such as Shusterman (1991), Brennan (1994), Dyson (1996), Potter (1995), Jacono (1994a) and (1998), Keyes (1996), some of the essays in Spencer (1991), many of the essays in Perkins (1996), and Rose (1994, Chapter 3), among others, concern themselves at points largely with validating rap music against the cultural biases which inform against it. And indeed, the project of explaining rap, against common misconceptions and racialised discourses, cannot be underestimated in its urgency. Rose, Potter, and Keyes, in particular, are eloquent about contextualizing the denigration of hip-hop culture and music in the history of Afrodiasporic musical aesthetics and their broader Western reception. And Jacono establishes the important point that the scope of such projects extends well beyond North American contexts. Further, such public expositions of rap's cultural value have facilitated the production of books such as this, by enabling me to assume the importance of the subject matter and continue from there.

The centrality of rap aesthetics raises further the question of music analysis. For the possibility, often suggested, that music analysis distances us from social reality, rather than illuminating it, would arguably be disastrous in the culturally powerful case of rap music. And, taken from another angle, if the validation of rap music depended on the music's being abstracted from its embeddedness in the world, then music analysis of rap could be pronounced something of a political and cultural dead end. So one of the major projects of this book is to argue that, taken a certain way, music analysis might be a way of thinking of rap's social embeddedness, not of producing (pseudo-) detached aesthetic enjoyment or a (pseudo-) neutral judgment of value or sophistication. Instead, and emphatically, the book is an attempt to understand rap music's cultural dynamics, at seeing how it works in the world and how its placement in societies is related to the design of the music. This last problematic – relating musical design to cultural workings in detail – is what may prove to separate this book from the other fine collections and monographs that already exist on the topic of rap music and/or hip-hop culture. Although in making that connection I knowingly risk charges of mystifying structure, abstracting from social reality, or aestheticizing real social phenomena, I also see the potential benefit as irresistible. For I aim here at nothing less than asserting that studying musical poetics can be a task of the greatest social relevance, even in some cases an indispensable (though never sufficient) part of the cultural study of music.

The book takes the form of five chapters which can be read more or less independently, but which are also designed to feed into each other. To begin with, any study that purports to combine music analysis with cultural theory must face directly a formidable obstacle: namely, that both the history of music theory (including music analysis) and some powerful critiques of it as a contemporary discipline force a serious examination of the motives and functions of discussing musical sound and organization. Chapter 1 presents a generalized discussion of the function of music analysis in any scholarship whose ultimate goal is to theorize more generally about culture. There, some of the basic critical objections to music analysis are discussed, and some recommendations are made, namely the redefinition of "music theory" to mean, simply, "theory about music," and the corollary specification of "musical poetics" as a subset of music theory, namely that which addresses the organization of sound as part of broader cultural processes. The chapter closes with an explanation of why musical poetics is particularly crucial to a certain conceptualization of rap music, to specifying its role in forming cultural identities.

Chapter 2 then performs a preliminary mapping of rap's musical poetics, namely a specification of a rap genre system. There, it is proposed that various styles, and topics, form a relational system, in which musical tracks, the MC's rhythmic delivery (or "flow"), rhyming style, texture, timbre, and semantic topics all contribute to a generic profile. That generic identity then in turn inscribes history, geography, ideology, and discursive regimes directly in sound. Chapter 2's genre system then forms a background for many of the discussions that follow it.

Chapter 3 focuses on a single song, Ice Cube's classic "The Nigga Ya Love to Hate," examining how identity can be formed on the level of the song. The focus there remains principally on texture and rhythm, by which the argument is advanced that Ice Cube establishes himself in the song as a particular kind of revolutionary African-American male subject. A detailed picture emerges there in which the musical organization of the song, particularly the musical tracks, outlines processes inseparable from the semantic reference of the lyrics. In other words, the sonic organization outlines complex processes of signification which nevertheless not only are graspable to a listener versed in rap style, but also are inseparable from a certain historical conception of a "hardcore" sound. This last notion, in turn, proves inseparable from the formation of a black revolutionary subject through rap sonic design and semantic reference.

Chapter 4 continues the proposition of Chapter 3 that musical poetics forms a crucial aspect of musical cultural formation and continues the focus on the level of the song. But the problematics of location and place are more central there, as an Atlanta group, the Goodie MoB, forms a specific geographic location via processes of word, sound, and image. There, a geographic formation particular to hip-hop's history and imprinted on rap music's present allows the group to foreground certain representations of geographic location, communal activity, and food consumption. That foregrounding is partially enabled by the construction of the musical tracks and other formal aspects of the song.

Chapter 5 shifts the focus outside the United States, illustrating how rap musical poetics may change according to local requirements, albeit always with reference to rap's African-American origins. In the case of Holland, where hip-hop culture has enjoyed a formidable presence since the early 1980s, rap music has developed in unique ways with respect to race, language, musical style, and institutional formations. At the same time, the inevitable presence of the international (principally American) music industry mediates the "locality" of Dutch rap music. One particular group, the Spookrijders, becomes the nexus of representations of "Dutchness," of Amsterdam life, and of a particular local genre called "Nederhop" ("Dutch-hop")

– this last genre being differentiated not only by language, but also by musical poetics. The other rap locality is Edmonton, Alberta, a site for, among other things, rap music of the region's native Cree population. One artist in particular, Bannock, articulates his own location and identity through his own ideas of musical poetics. The ways that he negotiates those poetics in his music intertwines ideas of cultural location with aspects of his personal history. Overall, Chapter 5 projects ways in which both the global and the local intersect in the sounds of rap music in vastly separated parts of the globe. What emerges is a picture of the ways in which locality intersects with history in the musical poetics of rap.

The trajectory from more mainstream and widely circulated rap music to what, to most readers, would be more far-flung and localized forms is not by any means meant as a validation of the latter at the expense of the former. On the contrary, one of the premises of the genre system elaborated in Chapter 2 is that apparently distantly related genres may, in fact, be intimately related. A corollary of such a notion is that the most localized forms of rap music are structurally dependent on a world (music) system whose most central and commercialized forms penetrate even apparently unrelated generic developments. The book's journey from center (the United States) to periphery is meant to be taken metonymically, to indicate only vaguely and elliptically a far more immense and complex system of dominant musical utterances and more contingent musical responses. The ways in which those utterances and counter-utterances are involved in forming cultural identities, and the role of sound in those processes, may then suggest other, more distant social processes not explicitly musical at all. In other words, the studies of this book are meant to connect music theory to the study of cultures.

Discussions in some parts of the book refer extensively to rap recordings. Since neither transcriptions of large numbers of songs nor an accompanying CD is a practical possibility, those not familiar with recent rap music may wish to insure the availability of as many of the recordings listed in the discography as is practically possible.

1

Music analysis and rap music

I am proposing here a poetics of music, addressing an intended audience of scholars of popular music and cultural studies, and music scholars generally, including those engaged with progressive musicology. In doing so, I confront a considerable historical burden and some formidable disciplinary obstacles. "Close reading" of music, here, means interpretation based on some conception of the musical piece as an object; and such a practice has become somewhat suspect in both musicology and popular music studies, although in the case of the former its problematic status is less entrenched. The field of popular music scholarship presents a more formidable challenge; those affiliated with fields such as communications, cultural studies, anthropology, and sociology, to name just a few, often voice suspicion about close reading of music under the rubric of the term "musicological."[1] Musicologists, on the other hand, often identify analysis with the rival discipline of music theory and have voiced some salient critiques over the past few years (countered by some, frankly, poorly informed conservative responses from music theorists).[2]

Musicological critiques of music theory and analysis have been launched by, among others and from quite different perspectives, Tomlinson (1993a), McClary (1985), Cusick (1994), and Kingsbury (1991).[3] In the case of popular music, music analysis is particularly suspect not only for eliding institutional facts and often avoiding questions of social relevance, but also for sidestepping the possibility that audiences might shape their own responses to music, challenging and reinscribing its cultural force and significance.[4] To such championing of audience activity – understandable, in the still powerful wake of Adorno – one could, of course, counterpose David

---

[1] Some of the limits to music analysis from the standpoint of communications theory are summarized in Manuel (1993), pp. 15–17.

[2] I discuss some of those responses in Krims (1998b).

[3] Reciprocated suspicion from, if not officially a music theorist, then certainly a scholar strongly upholding the standards of technical analysis can be seen in Agawu (1993).

[4] Chambers (1994) makes this point with particular force, arguing that audiences may inflect and revise meanings of musical (among other) texts.

Morley's (1993) important distinction in scale between audiences' abilities to inflect texts, on the one hand, and the culture industries' ability to encode texts, on the other. Whatever one thinks of the power of audiences to inflect music, the doubts "in the air" concerning music analysis are powerful and inevitable.

Some of the assertions about contemporary music theory coming from musicology may seem dismissive and do at times caricature music analysis, especially when the latter has been beginning to recognize some of its former blindnesses and take steps, however halting and clumsy, toward addressing them. Nevertheless, suspicions of close reading are a disciplinary fact that must be faced, and they form a considerable historical burden to those who venture to propose a musical poetics. Furthermore, many of the critiques must be accepted as perfectly valid and met seriously with something other than dismissal, angry denial, or silence.

My basic argument here is that cultural studies (and cultural-studies-influenced work in communications, media studies, and other fields) needs to reexamine its very understandable suspicion of close reading of music. Furthermore, I will analogously claim that the suspicion of music theory in some recent musicology, although well placed in view of the history of the former discipline, does not diminish the need to come to terms with music analysis and what will be called here "musical poetics."

Popular music studies against analysis

Popular music studies does not have a disciplinary center – e.g., widespread departments of popular music studies – and thus, it is always dangerous to speak of central disciplinary contentions in the field. Rather, the mix of scholars from communications, comparative literature, musicology (and music theory), Afro-American studies, area studies, English, sociology, and so many other established (or quasi-established) disciplines combines to make popular music studies an ever-shifting, irreducibly diverse ensemble of viewpoints and practices. It is difficult not to savor this environment, in which one may open a journal or book, or attend a conference, with a high degree of confidence that one is about to witness an interdisciplinary discussion, a set of multiple approaches, models, and constructions of the object. The flipside, of course, is that one always risks over-generalization when summarizing the objections to close reading. Nevertheless, there are some pronounced enough tendencies to venture a few words.

The notion is widespread in popular music studies that analyzing popular music in the "musicological" sense distances one from the

18

real engagements of both artists and audiences, both of whom presumably do not relate to any significant extent to the music as modeled (e.g., McClary and Walser 1990 – voiced by two musicologists, and thus perhaps implying a certain unfairness in the negative weight to the word "musicological"). A fairly narrow (though important) set of objections to technical analysis of popular music has to do with the inappropriate predominance of pitched parameters (especially harmony and melody), a predominance held over from the analysis of classical music (e.g., McClary and Walser 1990). Such criticisms are salient, especially given the importance of timbre, gesture, rhythm, and texture, in many people's reception of various popular musics. On the other hand, such problems are not insurmountable, as, for instance, Robert Walser (1993 and 1995) has demonstrated. The lesson to be learned here is the importance of delineating carefully what one considers the parameters relevant for consideration – a decision that will often be highly context-specific by genre – and of specifying (and supporting with evidence from the relevant parties) the *culturally salient* reason for doing so.

But there are also more fundamental objections to music analysis in popular contexts. The field is often the province of ethnomusicologists, or even more often (in North America) pursued in departments of communications or cultural studies (among many other possibilities); and in those disciplinary contexts, "close reading" has not always enjoyed canonical status.[5] Peter Manuel's view may be taken as representative:

> An analysis of popular music which concentrates only on the phenomena of composition and studio performance thus runs the risk of distorting reality by means of a sentimental and nostalgic reification of creative processes which are of secondary importance in media production as a whole.
>
> (Manuel 1993, p. 16)

And such is the aesthetic orientation of mainstream music analysis in general (and in particular its self-relating, structuralist procedures) that even an analysis which does *not* focus "only on the phenomena of composition and studio performance" may also run into similar problems. Manuel's statement accurately poses a problem, and it does so without reproducing the more puzzling adjective "idealist," which is often predicated of music analysis without (as far as I know) any explication of its relation to the more properly philosophical term "idealism." Reification, then, may be taken as a serious challenge.

One basis for the challenge to popular musical close reading is the

---

[5] Exceptionally, Covach and Boone (1997) present essays mainly by music theorists on popular musics.

claim that musicological analyses tend not to leave room for audience inflection. The argument asserts that such analyses treat the music as if it were some self-existent object whose meaning and social function can be determined outside creative and diverse responses of communities, subcultures, and the like. Furthermore, they ignore that what we sometimes treat as static texts might in fact be sites of negotiation that bear multiple social inscriptions (e.g., Lipsitz 1994). This critique is particularly prominent in communication studies.

Such objections are, in fact, excellent arguments for audience studies, and it should be borne in mind that some of the contentions of this book should benefit greatly from thoroughgoing ethnographic studies of audiences and their own constructions of musical content.[6] In the meantime, discussions of genres and songs in this book indicate, at various points, places that audiences have interpreted the music, and ways in which audience investment has made its way into sound, word, and image. In addition, the discussions of genres and songs are already multiple inscriptions and always in historical and geographic motion: they result from the constant feedback loop which implicates the music industry and its clientele (both artists and purchasers) in constant negotiation and development.

Other critiques of close reading from popular music studies overlap significantly with those from musicology and therefore will be elaborated in the following section. At the same time, it would be an exaggeration to say that music analysis is fully disreputable in popular music studies. Moore (1993) makes a forceful argument for the importance of rock analysis, and although his argument is not in all quarters (and disciplines) accepted, it stands as signs that music analysis occupies some discursive space. John Shepherd (1991) maintains the usefulness of music analysis as one parameter of understanding how music works in culture. Richard Middleton (1990) allows for musical structure as one of many possible levels of musical signification. And although not engaging music analysis himself, Simon Frith does suggest that sociological studies of rock and pop tend to underestimate the importance of sound (e.g., Frith 1983, p. 13 – cited in Shuker 1998, p. 208). Such studies, though important, remain in the minority.

Musicology against analysis

In musicology, as in popular music studies, it would also be an exaggeration to claim that music analysis universally bears the brunt

---

[6] Keyes (1996) performs such an ethnography for several African-American communities, for example.

of heavy suspicion. Even in the so-called "New Musicology," there are examples of simultaneous engagements of both postmodern theory and music analysis; it is useful to recall, for example, that arguably the first major monograph of "New Musicology," Susan McClary's *Feminine Endings* (1991), is itself replete with arguments culled partially from music-analytical observations.[7]

Nonetheless, some serious critiques of music theory as a discipline and music analysis as a practice have appeared in musicological work in recent years, and they are very much worth considering. One may find music theory reproached as "essentializing" (Cusick 1991) and "pseudo-scientific" (McClary 1985), and one may also find close reading charged as "pull[ing] us back toward the aestheticism and transcendentalism of earlier ideologies" (Tomlinson 1993a). Indeed, it is difficult to peruse any mainstream music theory journal without getting the impression that, while overstated at times, such characterizations are often true.[8]

Critiques of close reading in musicology (i.e., in the context of "Western classical" music) are rather similar to those in popular music studies; but musicological critiques tend to focus more explicitly on the technical and scientifistic features of post-1950s music theory (as in the McClary 1985 essay just quoted). The difference in emphasis may well stem, in part, from the greater tendency in the discipline of music theory proper (which, let us recall, tends largely to confine itself to "Western classical" music[9]) to develop far more elaborately technical analyses (and theoretical systems) than those generally deemed "musicological" in popular music scholarship. Music theory looks different from there.

But equally relevant to the differently flavored critiques from within musicology of musical close reading is the relative novelty of requiring that classical music scholarship yield an ultimate social significance. That is to say, it is largely through the so-called "New Musicology" that the world of "the social" has entered the problematic in full force, enabling criteria of cultural and political relevance and function now to be applied (at least for certain

---

[7] In fact, a small tradition of feminist music-analytical work continues today, involving scholars such as Suzanne Cusick, Marianne Kielian-Gilbert, and Ellie Hisama, to name just a few.
[8] Tomlinson's wording about "earlier ideologies" foregrounds an unhelpful aspect of many discussions about music theory, namely the tendency in much postmodern theory to assume a position *beyond* a certain historical/ideological point, from which perspective the labeling of "earlier ideologies" then becomes virtually a *de facto* critique – a disturbingly ahistoricist perspective.
[9] Exceptions include Covach and Boone (1997), and the various publications of Walter Everett on the music of the Beatles.

audiences) to judgments of scholarship.[10] Thus, the benchmark of cultural salience is not by any means a habit in the minds of all musicologists (unless one refers to "culture" in the older sense of cultivating the spirit). Yet that benchmark has been in force, to some extent, in popular music scholarship almost from the beginning. Hence, critiques of close reading in the latter discipline tend to rely more heavily on cultural-theoretical arguments, while those from musicology only at times do so.[11] Furthermore (and I would say, revealingly), specifically literary forms of post-structuralist theory have been more influential in "New Musicology" than they have been in popular music studies (which is not to say that there has been no literary-theoretical influence in the latter).[12] Thus, issues like pleasure and sexuality, along with manners of speaking culled to a large extent from French traditions, predominate more in the scholarship of classical, than of popular, music. The constellation of literary approaches, in turn, may at times, particularly in the case of musicology, instill habits of internalist interpretation more amenable to music-theoretical close reading.

In any case, much "hardcore" music theory and analysis, with its heavy reliance on the salience of "purely" musical relationships and experiences, fares rather poorly by standards of cultural-theoretical understanding. And, as new and at times literary as postmodern theory may be in "New Musicology," it may be said that the critiques of music analysis in musicology and studies of popular music overlap to a very significant extent. What is at stake in both, from the perspective of the present discussion, is the purpose of musical poetics, and its relation to social structures and actions.

Musicological critiques of close reading usefully identify a lineage of such musical aesthetics (via such figures as Schopenhauer, Schiller, and Hanslick) which survives without proper names, and with terms like "structure" and "coherence" as the cornerstone of a history replete with the ideology of the artwork and aesthetic transcendence.[13] Such a lineage, inextricable from the intellectual foundations of musicology, buttresses, in the case of Anglo-American music theory, an elaborated discipline whose emulation of scientific

[10] Krims (1998a) explores, from another angle, the problem of "the social" in music scholarship.
[11] Even Gary Tomlinson (1993), one of the musicologists most explicitly influenced by Foucault and thus, one might assume, most likely to engage arguments about political consequences of "close reading," instead sticks fairly closely to a postmodern epistemological point about reinscription of the "artwork" assumption.
[12] In Krims (1998a), I discuss at greater length the delights and dangers of literary theory (especially deconstruction) in musicology and music theory.
[13] Lippman (1992) gives an overview of post-Kantian musical aesthetics; Norris (1988), pp. 28–31, summarizes some of the major relevant developments.

and mathematical models virtually invites the resistance of humanities academics. But dismissing music theory, like dismissing any discipline, is too simple and undialectical a gesture to be acceptable to those who take history, and its ideological twists and turns, seriously.

In particular, such a dismissal would seem to miss the dialectical moment in history represented in the disciplinary development of music theory; in the 1950s the discipline in the United States underwent a turn whose direction may partially determine the current status of close reading.[14] Specifically, the drive in the era of American universities toward the correlation of scientific knowledge and industrial "progress"; the concomitant model of science as a mode of validation for university disciplines; the elaboration of music analysis as the source of precision and controlled complexity in music studies – all of these developments render music theory, in its current mainstream incarnation, not an object of scorn, but rather a rich source of historical knowledge, a living specimen of an era widely believed to have disappeared in the postmodern age but nevertheless very much with us.

Current critiques of music theory would gain from historicizing the current climate, in which music theory sometimes feels so odd; and film studies (to which we will return at greater length later) may serve as a contrasting example of how a field's *reception* of close reading *may itself be historically conditioned*. That is to say, the question to be asked here of musical formalism is not how it is that we can get over or around it, but rather how it is that it has come to play the role that it has in musical discourse. And there, the divergent development of academic theory in music and film can be marshaled to make the point that close reading is neither intrinsically mystifying nor intrinsically demystifying. Instead, the particular development of close reading in a particular disciplinary climate may influence our own retrospective assessments of it.

Film studies serves as an excellent counterpoise to music scholarship *qua* cultural studies, since film theory has developed, since the 1960s, its own tradition of close reading.

But a signal motivation of film-studies poetics, especially since the advent of efforts such as Mulvey (1975), has been the location of ideology in the construction of film. In Mulvey's case, for example, the construction of the gaze is precisely an effect of how the film is assembled, so that explaining just *how* that gaze is produced will have the effect of ideological demystification. In comparison to film studies'

---

[14] McCreless (1997) gives a valuable summary of the development of music theory as a discipline in the United States, beginning in the 1950s.

close reading, earlier *auteur* theory, with its emphasis on personal style as the origin of aesthetic effects, takes on the appearance of sheer art appreciation, the very avoidance of social engagement. So the advent of a tradition of reading poetics in film scholarship repre-sented, among other things, a coming into focus of ideology within what had previously been constructed as an artwork.

Such could not be said of music theory and its traditions of close reading, in which demystification and the location of ideology are far from standard projects. On the contrary, as we have seen, close reading in music theory falls prey to the charge of aestheticizing music and closing off avenues of ideological investigation. So whereas the advent of contemporary film close reading is widely received as a demystifying development, close reading in music theory enjoys no such prestige. The contrast might raise the question: is the practice of close reading mystifying or is it demystifying? Is it conducive to ideological critique, or is it an obstacle? The questions are abstract and hollow, because they fail to take into account that the ideological function of each discipline's poetics are residues of their specific histories, and of the situations in which close reading found its disciplinary location.

Other, often related, contrasts between film studies and music studies can be cited in their histories. The former languished for a long time without academic recognition and, in addition, has always lent itself rather readily to theories of representation; while music, by contrast, has long enjoyed academic prestige as an established discipline designed precisely to *remove* it from the field of representation. The point of observing such contrasts is that the value of close reading cannot be discussed as anything other than a position concerning history itself, and that the mere engagement of a poetics is not *inherently* progressive or regressive, mystifying or demystifying. A judgment about music analysis is a judgment about the result of a particular and contingent set of circumstances and developments. And just as the aestheticizing and mystifying function of much Anglo-American music theory had a birth only possible at a certain unique point in time, so may it have a death at another unique point. Thus, whatever the accuracy of reproaches to music analysis, such reproaches do not by any means exclude the value of music analysis categorically. Later in this chapter, film theory will once again come into focus in a more extended way; for now, an underlining of the historical contingency to musical close reading's poor reputation in some quarters should be the first offshoot of the comparison. From the standpoint of late 1990s musical academia, we may appreciate how possibilities of social engagement were lost to the emulation of Cold War era intellectualism.

24

From music theory's past into its future

Once music theory's dysfunctions are conceived historically, the gap between music theory's current and stunningly elaborated forms, on the one hand, and the postmodern ethos predominant in "New Musicology," on the other, does not simply speak to music theory's need to "get with the times" and become postmodern. True, postmodern epistemological and metaphysical critiques would certainly be a useful addition to music theory.[15] But unless we have no interest in knowing histories, even histories we do not like or enjoy, it might be more productive to observe music theory than to condemn it, and even perhaps to relish the trace of Cold War science it presents to us in astonishingly pristine condition.

But conceiving the historical emergence of music theory as a discipline is only half the equation; the other half is to ask why the discipline, throughout the last few decades, has been so resistant to paradigm change. For whereas the sciences (after which music theory often patterns itself) have been able to retain their methodologies while remaining industrially productive, humanities disciplines such as English have diverged, developing theories more conducive to post-Fordist production and culture.[16] Meanwhile, music theory, perhaps because of the exclusivity of its music-educated clientele and perhaps because of its still tenacious links to composition, has remained in, and developed to a breathtaking level, the models of precision and controlled, confined elaboration that now retain little prestige in the humanities.[17] The historical lapse, then, between music theory and the humanities as the whole, rather than simply being portrayed in moralizing terms, could perhaps more valuably be seen as a living legacy of a social vision that now seems quaint (seen from the perspective of cultural theory). For those more sympathetic to music theory, its 1950s social vision (or blindness) may seem, on the

---

[15] In Krims (1998b), I elaborate how this might be possible.

[16] "Post-Fordist" refers to the kinds of commodity and service production that have prevailed in industrialized countries since the advent of technologies such as computerization, high-speed and versatile communications, and container shipping. Geographers such as Harvey (1989) have attributed to such technologies fundamental changes in commodity production, for example, the ability to produce on short order and to sophisticated design specification. Such methods of production are "post-Fordist" in the sense of succeeding the older assembly-line methods pioneered by Henry Ford. Furthermore, and more suggestively for the present context, Harvey refers many aspects of postmodern theory to the time/space compression and spatial world order created by post-Fordist production. A good overview of theories of post-Fordism can be found in Amin (1994).

[17] Music theory's role in providing vocational training to composers has undoubtedly affected its procedural development, as has its contribution to "musicianship."

contrary, an obvious advantage, seen from a more popularized perspective; from that perspective, capital's immense global expansion in the last two decades or so implies the never-ending progress of science and individual freedom and virtue. For such advocates, the left-leaning (albeit more reformist than revolutionary) critique pervasive in the humanities is a mere muffled voice in the worldwide triumph of capital.

The substantial (and growing) subfield of cognitive science in music theory, and the energetic application of mathematical models retain an unmistakable connection with Cold War conceptions of academic knowledge. On the other hand, a more humanistic face of music theory (represented by scholars such as Carl Schachter, Scott Burnham, and Daniel Harrison) serves as a reminder of the humanities in that era, the age when New Criticism promised a redemption of the spirit from the domination of a greatly expanding capitalist instrumentality. Music theory, in other words, perpetuates, in a way otherwise impossible to reproduce, a dialectic – namely, of instrumental reason and of its spiritualized refusal – whose untimeliness promises a rare glimpse of humanities from an earlier era relatively unchanged and intact. When one can grasp the opportunity to glimpse a disciplinary field from the time of New Criticism and to compare it with the greatly changed disciplines of the present, does that not render all the greater an error any attempt simply to dismiss it? From that perspective, music theory as a discipline offers a history lesson, not a proper object of scorn.

The conception of music theory suggested here is, in my view, a more productive angle on the more common New Musicological critiques of music theory, which, relying as they do on feminist or post-Foucauldian theory, emphasize music theory's failure to meet contemporary standards of social engagement. While music theory may for the most part be missing that boat, simply to conceive it that way forgoes the opportunity to see *both* music theory and musicology as imbricated together in a contemporary dynamic. For both disciplines can be seen as symptoms of the growing autonomy of both a postmodern culture (and theory), and also a post-Fordist regime in which scientistic methods, and science itself, are seen as "beyond ideology." Our overlooking music theory's potential as a historical trace, including for perspectives on musicology, may also be attributed to our overemphasizing the similarity between musicology and music theory, namely their dedication to the model of the artwork.[18] Although that similarity is certainly significant, it misses

---

[18] In this sense, the labeling, in popular music studies, of analytic approaches as "musicological," though understandable, may be slightly off base.

the equally salient point that music theory never completely followed musicology into the realm of *humanistic* study, remaining instead in a (perhaps unique) cusp of the humanities and something between "hard" science and vocational training for composers. Otherwise put, music theory has retained its 1950s dialectic of the instrumental logic of industrial capital,[19] along with the humanistic critique of that logic that located spirituality in a conception of autonomous art. Understanding music theory as an unusually, and even valuably, frozen dialectic may lead to a further understanding of how it, as a discipline, never quite having followed musicology into full humanism, has found it so far correspondingly difficult to follow the New Musicology into post-humanism.[20]

Music theory and musical poetics

Grasping the significance of the 1950s climate in which "music theory" came about may also serve to introduce another distinction, namely one between music theory, in its current institutional form, and musical *poetics*, as it will be advocated here. And this book aims, first, to broaden vastly the scope of the term "music theory" to mean simply theory (including cultural and social theory) about music. And second, the book proposes to rename what is now called "music theory" – specifically, the designing of models of intramusical relations and analysis of particular pieces – as "musical poetics." The terminological modifications would allow "music theory" a much broader domain, while still retaining, as a sub-field, the possibility for music analysis and elaboration of aesthetics, styles, genres, and so on. Furthermore, and more important, the broadening of the term "music theory" and the redesignation of "musical poetics" would clarify the latter as merely one subset of the former, engaged explicitly with the question of how music works in cultures.

Thus, redefining "music theory" as "theory about music" would not be a mere nominalist (or idealist) ploy. Rather, given the scope of "theory" in the humanities, such a redefinition could offer the benefit of allowing music analysis to suggest the world of cultural theory itself. Imagining such adjustments in disciplinary practice will be facilitated by keeping in mind fields such as film theory, in which the

---

[19] The time of music theory's disciplinary establishment was a period in which many university disciplines were explicitly being modeled as sciences to support the post-World War II industrial expansion.

[20] Some exceptions are collected in Krims (1998c) and Schwarz (1997). Some publications of Kevin Korsyn and Brian Hyer also merit mention in this regard; in a different category entirely is the Marxist music theory of Henry Klumpenhouwer, especially Klumpenhouwer (1998).

engagement of a certain poetics is not at all disreputable. In fact, doing so might serve as a reminder that music is, in a sense, the historical oddball. For "music theory" as practiced now is, by and large, coextensive with what here is being called "musical poetics," whereas what is called "theory" in most other areas of the humanities tends to embrace the more recent models of "theory" following the semiotic (and post-structuralist) revolution in the humanities. In other words, the scope of the term "music theory" proposed here is already assumed in the case of film (not to mention close reading in disciplines such as English). In the meantime, the field of musical poetics is already elaborated by what is now called "music theory," although it is a separate question how much of current music theory one would want to deem useful to the project of mapping the social place of music. It would certainly be senseless to deny the relevance of *all* current music theory; that denial would be no better than a blind counter-reaction, disposing of some work that may indeed bear information on culturally significant phenomena and processes. Indeed, it would seem problematic to maintain that we may safely dismiss music theory as "false consciousness" and presume that music exists apart from its constituent theorizing. Such a position would itself hardly take into account Marxist and postmodern lessons about the discursive constitutions of artistic production and reception. Careful (and methodologically informed) explorations of music theory are necessary to understand the social constitution of "music," and to see the multiple ways in which that constitution plays into wider circuits of power. Even musicological (postmodern) critiques of music theory suggest that whatever kind of practice "music" is in Western society, it performs certain social functions.[21] In that case, some poetics is necessary: if cultural life is to be mapped, then it is important to recognize that representation (in its broader meaning within critical theory) is not simply a "what," but also a "how." In the case of music, it is difficult to deny that the "how" involves, at least, the particular arrangements of sound. To assert that talk about "structure," "form," "unity," and the like is "just discourse" is to miss the point: regardless of whether such terms have "real referents," social action is profoundly affected by them. And it is for this very reason that bracketing musical poetics risks ignoring social processes by which musical actors (performers, composers, producers, and so on) model, invoke, play against, or in some other ways make use of musico-poetic discourse. Setting aside musical poetics would be no less a mystification than the more traditional

---

[21] This, in fact, is one of Tomlinson's (1993) most salient points. Kingsbury (1988) and (1991) shows how the notion of "music" functions in a conservatory setting.

practice of treating musical poetics as socially isolated or autonomous. In both cases, the text/context dichotomy remains deeply inscribed in our conceptions of music, hypostatizing both text *and* context.

Musical poetics, then, conceived as I suggest here, may be recognized as simultaneously crucial to (a broadened) music theory and incomplete without what other "theories" in the humanities must encounter at some point, namely the twin problematics of culture and representation. Once one has encountered those problematics, it becomes especially clear that forming, engaging, and judging musical poetics can never be a complete process without more generalized theories of societies, ethnicities, histories – in short, those things to which music analysis has often resolutely refused to direct its attention.

Some important consequences follow from the terminological (and methodological) changes I propose here. If one accepts some of the "New Musicological" critiques of music analysis, then it follows that music theory and analysis, in their current institutional state in North America and the United Kingdom, err in stipulating musical "structure" for the sake of aesthetic consumption. Here, the word "aesthetic" is meant in the strictly Kantian sense of invoking the value of disinterested pleasure and the free-play of the faculties.[22] It is thus not coterminous with questions of pleasure, "leisure," and other problematics that may well lead into social engagement.

Music theory, within the redefinition proposed here, could offer, given sufficient elaboration, a formidable response to musicological critiques. At the same time, critiques coming from popular music studies, involving the distance of music analysis from either performers' or listeners' realities (not to mention institutional ones), are not necessarily salient, if music theory may be taken to encompass problematics from communications theory, cultural studies, ethnomusicology and the other disciplines forming popular music studies.

Conversely, some kind of musical poetics would have to form an indispensable part of music theory. For the project of this book extends beyond the mere assimilation of music theory to cultural theory, to argue specifically that musical organization must be taken seriously, precisely because *artists, the music industry, and audiences of popular music take it seriously.* That is to say, there is evidence all about that the cultural force of popular music sought by theorizing on the topic lies, in part, in artists', audiences', and institutions' investment

---

[22] The phrase "free-play" here hints at something elaborated in Krims (1998a), namely the possibility that the slowly increasing vogue for deconstruction in music theory and analysis may in fact simply be reinforcing existing disciplinary practices.

in kinds of sounds, in distinctions among sounds, and in events of particular genres and songs. Such evidence can be culled from discussions one may have with consumers of popular music, in public statements and advertisements of artists and record companies that cue musico-poetic aspects of music, and in discussions with artists concerning their notions of their audiences and (sub)cultural location. Now, the variability of the investment in musico-poetic processes may well explain in part why the specificity of sound is so often sidelined in cultural studies of popular music. And indeed, the visual cues and verbal discourse to which most cultural theory is directed rarely provide significant clues about the functions of sound and musical process.

But the last point – the disciplinary orientation of cultural studies to verbal and, secondarily, visual discourses – is precisely the reason that a parallel, and, I would argue, equally significant body of cultural theorizing should base itself on the musical (i.e., aural) poetics of popular music. This would not, by any means, be to sanctify the "musical" as somehow an interpretive bottom line displacing other points of interpretive entry, with disingenuous arguments that we are, after all, talking about music; rather, it would be to place musical poetics – i.e., the discussion of musical design – in a place *parallel* to, and always bearing a complex relation to, other aspects of the social imbrications and functions of popular music. Admittedly, in the pages that follow, analytical attention will be focused more on musical texts and producers than on audience studies to make that point; and audience studies concerning musical poetics would form an important counterpart to the discussions in this book. But at the same time, the dynamics of producer, media content, and consumer are never discrete, and at least in the case of rap music, the media investment in musico-poetic features of the music cannot occur in isolation from a responsive audience and often changes in response to audience articulations. Just *how* that audience responds to (and inflects) the media content is a project whose exploration may well await more ethnographic work.

An argument running parallel to all this is that audiences often listen in more sophisticated ways, and *invest* more in that elaborated listening, than one might infer from those critiques that accuse music analysis of representing an unpalatably high act of abstraction. On the contrary, my own observations reinforce Simon Frith's (1996) notion that fan culture often involves sophisticated and genre-specific judgments little recognized in academic literature. The question of just *how* to engage those judgments, on the other hand, is not an easy one. It most likely does not necessarily involve the pitch-structuralist systems that inform many "musicological" analyses of popular musics, such as those presented in Covach and Boone (1997).[23] Instead, the analyses in this book take, as a starting point, remarks by, and what seem to be the concerns of, artists, institutions, and audiences, whose views on aesthetic issues in rap music often correlate extremely closely. Thus, rather than concerning oneself with notions like "middleground *Zugs*" or particular re-harmonizations of melodies, close readings of rap music might engage an effort to model what makes a given genre (or song, or artist) "hard" or "hardcore," or how it is that a song might project "Brooklyn-ness" (or, as discussed in Chapter 4, "Southernness"). It is precisely terms such as these that form part of the consciousnesses and cultural engagements of those that produce and consume the music. And, equally important, those same terms are invested directly in types of sound.

As an illustration, Rakim Allah (formerly of Eric B. and Rakim) explains in a 1997 interview what he means by "hardness" in rap music:

"Hard," to me, is a sound. This is music, you know what I mean? It ain't about chewing on nails, swallowing glass, screw face in the cameras and knocking 'em. It's not about that, you know what I'm saying. Being this is music, we express the hardness through sound: delivery, bass kicks, the mood of the tracks or the samples that we chose. That's what hard hip-hop is to me, you know what I'm saying.   (Allah 1997)

Given the validatory status the word "hard" has in hip-hop discourse, it would seem sheer folly not to see tremendous force in questions of musical style and organization involving "hardness" in rap music. Nor will it do to dismiss Rakim's words as "simply" publicity-oriented or as inauthentic (or insincere) because media-directed. On the contrary, that Rakim elucidates his own musical poetics of "hardness" for public consumption should suffice to indicate that questions of sonic organization permeate the circuit of producers and consumers. Or, to use language more current to cultural studies, the music, and Rakim's discussion of it, becomes a site of negotiation for musico-poetic definitions of hardness.

Music, musical closure, and film theory

Rakim's commentary (and many others like it) suggest that some poetics is necessary to understand the cultural force of music, no matter what problems music theory may have developed as a disci-

---

[23] This is not to say that artists and fans are inattentive to parameters of pitch, or even to pitch-structural judgments. The degree to which fans focus on pitch probably varies greatly by audience group and by genre. Hence the analyses of rap music in this book assume a normally greater salience for rhythm and texture.

pline. But something *proper* to music analysis may itself present an obstacle to further cultural study. One of the most common quandaries a socially oriented analyst may encounter is what I will call the *problem of musical closure*. By this phrase, I mean to refer to the fact that the only commonly accepted references of musical features are, for the most part, other musical features.[24] Being a notorious dilemma of musical semiotics, the problem of musical closure has, as one of its effects, the music-analytical practice of modeling songs as inwardly (or self-) articulated. The inexorable and exclusive logic of musical explanation thus mounts its own formidable resistance to the analyst interested in music analysis as cultural studies.

Indeed, once some music-structural assertions have been posited, the task of convincingly implicating other levels of social life faces its own daunting obstacles. The closure of interpretive systems – of which it should be clear by now that music is only a particularly intransigent case – is particularly daunting for those who (for whatever, presumably localized, reason) start out with a musico-poetic issue with the intention of opening the discussion into broader cultural processes. This is not only because of the strong resistance music-analytical discourse poses to "external" determinations. It is also because an interest in music as a cultural force tends to carry with it the presumption that either more semantically decipherable discourses (in the case of postmodern cultural theory) or relations of production (in the case of Marxist theory) are more desirable interpretive places to be. So closure in musico-poetic relations does not simply confine the analyst to one domain; it confines the analyst to a domain that is counted as, if not trivial, then somehow damningly preliminary. One has not yet achieved the "material" level – whether by that term one is thinking of the post-Foucauldian materialism of genealogy or of a more properly Marxist historical materialism.

One may easily slip into some form of expressive causality, in which some aspect of social life is seen as somehow "causing" the musical poetics to take a specific form. The music thus ends up either epiphenomenal to, or homologous with, other aspects of culture for reasons left inexplicit. The latter possibility then may slide quickly into idealism.

Another option frequently deployed – inserting an "extra-musical" interpretation at the point of some musico-poetic anomaly, or some other remarkable moment, to which the rest of the musical structure then is subordinated as ground to figure – has the virtue of boosting

[24] Undeniably, some conventional references may be posited between musical parameters and, say, certain emotions or ideas. But such references are not generally treated as systematic, or as capable of forming structural elaboration or design in music-analytical contexts.

the analyst out of a methodological aestheticized isolation. But the analyst's choice of "extra-musical" interpretation (from among the many possibilities) then itself secretly becomes a matter of homology. Thus one might want to designate, for example, a jarring pitch-interval as a sign of social conflict, with the hidden premise that some social agency bears an analogous relation to society that the interval in question does to the tonal order. But the apparent interruption of musical argument nevertheless relies on a background of its self-relationality, and the musical object ends up seeming no less isolated than it had initially, related to the rest of culture by metaphor or simile, or in the best case, metonym.

The problem of musical closure is in some ways not much different from the problems of correlating relations of production to cultural practices.[25] And if music theory is to include those two factors in addition to musical poetics, the problematic then becomes (at least) three-leveled. We are then faced with the challenge of finding ways to figure the relations of the production (in which we would include, among many other things, the music industry itself) to the webs of discourse that are more properly the object of much current critical and cultural theory. To model the dynamics of those two levels, we may well accept as at least a provisional principle some form of so-called "relative autonomy," while at the same time recognizing that the oxymoron of the term itself betrays its status as a problem, rather than a solution.[26] In the meantime, a third factor enters the equation, though eventually we will want to collapse it into the discursive level; namely, the world of musical poetics, in which music appears to be arranged, to quote Martin Stokes (1994), in

a patterned context within which ... complex aesthetic vocabularies, or single terms covering a complex semantic terrain point to minute and shifting subtleties of rhythm and texture which make or break the event. (p. 5)

Thus, the close relation of the "event" to an aesthetic vocabulary, with its attendant relative autonomy, militates that the aesthetic (or, to use the present terminology, "poetic") language be taken seriously, if only as a moment of interpretation among many others. Therefore, although one of my principal arguments here is that musical poetics need not be conceived as anything other than a specialized case of representation, for the time being it will be useful to keep it separate and think through its relation to discourse in general.

---

[25] Here, I purposely avoid the terms "base" and "superstructure" in order to avoid implicating my discussion in widespread misrepresentations, in postmodern theory, of the meaning of those terms.

[26] Garofalo (1987) works through some of the problem of relative autonomy in relation to popular music.

If the dilemma of musical poetics seems to be its own inexorable momentum toward closure, and if that momentum seems inevitable in the face of well-intentioned attempts to avoid it, then we may nevertheless take heart from the fact that musical poetics may not be alone in this respect. Thus, we might want to approach once more the problem of musical closure from perspectives afforded in other situations. We might look specifically for cases in which a social practice might instantiate some poetics of its own, while it simultaneously remains conspicuously involved in ideology and social formation. Film offers precisely the desired circumstances, and it also has the signal advantage of an allied academic field – film theory – in which discourses both of poetics (i.e., the "how" of film representation) and of social relations are well articulated. (Indeed, the compatibility, even interdependence, of poetic and ideological theory has often been assumed in film studies, as I will discuss presently.)

This is not to say that film poetics has never been at odds with other aspects of film theory; on the contrary, the practices of focusing either on poetics or on technology have indeed generated tension and debate in the field. Fredric Jameson, in his (1990) essay "The Existence of Italy," offers the occasion to think film poetics and technology in a way that will bear directly on the problem of musical poetics. Jameson opposes what he regards as the more strictly "theoretical" discourses about film to technological explanation.[27] The latter involves such "interventions," to borrow his term, as explaining the composition of shots, formerly attributed to some aesthetic principle, as a result of a material necessity of the then current state of film stock. In other words, where an intrinsic poetics had formerly seemed to prevail, a brute contingency of material life now rudely intervenes. The technological register, for Jameson, tends to work best as "demystification, generally in the service of a materialist philosophical position ... [It] comes as the therapeutic revelation of an *outside* to the work itself ... suddenly show[ing] up the shabby idealistic pretenses of an older intrinsic criticism" (p. 178; emphasis Jameson's).[28] The moment when technology intervenes demonstrates

---

[27] In the following discussion of Jameson's essay, page-numbers only will appear in the text, all referring to Jameson (1990). The word "theoretical" also appears in quotation marks in Jameson's text, indicating, one might assume, that he does not mean to imply that technological explanation somehow escapes the category of theory. Indeed, his discussion makes clear that "the technological" turns out to constitute its own theoretical realm.

[28] It might be proposed that some recent musicological critiques of music theory (in the narrower, currently institutional sense of the term) are themselves attempts to point up a similar idealistic pretense to the intrinsic criticism known as music analysis.

that the intrinsic (or poetic) interpretation had "drawn [the material condition] inside the text and endowed [it] with meaning of a more properly aesthetic kind" – a forced shift of perspective that can be "pitiful and humiliating" (p. 178).

The technological fact, however,

does not stop at this moment of demystification and intervention; it leads on into a new kind of discourse in its own right (which can be called techno-logical determinism for shorthand purposes) ... [And that discourse] will now begin to reproduce all the dilemmas generated by the history of forms, and very specifically that of the opposition between the intrinsic and the extrinsic ... (p. 179)

The technological discourse, then, will eventually outline the very same (and equally idealist) closed system. At the point where such a process seems in danger of imposing itself, further interventions would be needed, be they once again from the "theoretical" register, or perhaps from some register not yet appearing in the process. In the case of film, mutations in audience and/or class structure, or new institutional modes of function in the industry might impose them-selves as explanations, while surely the oft-observed new horizontal organization of global-culture industries in general might intervene at some point, at least for recent contexts.[29] What is being traced here is not at all a paradox, but rather the tendency of modes of analysis to totalize the field of objects (or systems) under study, together with the concomitant need to show the sublime and shocking "outside" to whatever enveloping modes of thought one develops.[30]

Jameson's discussion is particularly useful because musical poetics poses (possibly even more forcefully) the same daunting challenge as film poetics: it imposes an almost irresistible force toward closure, toward insisting, in a sense by its own momentum, on explanations within its own systematic context for problems that had initially been posed there. In other words, questions of film-aesthetic provenance tend to insist on locating their answers in film aesthetics, and similarly for film-technological questions, while questions of music-structural provenance tend to lock the interlocutor into answers about musical structure.[31]

[29] Burnett (1996) describes horizontal organization in the case of popular musics.

[30] This is quite a ways, of course, from rejecting *all* totalizing categorically; instead, one might avoid a *premature* totalizing of an isolated explanatory level, which would have the effect of closing down investigation. Such distinctions should not be equated with the unfortunate tendency, particularly in much postmodern theory, to use the word "totalizing," often in an uninformed way, as an index to denigrating Marxist modes of thought.

[31] In retrospect, it would have been useful to emphasize this dilemma in my (1994) discussion of Joseph Straus's adoption of Harold Bloom's theories. It is central to Krims (1998a).

35

Now, the particular opposition in the case of music has not always tended to be poetics (or "theory") versus technology.[32] There is no reason it could not have been precisely that opposition in the case of popular music studies. But just as often there, and far more often in the case of "art" music, the oppositions have been between poetics and some other register, such as discourse, institutional configuration, or perhaps some conceptions more specific to music studies, like the cultural formation surrounding rock.[33] But the specific discourse of the technological is less important to this scenario than the opposition at which Jameson arrives in the last quoted phrase, between the "intrinsic and the extrinsic." The dynamic that film studies and music studies share is the tendency of a strategic and localized intervention in one realm to become hypostatized, to perpetuate its logic in a deterministic way contrary to the spirit of its initial demystifying function. Technology in film theory may easily stand for "society," "culture," "gender," or even "resistance," as much as it may for musical poetics, or whatever, in music theory. In any case, Jameson's framework would retain its vital relevance.

In the case of music theory, systems of "purely musical" determination – in other words, matters of what is here being called "musical poetics" – threaten the same methodological mystification as "theory" had in the case of film, reinforced still more strongly by discourses of musical autonomy (and its presumed superiority for being autonomous) with which any cultural-theory-oriented music scholar is only too drearily familiar.[34] The intervention of extrinsic determinations (including, perhaps, technology, as in the case of film – an underexplored possibility) may then expose the "shabby idealism" of the musico-poetic analysis.[35] The continued development of determination levels may then pose a counter-image, in which the musico-poetic discourse is itself obscured, and the specificity of that

---

[32] In fact, technological explanation may well be an underexplored option for rethinking some aspects of "art" music history (and preferably in ways that take a broader view of technology than the so-called "historical performance" movement). Chanan (1995) may be a good starting point for beginning such an investigation.

[33] Grossberg (1993), for example, addresses cultural formations of rock, as well as their possible end.

[34] Norris (1988), pp. 29–37, gives an interesting philosophical background to the rise of the superiority of music, and the contingency of that superiority on its presumed non-representationality.

[35] Here, of course, the parallel to Jameson's film argument breaks down, as, though he does not specify which "theory" he means, it is most likely to some extent "social," in the sense of modeling discourse. That even the posited initial state of film theory needing demystifying should be already socially embedded, whereas the initial state of music theory is not explicitly so, shows how much more urgently something like Jameson's process is called for in music studies.

register of cultural action is lost. At that point, one might be tempted to marshal as a new intervention the field of musical poetics – not how "well put together" something is, but how musical organization develops as a culturally significant field, with material consequences. The point here, of course, is to allow the objects created by methodological fields to assault and destabilize each other, while simultaneously retaining the explanatory pathways one has already developed, never abandoning or considering as obsolete previous determinatory stages. (This last clause itself may serve as a reminder that we are not here considering a nihilistic project, or a radical skepticism, but rather a cumulative course of research.) The process of continuing interventions suggests that there may well be no ultimate and stable solution to the forceful drive of musical poetics toward closure. But music analysis is not unique in that respect; although it may well appear that way because of the hardened layers of mystification that have settled over music theory, especially since its institutional separation from musicology.[36]

The successive methodological interventions, in the case of music, probably come as even more of a rude shock than in many other cultural realms, because of the accepted separation between musical poetics and other discourses of music – a separation well established institutionally in the current climate by graduate degrees, university positions, professional organizations, and university curricula. And the present study is not likely to change the brute force of the shock to any great extent, perhaps not at all. But the brutality of the shock may be all the more therapeutic for those used to thinking of music theory as an aestheticizing exercise.

On the other hand, levels of the intrinsic and extrinsic need not be engaged in a static back-and-forth series of substitutions; rather, the categories themselves may be seen to transform themselves and problematize their mutual separation. One might notice, on reproducing series of interventions, that the methodological fields begin, if not exactly to look like each other, then at least to lead into each other in ways about which one can begin to talk, or for which one may even begin to invent terminology. At that point, of course, one is merely beginning another methodological field whose stability itself will eventually have to be challenged, but which nevertheless represents, in its own moment, a break into significant new territory. The theories of rap music and its cultural workings in the chapters

---

[36] Brown and Dempster (1989) is a notorious example of such a mystification, in which music theory is proposed to be modeled after science. But perhaps more eroding of intellectual life are the essentialisms and mystifications that do not so overtly announce themselves, such as Galand's (1995) claim that his Schenkerian graphs might uncover historical knowledge about classical rondos.

that follow lie somewhere in the midst of this whole process. As an example, one may see formations of youth and ethnicity, and regimes of authenticity, as well as imagined geographies, invested in certain genres of rap music. All of those aspects of identity, in turn, can be traced half-formed in remarks by audiences and performers, in song lyrics and musical events, and in media articles and record advertisements. At that point, one is watching musical poetics contribute to forming identities and discourses, through groups who produce, distribute, and consume music. Tracing all the aspects of identity formation back and forth through successive methodological interventions is one of the challenges of what music theory could potentially become.

Musical poetics of rap

The arguments and proposals here about close reading and musical poetics have not yet been specific to rap music. But there is a surprising consensus among scholars that some exposition of rap's music poetics is very much called for. Such diverse scholars as Tricia Rose (1994), Paul Gilroy (1993), Tim Brennan (1994), Richard Shusterman (1991), and Robert Walser (1995) have called for elaborations of rap's musical poetics, despite coming from quite differing disciplinary and ideological locations. Thus, attitudes in rap scholarship seem to defy the overall context of popular music scholarship in their calls for musical poetics.

The rationale that each scholar gives for the desirability of a rap poetics varies greatly; but it is difficult not to see at least a couple of common threads in their thinking. First of all, there is the simple matter of musical validation. Because of its obviously very different means of organization, rap music has provided a perfect opportunity for those already predisposed against African-American musical traditions – and even some, like Wynton Marsalis, sympathetic to earlier African-American traditions – to dismiss it as degraded, even at times as random, ugly noise created by unsophisticated (non-) musicians.[37] Certainly, elucidating a poetics for this genre, if effective, would go some way toward demonstrating that rap music is a cultural practice invested with articulated meaning and sophistication; it could allow rap music the cultural capital to take its place alongside a great tradition of African-American music.

---

[37] Not atypical of the popular denigration of rap music is the view of a childhood friend of mine, who, when I told him I was specializing in rap music, asked me in a tone of disgust, "But is that *music*?" Keyes (1996) points out, on the other hand, that not all rap artists covet the title "musician."

Although I am very much sympathetic to this line of thinking, I also see some dangers to it. Great care must be taken with the notion that there is something objectively defined as "music," which constitutes an unchanging standard against which new practices can be measured. What would be the consequences if we somehow (how?) determined such a standard and found that rap is not music (or is not good music)? Are its pleasures then to be forbidden, its admirers denigrated and its cultural effects dismissed? Would the standard then be deemed transhistorical and thus be posed as a challenge to the validation of any future artistic practices? Such a prospect holds pitfalls that articulate a larger point, namely that artistic validation is a route strewn with mystificatory and de-historicizing logic, perhaps of a local strategic value but, if one is not careful, potentially costly.

But on a different track, many of the authors named above, particularly Tim Brennan, emphasize that so publicly has rap music been debated in terms unrelated to its musical aspects – and so often in connection with a purported social dysfunction, especially of young black men – that a discussion of rap as *music* might be a valuable reminder that it is sites of pleasure and artistic production that we are stigmatizing, and experiences of profound investment and artistic engagement. To this argument I am more sympathetic (although I grant that it can be closely related to the validation argument in many contexts); and it is, in fact, something very much along those lines that is articulated by Robin D. G. Kelley in his groundbreaking book *Yo' Mama's Disfunktional!* (1997). Kelley, while acknowledging the valuable scholarship that has already been produced on hip-hop and rap music, is highly critical of the inattention to what is here being called "poetics" of the music:

By not acknowledging the deep visceral pleasures black youth derive from making and consuming culture, the stylistic and aesthetic conventions that render the form and performance more attractive than the message, [hip-hop scholars] reduce expressive culture to a political text ... [W]hat counts more than the story is the "storytelling" – an emcee's verbal facility on the mic, the creative and often hilarious use of puns, metaphors, similes ... (p. 37)

To which might be added (and I am sure Kelley would agree): the DJ's (or producer's) ability to create great beats and musical back-drops. In fact, Kelley goes so far as to contend that "[f]or all the implicit and explicit politics of rap lyrics, Hip Hop must be under-stood as a sonic force more than anything else" (p. 38). Throughout his first chapter, tellingly entitled "Looking for the 'Real' Nigga: Social Scientists Construct the Ghetto," Kelley upbraids those who ignore the aesthetic aspects of black expressive culture; not because he denies the broader socio-political significance of black culture – anybody familiar with his work knows that to be an impossibility – but because he is wary of collapsing sites of pleasure and creativity into dysfunctional cycles of racism and poverty: "Few scholars acknowledge that what might also be at stake here are aesthetics, style, and pleasure" (p. 17).

While, as explained in the Introduction, this book does not purport to analyze black expressive culture per se, but rather a media content derived mainly from black expressive culture, Kelley's point nevertheless remains highly relevant to the project undertaken here: to talk about rap music without coming to terms with its function in the spaces known as (among other things) "music" and "aesthetics" – maintaining, of course, at all times the understanding that those are socially constructed categories, but categories that are lived and thus culturally functional – is to miss an important level at which rap is working. Furthermore (and this is more to the point of Kelley's discussion) to discuss rap without indicating its musical organization is to slight the views of those who create it and those who consume it; in Kelley's eyes, such a slight is merely among the most recent in a long line of not taking black self-representation seriously.

My own concept of this problematic might not overlap Kelley's entirely – when I call musical poetics a "level of mediation," I am clearly invoking a history of Marxist thought for which Kelley's sympathies are mixed, especially with regard to African-American studies – but it adopts (and adapts) Kelley's important point that rap music can never be collapsed into verbal or visual cues or systems of representation. One must, at some point, work through its musical poetics as well, not to aestheticize it or abstract it away from social life, but *precisely to factor in that the people one is studying are taking the music seriously, as music* – and that their cultural engagement is mediated by that "musical" level.

The enterprise of this book, then, will be to open rap musical poetics onto the terrain of cultural politics in which it is situated and which it helps to create. Walser (1995) begins that modeling in a promising way, at the level of the song; the remaining chapters of this book will generalize the project, maintaining the focus on close reading of rap music, while proposing different and more generalized models of musical processes, and different cultural contextualizations. In addition, it is a central contention in the following pages (particularly Chapter 2) that the cultural force of sound in rap music requires conceptions of style and genre. The poetics occurs, in fact, at several different levels at once (as with other kinds of music): this book will focus principally on the levels of style/genre and the song. The next chapter will take up the former, and Chapters 4 and 5 will take up the latter; a word should be said here, though, since there is the recognizable danger that analyzing songs can slip imperceptibly into appreciation of the artwork and thus undermine the present project.

Here, the salient point is that the existence of the "song," though certainly impossible in isolation from other contexts, is nevertheless culturally widespread and widely "lived." For broader public discourses about music can be just as formalist as those of music analysis, and, regardless of the suspicion that we may hold as academics toward the ideologeme of the "artwork," the fact is that audiences talk and think of rap music largely in terms of songs. Thus, in the same spirit of taking seriously audience (and artist) discourses that leads one to musical poetics in the first place, one is constrained, however provisionally and contingently, to think at the level of the song in order to conceive rap music's workings.

One may say, for example, that Ghostface Killa's (and the RZA's) "Camay" (from Ghostface Killa 1996) exemplifies the expansion of the hip-hop sublime (to be described in Chapter 2) to a topically anomalous context. In such a statement, the status of "Camay" as a formally delineated song only serves as a moment in the process of interpretation, a moment which is eventually left behind in the ambition to describe a broader socio-poetic process. But nevertheless, the status of "Camay" as a formally delineated song – complete with the attendant discourses of self-relation, internal determination of poetic elements, and so on – remains a moment in the broader process of cultural interpretation (as the interpretation, so to speak, thickens). And like any moment, the intrinsic status of "Camay" – its poetics – is "true" *as a symptom of its social determinations*. The topically anomalous context mentioned above, for example, is the situation of "macking" (in this case, picking up women) more generally associated, in rap music, with "smoother" R&B sounds, i.e., a slower tempo, tonally commensurate (and, within jazz harmony, diatonic) pitch relations, live instruments with few or no samples, keyboard-heavy textures, and little sudden or drastic textural contrasts within the song. "Camay," though, is set to musical tracks of a contrasting, more "hardcore" style, in a combination of incommensurable musical layers that one might refer to as a "hip-hop sublime." Recognizing this topical/stylistic incongruity forces numerous questions of representation, of the relation of "hardness" to macking, of the various ways and modalities in which the two discursively loaded worlds come together.[38] And it has been widely remarked how

---

[38] This is not to say that those two worlds have never come together; they certainly have, for instance, in much of the music of Ice-T, Smoothe Da Hustler, and quite a few others. But the particular blend of the RZA's sublime style and an overtly macking song is exceptional, and, given the prominence of this particular production

crucially and thoroughly questions of masculinity, race, and class, to name just a few factors, figure into the kinds of representations involved in both of the topics/genres that come together here. The *song* "Camay" is the locus for this generic and discursive encounter, thus rendering analysis at the level of the song an appropriate way to open "Camay" into the world of social relations and cultural representation. Further, some plainly sonic aspects of the song are implicated in the encounter; for instance, the RZA integrates a Teddy Pendergrass sample, foregrounded as a refrain (and very much recognizable, while radically recontextualized tonally), introducing its own cultural/historical connotations. Meanwhile, Ghostface Killa's vocal climax near the end of the song, "You sexy motherfucker! Goddamn! … Goddamn!," cannot be ignored as a significant moment of the discursive confrontation, especially when one keeps in mind that it is also the climax of a particular fantasy, namely that the addressee of the verse (the object of the macking) is cooking for Ghostface a variety of his favorite foods. In a song where two paradigms of masculinity confront each other, the overwhelming excitement at the image of such a highly gendered role (and in such a sexualized context) invites serious engagement. And engaging seriously such developments forces consideration of the moments of "music" and "the song" in all their specificity, as levels of social mediation.

This is not to say that analysis at the level of the song is the *only* way to open music into the broader world of discourse and social life. On the contrary, it may often be more heuristically useful to begin at the level of genre – which is why the next chapter is devoted precisely to the outlining of a rap genre system. But the temptation of song analysis toward aestheticizing and closed interpretation cannot serve, in any permanent way, to discourage the cultural theorist from taking songs very seriously, and from discussing their poetics.

A principle behind this claim is, in fact, taken for granted in the vast majority of work in cultural studies: namely, that the purpose of mapping discourses is not to expose them as "false," but rather to show how they are involved in forming various aspects of shared knowledge and relations of power. The strategic necessity then becomes that of insuring that the "song" receive the same exacting, detailed, creative and thoughtful attention as any other discursive network involved in the social construction of music.

In rap music, style may connote not only genre (or, as will be

style in recent rap history and the Wu-Tang Clan's commercial status, it is a noteworthy event. (The song was, in fact, released both as a single and as a music video.)

discussed in Chapter 4, geography) but also temporality; and herein lies an aspect of rap musical poetics which is crucial to many of the representations discussed in this book. For not only has it often been observed that rap music is often "about" African-American music and musical memory in general;[39] but it must be added that rap is often also about specifically *rap* music and its own history. This is especially true since 1993 or so, when, simultaneous with a growing exasperation with gangsta rap's commercial domination, a large segment of rap consumers started despairing that the music had wandered too far from the aspirations of its origins. It was just around this time that many mainstream artists (like 2Pac Shakur) started featuring tribute songs to the "old school" (or, like The Notorious B.I.G. on the "Intro" to *Ready to Die* 1994, portraying their own personal histories as inextricably bound up with that of rap music generally).

Representations of history also engage style, and a certain "old-school" style may stand in for the diverse uses to which history may be put. For both the musical tracks and the rhyming style of rap music have changed, in most genres, substantially since its early recorded history.[40] In particular, rhymes since the "old school" days have increased in density (with more internal rhymes), have become more irregular (with many lines having no end-rhymes at all, and rhyming syllables on offbeats), and increased in quantity (with more than four or five rhyming syllables often occurring within a rhyme complex).[41] The rhythm of rapping has become more irregular and "jagged," sometimes more closely approaching the rhythms and cross-rhythms of speech than the more regular and repetition-based "musical" rhythms of the early delivery. In general, recent styles often deliver lines more rapidly, as well.

Although the summary just given of the changes in rapping style is most certainly my own, and some rap listeners might disagree with some details of it, it is most certainly true that something like what I describe has become widely recognized in the rap world. An item of media coverage should suffice to illustrate this. Hip-hop journalist Robert Marriott reflects a widespread recognition of what is being advanced here. In an interview/article with Rakim Allah (of the

---

[39] Gilroy (1993), for example, argues this convincingly.

[40] I use here the phrase "recorded history," since it is sometimes claimed that rap live performance styles in the early days of the music varied greatly from the styles recorded and commercially available, and furthermore that they were generally more similar to present-day styles. Although it is a fascinating and suggestive notion, present-day representations of older rap, the focus of this discussion, are at any rate mainly based on recorded music.

[41] I use the term "rhyme complex" to describe a section of a song in which any one rhyme predominates.

now-reunited legendary duo Erik B. and Rakim), Marriott speculates about why it is that Rakim has had difficulty reviving his career: "Hip-hop is something different now. There's a new generation raised on Mobb Deep and Snoop Dogg. He's up against faster cadences, new rhyme patterns" (Marriott 1997, p. 68).[42] The notion that rhyming style forms such an overriding context for the career of an MC demonstrates not only to what extent the music industry assumes that its audiences are attuned to rhythmic stylistic innovations and differences, but also that those differences are crucially determinate of large-scale audience response and commercial developments. And indeed, among the rap fans and aficionados that I know, the rhythmic style and the MC's delivery – or, to use the more common jargon, an MC's "flow" – are paramount not only to appreciation and pleasure, but, as will become clear in the course of this book, also to individual and group identities.

The historicity of styles in rap music, in fact, is one of the great untold stories of scholarship on the subject, and yet it is one intimately familiar to most rap fans. It is not at all an obscurity, among listeners, to refer to someone as having an "old school flow," or even a "early 90s West Coast flow," or a "new-style Queens flow." [43] Such terms are fodder for record company ads, artist interviews, song lyrics, and discussions among fans. The last two quoted terms also suggest a point that will be elaborated in Chapter 4, namely that temporality and geography are inextricably related in rap music. And furthermore, producers and consumers of the music tend to locate them both in sound. Some kind of musical poetics of rap music, then, is needed in order to reflect realistically behaviors and attitudes of those for whom the existence of objective musical properties is a firm belief.

What follows, in the remaining chapters, is by no means a complete poetics of rap music – a project, which, even if the music were to stand still for scholars to map, could not be completed. Instead, the next four chapters will indicate some directions that might be taken in that project. One aspect of rap musical poetics *not* dealt with at length in this book but nevertheless requiring serious discussion is the role of

---

[42] The choice of Snoop Doggy Dogg as an exemplar of new style seems puzzling to me, since his delivery is, in fact, slow and end-rhyme-dominated, by recent standards. Perhaps Snoop is an appropriate reference, in that he is obviously popular and therefore influential; and given that the tone of the article is (justifiably) laudatory toward Rakim, Snoop may also be an effective choice to imply that the difficulties of the new style do not guarantee that commercially successful MCs will be highly skilled.

[43] A good number of rap songs, in fact, play off fans' awareness of historical style, such as the Alkaholiks' song "Flashback" from Alkaholiks (1995).

timbre in musical organization (crucial in rap music), and its relation to technological reproduction (both means of, and degrees of, sonic reproduction in the DJ's mix). Part of the reason for that is simply the greater ease of calibrating a parameter to which I devote more attention, namely rhythm. But ways of talking about timbre in rap poetics can and should be found, as it, too, is of crucial musical and cultural importance to those who produce and consume the music.

It should also be noted that in the following discussions, I tend to assume and refer to dichotomies between the rapping (or MCing, as I more often call it) and the "musical" tracks. I have been extremely hesitant to use the latter term, since it can easily be taken to imply that rapping is not musical, and thus that rap music consists of some music, plus something else non-musical. It is not at all my intention to imply this, as it would surely reinforce some dichotomies that have always been harmful to the valuation of African-American musics, most immediately, a dichotomy between music and non-musical noise, which, in turn, often turns on the question of whether a music is principally organized (or analyzed as organized) by the calibration of pitch. I have retained the terms "MCing" and "musical tracks" simply because I could find no way to introduce other terminology without, at some points in the book, leading the reader into tortuous prose. I hope it is nevertheless clear that, in addition to the fact that rap can be seen very much in Afrodiasporic musical-aesthetic traditions (as Keyes 1996 has pointed out), it is music simply because it is received as music. The chapters that follow will flesh out some consequences that rap's status as "music" might have for the cultural processes and identities it helps to create.

2

A genre system for rap music

If, as argued in Chapter 1, musical poetics may be conceived as a level of social mediation, then presumably consideration of its internal structuration will be crucial to grasping rap music's social functions. Indeed, the genre/style system to be drawn here is assumed as a background to the discussions of rap that follow, both of particular songs and of broader cultural processes. It will, of course, never be more than a consideration of one among quite a few levels of musical mediation; but it seems safe to say that, at this point in hip-hop scholarship, consideration of this *particular* level of mediation is underexplored compared to, say, the burgeoning and distinguished scholarship already produced concerning gender, race, and class in rap music and hip-hop culture. Thus, the following discussion of what I want to propose as a rap musical genre system is meant to complement that already-existing scholarship. The musical poetics discussed here (and also, in my view, in scholarship such as Walser 1995) complements discussions of gender, geography, class, race, and so forth, not as a discrete and externalized dynamic, but rather as a moment of symbolic production that *internalizes* the other levels of mediation. In other words, musical poetics in some sense transcodes the social dynamics that are otherwise considered external to it; and a relational map of the social world is chartered within the genre system to be described here, invoking African-American traditions, pre-existing genres, gender relations (and gender domination), class relations, and the possibilities more generally of (especially American) urban life. Perhaps most directly telling of how social life, writ large, is internalized in musical poetics are the multiple points at which simply describing a genre involves reinvoking not only the entire context of rap music, but also the equally (relatively) autonomous world of discourses that surrounds the latter – and, not too indirectly, reinvoking aspects of the (late) capitalist mode of production itself.

The use of "style" in my discussion departs from some mainstream musicological (or music-theoretical) notions of style, in that here, "style" becomes not an objective property of music, but rather a matter of social discussion, behavior, and negotiation. In other words, it becomes discursive. Furthermore, it is subject to local variations, as we will see in later chapters. And of course, ideas of style are constantly changing in the rap and hip-hop worlds, and not only because of "stylistic innovation," but also because of reconfigurations of internal relationships between and within styles. More will be said about this at the end of the chapter; before that it will be useful to give an overview of the current state of the rap genre system.

The current North American genres of rap music, always in flux, have nevertheless shown a reasonable degree of stability since roughly some time in 1994. I choose that year, with of course a great deal of imprecision, because it seems to mark a time of important shift. A substantial decline in the dominance of classic gangsta rap had become evident by that time, not only from declining sales of some of the figures most associated (rightly or wrongly) with that term (such as Ice Cube), but also from such films as *CB4* (1993) and *Fear of a Black Hat* (1994). Those films both reflected and reinforced public exasperation with the lurid and commercially flaunted "rawness" of the artists.[1] The earlier commercial dominance enjoyed by gangsta rap guaranteed that its partial overshadowing, by either mixed-genre artists like The Notorious B.I.G. or more dance-oriented "commercial" artists like Puff Daddy, would have substantial repercussions. And the genre system resulting from the dispersion and division of the classic gangsta style and image forms a substantial context for present-day hip-hop culture's creation of cultural identities.

The following enumeration of rap genres is, as one might expect from such a project, culled and inferred from an extremely wide variety of sources, ranging from articles and advertisements in popular magazines (such as *The Source*, *Vibe*, *Rap Pages*, and *XXL*), to interviews with artists (either first-hand, or published), to music listening and conversations with fans. Despite the great variety of sources, though, there is a remarkable consistency in how the field of possible rap music is divided and what characteristics are attributed to each division and subdivision. Still, the generic/stylistic labels are selected by me from perhaps several labels that I have heard and/or read at different times. For instance, what I am calling "mack" rap could just as often be called "pimp" or "player" rap, and so on; and in some political contexts, what I call "jazz/bohemian" rap might be referred to, somewhat denigratingly, as "college-boy" rap, or with more historical consciousness, Native Tongues style. Nevertheless, the

---

[1] The eclipse of gangsta rap is taken for granted by many rap fans. As one observer puts it, "[G]angsta rap has been said to be on its last legs," by way of remarking that one group (Allfrumtha I) is "going against the grain by trying to continue the gangsta tradition" (Davis 1998, p. 83).

divisions described here should be familiar to most informed fans, and, importantly, they are aptly reflected in the wider body of rap musical poetics.

Each genre, in addition, carries its own regimes of verisimilitude. In other words, if one of the principal validating strategies of rap music involves "representing" and "keeping it real" – in other words, deploying authenticity symbolically – then that ethos is formed (and reflected) differently in each genre. In fact, fans of each genre not infrequently tout theirs as the true rap genre, asserting likewise that fans of other genres have somehow betrayed something essential about rap music, perhaps hip-hop culture as well.

Some rhythmic-stylistic terminology

A first step toward outlining the genres themselves will be to introduce some terminology for describing rhythmic styles; those terms will be invoked throughout this discussion and those of later chapters. The rhythmic styles of MCing, or "flows," are among the central aspects of rap production and reception, and any discussion of rap genres that takes musical poetics seriously demands a vocabulary of flow. Rhythmic style marks several dimensions of rap music at once for artists and fans – history, geography, and genre all at once, not to mention the constant personal and commercial quest for uniqueness. It thus cannot be separated from an exposition of rap genres and styles. At the same time, unlike the case of musical tracks, there is little common language that I have been able to observe to describe flow. Just about any rap artist or fan that I have encountered has well-developed notions of (and preferences for) rhythmic style; but artists and fans tend to refer those notions sometimes to particular artists, sometimes to history or geography, even sometimes to particular songs. So many different frames of reference have rendered popular terms for flow diverse to the point where generalization becomes confusing.

Accordingly, I have designed my own terminology to describe some basic distinctions of flow, with no pretense that they are the actual terms used by rap artists or audiences. I would, however, retain the claim that something corresponding to the terms is widely recognized and referred to by both listeners and (in media aimed at consumers) the rap industry. Robert Marriott's description of Rakim's situation, for instance, quoted in Chapter 1, shows how central poetics of flow are in rap reception, as will much of the discussion in Chapters 4 and 5. Thus, unlike the case of the generic and stylistic labels, which would be familiar to a great many rap fans, the rhythmic-stylistic terminology to be presented here is my own abstraction – albeit from some very concrete conceptions and actions.

Contemporary rap aesthetics is far distanced from those of the earlier styles. The flow of MCs, in fact, is one of the profoundest changes that separates out new-sounding from old(er)-sounding music, or "new-school" from "old-school" (both of those last terms themselves constantly shifting with rap styles themselves). Roughly speaking, both an antecedent/consequent couplet and the matching-beat-class end-rhyme were stylistically *unmarked* features of rap music during the first ten to fifteen years of its existence.[2] From Grandmaster Flash to Biz Markie to Queen Latifah, classic and revered MCs have frequently deployed a rhythmic practice that, from today's standpoint, might sound "sing-songy," an "old-school" flow. It is widely recognized and remarked that rhythmic styles of many com-mercially successful MCs, since roughly the beginning of the 1990s, have progressively become faster and, as it is often put, more "complex"; even public statements by MCs such as Queen Latifah and Guru of Gangstarr (about changes in their own techniques) attest to this. The trend would be exemplified by artists such as a number of members of the Wu-Tang Clan (especially Raekwon, Ghostface Killa, the RZA, and Ol' Dirty Bastard), Nas, AZ, (the) Big Pun(isher), and Ras Kass, to name just a few. The complexity referred to involves multiple rhymes in the same rhyme complex (i.e., section with consistently rhyming words), internal rhymes, offbeat rhymes, mul-tiple syncopations, and violations (i.e., overflows) of meter and metrical subdivisions of the beat. At the same time, older styles persist (and new *kinds* of complexity develop), thus affording an opportunity for rhythmic-stylistic contrasts to open up into historical, geographic, political, and other kinds of signification. It is thus important, given the project of delineating a genre system, to provide at least some rudimentary way to speak of rhythmic styles.

I will use three different terms to model styles of *flow,* or rhythmic delivery; the terms describe directions along spectra, rather than well-defined and separable points. The three terms overlap somewhat in different respects. One style I will call "sung" rhythmic style, referring

---

[2] I use "beat-class" in the same sense as Babbitt (1962), to refer to a recurring metric spot in some recurring meter (e.g., the "one" beat, or the "four-and-a-half" upbeat). Thus, a matching-beat-class end-rhyme would consist of a syllable at the end of a metrical unit (usually followed by a caesura), followed by a new line in the next metrical unit; the new line would then itself end with a syllable that rhymes with the first line and falls on the same beat-class. A well-known example of the phenomenon would be the first two lines of a limerick, such as "There once was a man from Nantucket / Who would gather his clams in a bucket," in which "-tucket" and "bucket" would be matching-beat-class end-rhymes.

to rhythms and rhymes equivalent (or parallel) to those of much sung pop or rock musics. Too $hort often provides clear contemporary illustrations of sung style, as does much early rap, such as Grandmaster Flash and the Furious Five (e.g., in "New York, New York," from Grandmaster Flash and the Furious Five 1994). Characteristic of the sung style are rhythmic repetition, on-beat accents (especially strong-beat ones), regular, on-beat pauses (in this case, on what I will call BC 3, i.e., the beginning of the fourth beat [see p. 60 below]), and strict couplet groupings. All these may be taken as characteristics of the sung style.[3] The Beastie Boys often exemplify sung delivery, with end-rhymes falling predictably on the fourth beat, shouted by two or three group members in unison, followed by a caesura, and falling into regular couplets.

The other two rhythmic styles will both be labeled as "effusive" styles, one of them "percussion-effusive" and the other "speech-effusive." The common term between the two refers to a tendency in rap music to spill over the rhythmic boundaries of the meter, the couplet, and, for that matter, of duple and quadruple groupings in general. Some early pioneers of the two effusive styles, beginning somewhere since the late 1980s, are MCs such as Chuck D (of Public Enemy), the MCs of the Freestyle Fellowship, KRS-One, and Ice Cube (then of NWA). The spilling-over of rhythmic boundaries may involve staggering the syntax and/or the rhymes; it may involve relentless subdivision of the beat; it may involve repeated off-beat (or weak-beat) accents; or it may involve any other strategy that creates polyrhythms with four-measure groupings of 4/4 time.[4] Speech-effusive MCing also breaks up the regularity of large-scale formal divisions: it has become almost a stock figure to begin a new four-measure unit with either the ending of the previous syntactic unit (and/or rhyme complex), or a new, truncated one. Either technique results in a caesura within the first line of a new four-measure unit.

Speech-effusive style may be opposed to percussion-effusive style. The latter is that which tends to elicit the observation that a given MC is using her/his mouth as a percussion instrument.[5] Involved in percussion-effusive style is a combination of off-beat attacks with a sharply-attacked and crisp delivery that accentuates the counter-

[3] Not everything here called "sung style" will instantiate all of these characteristics; it will suffice for some of those characteristics simply to be prominent.

[4] Keyes (1996) makes the important point that the building of polyrhythms, long associated with many sub-Saharan African musical strategies, is also central to rap music. Chapter 3 will explore this in more detail.

[5] Keyes (1996), for example, cites this as an Africanism in rap music, along with the practice of beat-boxing, in which one effects direct verbal imitations of percussion instruments.

metric gestures. Percussion-effusive flow is not necessarily quick and may even fall into fairly regular and predictable rhythmic patterns; what marks it out are the focused points of staccato and pointed articulation, often followed by brief caesuras that punctuate the musical texture and subdivide regular rhythmic units. An easily recognizable practitioner of percussion-effusive delivery is B-Real of the group Cypress Hill. Speech-effusive styles, by contrast, tend to feature enunciation and delivery closer to those of spoken language, with little sense often projected of any underlying metric pulse. The attacks need not be particularly sharp or staccato, since that would be more the province of percussion-effusive delivery. But the rhythms outlined are irregular and complex, weaving unpredictable polyrhythms. The polyrhythms, in turn, trace their elaborate patterns against the more regular (albeit often themselves complex) rhythms of the musical tracks. Also notable in many speech-effusive performances are large numbers of syllables rhyming together, so that once a rhyme is established, quite a few rhyming syllables will be produced before the next series of rhymes begins. An easily recognizable practitioner of speech-effusive delivery is (the) Big Pun(isher), an MC of Puerto Rican descent from New York; his (1998) first album illustrates what, in popular media, is often spoken of as "new-style" flow.

Several things need to be said at once of these two "effusive" styles. For one thing, they are clearly not exclusive of each other: it is perfectly possible for an MC to alternate between the two, or for that matter, to instantiate the two at the same time. Also, the term "effusive" does not necessarily refer to an effusion of syllables, but rather to an effusion of rhythmic patterns and polyrhythms. In fact, the percussion-effusive style often works by placing sparse groups of sharp attacks strategically; much of B-Real's performance (generally with Cypress Hill) pointedly instantiates percussion-effusive style, and yet his delivery is often sparse. The same could be said for much of Ice Cube's work (for example, on *The Predator* [1992]). The speech-effusive style, on the other hand, does indeed more frequently involve a profusion of syllables. That profusion, in turn, can be historically marked, since speech-effusive delivery has become increasingly common in recent years, and increasingly extreme. One can see this in such new-school artists as Bone Thugs 'N' Harmony, Nas, Ras Kass, quite a few members of the Wu-Tang Clan,[6] Twista (formerly Tung Twista), Big Pun, and AZ. At the same time, the sung style most

---

[6] This especially applies to Raekwon, Ghostface Killa, and the RZA. Method Man would be an exception here, his style generally being slow and percussion-effusive, and the GZA would also be an exception, for similar reasons.

certainly lives on, as may be illustrated by Timbaland and McGoo's "Up Jumps the Boogie" and Mack 10s "Backyard Boogie" (in the latter of which the sung style often slips effortlessly into singing itself). One of the rare MCs consistently able to maintain both percussion- and speech-effusive styles simultaneously is Treach of Naughty by Nature. The RZA of the Wu-Tang Clan, by contrast, is capable of engaging extreme speech effusiveness with very little percussiveness. In the song "Wu-Gambinos" from Raekwon's (1995) album *Only Built 4 Cuban Linx*, for example, his delivery veritably overflows with complex polyrhythms, but in something approaching a monotone.

Although my terminology implies, in a sense, a relationship between percussion- and speech-effusive styles – namely, one of polyrhythm, which is certainly extremely important – there is at least as much reason to associate the percussion-effusive with the sung style. That association would then pair off the more "musical" (for current lack of a better term) manners of MCing against those closer to "natural" speech. The pairing would also carry some historical weight, as the dense style of rapping most often thought of as contemporary is most often the speech-effusive one, while the sung and percussion-effusive styles co-existed for many years previously.[7]

The styles of MCing, unlike (in the vast majority of cases) the much broader categories of genre, may change within a song. In fact, quite a few rap verses begin with a sung style and then proceed gradually to a speech-effusive style. This kind of "rhythmic acceleration" – as I will call it, referring to the increase in attack density and greater variety of rhythmic intervals between rhyming syllables – belongs to the basic repertoire of rhythmic techniques for quite a few MCs. Aceyalone (formerly of the Freestyle Fellowship) refers to this practice when he begins the first verse of "Mic Check" (from *All Balls Don't Bounce* 1995) with "I start most of my raps off kinda slow / Just so you can see exactly where we're gonna go"; the RZA's verse in "Wu-Gambinos" also serves as an excellent example of rhythmic acceleration.

As in much popular (and other) music, measure groupings of four are often a norm in rap. In other words, the length of verses, the length of choruses, the layering techniques, caesuras within verses and choruses, harmonic and melodic patterns, drummed upbeats and downbeats – whichever of these aspects might be applicable in a

---

[7] In fact, it is not uncommon for MCs to refer to their styles as somehow updated or "take[n] to another level," referring to increasingly effusive rhythms; for example, Guru's introduction to the album *Moment of Truth* refers to a change in MCing style, and indeed, his MCing is more effusive on that album than on previous Gangstarr releases.

given song will, most likely, be organized in four-measure cycles and groupings evenly divisible by four.[8] Such a statement should come as no surprise even to those not at all familiar with rap music, since four-measure groupings are well-known and widely recognized in many, if not most, genres of rock, dance music, funk, blues, and so on. Higher-level groupings of four-bar units into sixteen-bar units (i.e., four four-bar units) are also not unusual in rap, although they are not as pervasive as the basic four-bar groupings. There are certainly cases in which, for example, a couplet may be attached to four-bar groupings (especially at the end of a verse), and there are also cases in which odd-numbered measure groupings may occur; but groupings into four bars, articulated somehow by the parameters just mentioned, tend to be more the rule than the exception. The duple and quadruple groupings being described here not only suggest rap's lineage from funk and disco; they also have enabled substantial interactions between rap and other genres of music, such as rock and R&B. Quadruple organization constitutes one of the relatively predictable aspects of rap-music rhythm, against which the other, more irregular aspects of a song may trace out elaborate polyrhythms.

Rhythm is itself ultimately inseparable from timbre. My own discussion in this book will necessarily fail to represent adequately the ineluctably close relationships between timbre and rhythm, largely because I have not yet developed what I consider suitably informative ways of talking about timbre in rap contexts. The limits of timbral representation in Western discussions of music are well known; and such limits cannot but hinder some consideration of rap poetics.[9] But the crucial role of timbre in rap musical organization can nevertheless be approached obliquely. For example, one of its functions that is most relevant to some of the rhythmic poetics discussed in this book is its use to separate out and maintain as discrete the layers of recording that comprise the various samples used in a song. Mobb Deep's "Drop a Gem On 'Em," from *Hell on Earth* (1996), for example, demonstrates how crucially timbre separates out the voice-sample's "vinyl-like" surface noise from the rest of the texture, including the piano loop, which carries its own timbrally distinct hissing "noise"; and simultaneously, the bass and drums themselves stand out as less timbrally "distant." These timbral

---

[8] "Layering" is a term defined in Rose (1994), pp. 38–9 and often used in discussions of rap music. It refers to the practice of building up the musical tracks via the assemblage of disparate musical sources (or "layers"), creating polyrhythmic (and polytimbral) textures. Layering will be a principal focus of Chapter 3.

[9] I am not satisfied that spectrographs, or other such "scientific" measuring devices, give the kind of *culturally* relevant information that I would ultimately like to convey about timbre.

distinctions, in turn, are crucial in maintaining the separation of the recorded sound layers; and those layers enable the polyrhythmic relationships to work their way throughout the song. The striking, specifically rap aesthetic – later in this chapter to be called the "hip-hop sublime" – in which massive, virtually immobile and incompatible layers of sound are selectively and dramatically brought into conflict with each other, would surely not work, were timbre not available as a crucial means of organization. Thus, timbre lies as a factor behind much of the rhythmic discussions here, even when it is not explicitly mentioned.

One final term, addressing simultaneously timbre and rhythm, will be basic to most discussions of rap genre: layering. Layering generalizes the notion of "break beats" well-known to rap scholars.[10] The generalization describes entire songs, though, not just selected parts. Specifically, layering refers to the practice of building musical textures by overlapping multiple looped tracks.[11] It also refers to the ways in which the density and other aspects of the resulting texture are manipulated for certain effects. More will be said about layering in Chapter 3, and especially about how it can be used to project formal structure within a song.

The genres

The degree to which one elaborates the system, specifically how far one goes in breaking genres down into sub-genres, will, of course, effect to a great extent one's discussion. The following brief exposition of a genre system will err on the side of having small numbers of genres, in fact only four principal ones. Certainly, for each one explained, many sub-genres could be fleshed out, and what at one level is described as relative homogeneity may secretly bear within it the greatest variety, a number of objects whose resemblance can be posited but whose difference is also patent. Thus, the genre system to

[10] Rose (1994), for example, discusses "break beats," pp. 73–4. A break beat is a part of a hip-hop song where the rhythm section (and possibly some other ostinato elements) is isolated and foregrounded. Originally, such events served as opportunities for break dancing; now, the latter practice is rare, although it has recently enjoyed a comeback, along with a general historical self-consciousness in hip-hop culture. A Cree MC (rapper) with whom I work refers to these as "break-down beats." Rose (1994) also refers to "layering," though her use of the word is somewhat less generalized than mine.

[11] Rose (1994), for example, discusses this, pp. 88–90. As one might expect, the producer of a recording thus occupies a crucial role in the construction of its sound. Many producers in hip-hop, such as DJ Premier, Dr. Dre, and the RZA, to name just three of many, acquire stature simply by producing records for others (although the latter two are also known as MCs).

54

be described is very much a blunt instrument. But in my view, it is a necessary step in grasping representation in rap. In the meantime, the system to be described must serve at least two crucial purposes. First, it must lay a framework for musical poetics in its formation of identities. And second, it must outline some important parameters in which the poetics may function.

The basic parameters that outline the genre system are as follows: (1) the style of the musical tracks; (2) the style of MCing (or "flow"); and (3) the topics commonly dealt with (i.e., the semantic aspects of the lyrics). Although other parameters could easily be offered (e.g., more visual cues concerning dress, video style, and so on), the stress on the more properly "musical" parameters will more effectively reinforce the points that the sonic aspects of the music are replete with social function. Those sonic parameters not only reflect culture, they also form it. For that reason, the initial section on each genre will explain that genre's social situation(s) and function(s); musico-poetic descriptions will then follow, including musical style, flow, and topics.

Party rap

A genre that remains from the very earliest history of what is now recognized as rap music can be called "party rap," designed for moving a crowd, making them dance, or perhaps creating or continuing a "groove" and a mood. A good argument could be made that rap originated from this genre, since the (Jamaican, but also African-American) tradition of DJ toasting and rhyming often served similar purposes in similar contexts.[12] In fact, a recent historicist movement in hip-hop culture conspicuously laments the relative decline of party rap, claiming that hip-hop was originally a culture of entertainment and fun, and that the fun has been lost.[13] So, like any genre in rap music, party rap carries its own connotations of history, historicity, and social situation. Party rap's claim to authenticity is inseparable from the aura of origins that surrounds it, and it is also inseparable from the connoted idea that so-called "gangsta" rap and other more recent genres represent some kind of fall from an early innocence. Thus, the deployment of the genre may often project an identity that claims authenticity and historical validation. But the

---

[12] David Toop's (1984) discussion of hip-hop's origins also emphasizes this connection.

[13] Such historicist movements in hip-hop have proliferated in recent years, at a dizzying pace. An example of the nostalgia for the "hip-hop for fun" ethos can be found in an article on the Beatnuts (from *The Source*), which refers that group to "the pioneers [of rap] who chanted their rhymes and scratched their records simply for the pleasure ..." (Everett 1997, p. 116).

self-consciousness with which the genre is invoked varies greatly: for the flipside of party rap is that it is also seen as one of the most "commercial" forms of the music. Its generally optimistic tones and faster, often more dance-oriented beats have an appeal that crosses over from hip-hop audiences into the more general record-buying public, and therefore, those for whom rap is a form of subcultural capital may shy away from the party genre. If what has just been said about party rap seems contradictory, it is because the genre does bring with it precisely such contradictory social dynamics. Some artists manage to negotiate the tensions between authenticity and "commercialism" rather successfully, and over long periods: Doug E. Fresh, Biz Markie, and at times even LL Cool J could be adduced as examples.

Musical style

A fact not generally discussed in hip-hop scholarship – and one central to the purpose of this chapter – is that "party rap" carries its own musical *style*. In particular, the genre marks the dance function with a prominent rhythm section and (by rap standards) minimally layered textures. It is not uncommon for the rhythm of the musical tracks to be particularly quick in this style; much music of Will Smith would exemplify this, such as his song "Summertime" (from DJ Jazzy Jeff and the Fresh Prince 1991). In fact, quicker, upbeat R&B styles often can more generally suggest the ethos of early rap music, since in that earlier style, the disco and funk samples used were often quicker than present-day samples. But most generally, the musical ethos of party rap is consistent with the goal of "moving the crowd," getting heads nodding and bodies dancing (depending on the situation of reception). This explains not only the tendency toward faster beats, but also the tendency in the genre that musical-track rhythms be foregrounded and compelling, and that pitch combinations be relatively consonant (at least by the standards of jazz or rock harmony).

Flow

The MCing also marks the style, coming as close as any rap genre does to exemplifying sung flow. As the earlier discussion of rhythmic styles would indicate, this translates into a relatively high incidence of end-rhymes, few internal rhymes, and frequent two- and four-bar groupings. The rapped rhythms in this genre are thus also more conducive than many to audience memorization and sing-alongs (especially in the choruses); and DJs in dance clubs not surprisingly often value party rap for its ability to incite enthusiasm through listener (and dancer) participation. Along with the foregrounded rhythm section and sparser texture, the more sung flows are also more generally conducive to, or at least suggestive of, dance. The connection between the relative stability and repeatability of party-rap flows, on the one hand, and the requirements of dance and sing-along, on the other, may also go some way toward explaining how it is that the party-rap genre often produces successful singles and opportunities for cross-over.[14]

Topics

The topics of party-rap lyrics can vary greatly, but they are generally consistent with analogous genres in popular music, that is, those that focus semantically on celebration, pleasure, and humor. As with many other genres of popular music, the topics of romance and sex are extremely common, either in a celebratory mode or perhaps in a humorous, even self-deprecating one. In the latter category, Biz Markie's "Just A Friend" (from Biz Markie 1995) is well known, but more recently Skee-Lo's (1995) "I Wish" enjoyed much success as a single, precisely, one might speculate, for its disarming self-parody. Party rap simply about parties, celebrations, drinking, and dancing is not at all uncommon, and such topics can seamlessly shade into celebrations of rap music and hip-hop culture themselves, as in Naughty by Nature's "Hip Hop Hooray" (from Naughty by Nature 1993).

Like any genre of hip-hop, "party rap" may quickly, in any given instance, turn into its own representation, quickly fall into "quotes" and deploy its own stylistic markers self-referentially. And characteristically of hip-hop culture overall, it may then signal its own narrative of authenticity. Doug E. Fresh, for example, enjoyed a brief revival of popularity with an album significantly entitled *Play* (1995), capitalizing on the fact that he had been engaged in this genre of rap since the music's early days. The album's lyrics focus on "back in the day" narratives of hip-hop's early days, while numerous guest MCs are featured who were prominent in the formative days of rap and have hardly worked since (like Lovebug Starsky). Indeed, here is one of the points where social function and musical poetics work most visibly in tandem: the deployment of party-rap musical tracks and MCing may instantly invoke publicly shared discourses of hip-hop authenticity.

---

[14] Similarly, the MCing style of party rap frequently characterizes whatever MCing may appear at times in otherwise non-rap dance-oriented genres such as house.

In fact, there is a considerable subset of rap audiences for whom certain party-style artists represent the "true" ethos of rap music. Such audiences often refer to themselves as "hardcore" fans, in an interesting contrast to the other (probably better-known) usage of "hardcore" in rap music, namely that which refers to reality rap styles (about which more will be said shortly). These hardcore fans, by contrast, consider themselves closer to what they regard as the original spirit of hip-hop culture, namely entertainment and the love of the music. Artists often invoked in connection with this, and exemplifying the party style in many cases, include the Beatnuts (e.g., their song "Props Over Here" from Beatnuts 1994), the Pharcyde (especially their first album, *Bizarre Ride to Pharcyde* 1994), and, in a more extreme case, Doug E. Fresh himself. Some more "crossover" artists, as well, produce music in this genre, such as Will Smith and Heavy D. The strategic deployment of party rap can perhaps best be illustrated in a context where, in fact, styles are mixed and thus the party genre is differentially highlighted. Brooklyn MC KRS-One, a prominent MC for over a decade, can provide an illustration, since he ranges over a number of styles; and in his music, the party genre is often invoked conspicuously to frame topics that refer to his longevity, the earlier days of rap music, and his longtime (self-proclaimed) supremacy as an MC. It is worth pausing, then, a moment to consider his successful single of 1995, "MCs Act Like They Don't Know" (from KRS-One 1995), and the ways in which it deploys "party rap" as a recognizable and significant genre. The opening couplet is delivered almost *a cappella*, with only handclaps to accompany his voice; the texture, then, is already marked, for any rap style. But KRS-One's rapped rhythm signifies with equal force its generic situation. Figure 2.1 illustrates, marking out the beat-classes (henceforth: BCs) and marking with an "x" each successive attack of a syllable.[15] The first line counts out quarter-note values from 0 to 3, while the next line counts out sixteenth notes within each quarter note, again from 0 to 3.[16]

---

[15] The figure does *not* indicate note-lengths, which are difficult to distinguish in MCing and, at any rate, are beside the point being made here, which is about the placement of syllables and rhymes. The more salient information is the distance between attacks, regardless of where one might speculate the voice completely drops off. The avoidance of note-lengths also accounts for my not using standard musical notation for this figure.

[16] The reason for numbering from 0 to 3, rather than the 1 to 4 to which many people are accustomed, is (to explain very informally) that intervals *between* lines work in more mathematically predictable ways with numberings that have a zero.

Figure 2.1: The opening four lines of KRS-One's "MCs Act Like They Don't Know"

0				1				2				3			
0	1	2	3	0	1	2	3	0	1	2	3	0	1	2	3
	x		x	x		x	x	x		x					
	x	x		x					x	x		x			
	x	x		x	x		x			x	x		x		x
x		x	x	x			x			x	x				

Text
Clap your hands, everybody / if you've got what it takes / 'Cause I'm K-R-S, and I'm on the mike / and Premier's on the breaks![17]

Saying the words out loud to the rhythm marked out in Figure 2.1 will help to make the two principal points, here. First, the rhythms are "sung," as the term has been characterized here. One might note, for example, the consistency with which the first three lines begin on BC 1 in the first quarter note, as well as regular caesuras on BC 1 in both the second and fourth lines. Second, the rhyme involved ("takes" and "breaks") not only occurs as end-rhymes in a couplet, and further at an even distance of two lines; it also falls on the final beat (though a sixteenth-note early in the second line), followed by a caesura. Such characteristics are typical of "sung" style and are details that would be recognizable to quite a few rap fans.

The "sung" rhythm (especially on "clap your hands" and "I'm on the mike"), then, combines with the single end-rhyme to mark out a "party rap" style. Furthermore, the couplet is isolated in the song by the subsequent beginning of the musical tracks that will accompany the rest of the song. The song proceeds with KRS-One's rapping style progressively moving from "party rap" style to other styles, as two excerpts will show. The first excerpt, Figure 2.2, transcribes the first couplet (with upbeat) of the first verse, which remains more or less squarely in the same style.

The style of these lines lies somewhere between that of Figure 2.1 and a more effusive style. It is certainly not so regular as the earlier excerpt, and significantly, it has fewer pauses and something closer to a busy effusion of syllables. On the other hand, the (complete) lines form even caesuras on the third sixteenth of BC 3. And furthermore, the two lines' first two quick caesuras are in closely analogous places; the second line presents something of a loose temporal transposition of the first line's first two caesuras (i.e., plus-two-sixteenths, then plus-one-sixteenth). Thus, though not as clearly in "sung" rhythmic

---

[17] "Premier" is DJ Premier, the producer of the song and one of the best-known producers (and DJs) in the rap music industry.

Figure 2.2: First couplet, first verse, of KRS-One's "MCs Act Like They Don't Know"

```
0           1           2           3
0   1   2   3   0   1   2   3   0   1   2   3   0   1   2   3
_____
                                        x   x   x
x   x   x   x           x   x       x   x   x   x   x           x
x   x   x   x   x   x       x   x       x   x   x   x           x
```

Text
If you don't / know me by now, I doubt you'll ever know me, I / never won a Grammy, I won't win a Tony. But ...

style as Figure 2.1, Figure 2.2 does not yet squarely model any speech-effusive style.

The case is different in the lines transcribed in Figure 2.3, which are taken from the third (and final) verse. (Note: the unevenly spaced first three attacks and the "–3–" above them indicate a triplet figure.) Here, there is very little of the sung style left, and we are well into speech-effusive territory. Not only does an irregular rhythmic figure – the triplet – appear, but it appears on a strong beat.[18] Syllables come more quickly here than in the earlier passages. The caesuras are infrequent, and the only repeated one – on the last sixteenth of BC 2 – is short in duration and in a rhythmically weak spot. And equally important, multisyllabic words spill over each line into the next, a frequent characteristic of speech-effusive delivery (and also, incidentally, producing an offbeat caesura).

Figure 2.3: Two (plus) lines from the third verse of KRS-One's "MCs Act Like They Don't Know"

```
0           1           2           3
0   1   2   3   0   1   2   3   0   1   2   3   0   1   2   3
_____
-  3  -
x   x   x   x   x   x   x   x       x   x   x       x   x   x   x
x       x   x   x   x   x   x   x   x   x       x   x   x   x
x   x
```

Text
Comin' around the mountain, you run and hide, hopin' your de- /fence mechanism can divert my heat-seeking lyri- /cism

In the latter excerpt, we have clearly moved into another rhythmic style, in which multiple rhymes, internal rhymes, non-coordinated semantic and rhythmic parameters, and effusive rhythms combine to

---

[18] The strong-beat triplet, or more generally a rapid effusion of syllables on the downbeat, is actually more characteristic of non-New York MCs than it is of KRS-One.

mark out "new style" speech-effusive flow. And significantly, that new style is itself a position that is both commercial and more broadly discursive. What links its commercial and discursive aspects is the very paradigm of stylistic newness, in which a veteran MC like KRS-One shows his ability to adapt to new styles and still, presumably, maintain his authenticity as a fundamentally "old school" MC.

But an equally important context is the stylistic progression of the song. There is a progression from the party genre to one whose historical predominance is more recent than the former.[19] For one of KRS-One's principal claims to authenticity is his connection to early hip-hop culture. Indeed, he began his recording career in 1986, at a time when the "party" genre was a good deal more prevalent than it is now, arguably dominant. In that sense, KRS-One uses the occasion of the song's beginning to signal his own historicity with the party genre (complete with hand-clapping). Signaling his own historicity is even a well-known tactic of KRS-One, who rarely misses the chance in interview situations to remind audiences how long he has been a rap artist. Another temporal signal appears in the form of his frequent, even insistent, validation of live performance and freestyling; for both of these are widely lamented "lost" (and perpetually revived) aspects of early hip-hop culture among rap audiences. He even goes so far as to include, in the album *I Got Next* (1997), several live cuts, the first of them introduced with the admonition: "Anyone in here with tape decks, right now, turn 'em on ... I wanna add authenticity to your tape, so when it's sold out in the street, you all can know this was a real party" (KRS-One 1997). Particularly notable here is the explicit linkage of live performance, partying, and authenticity. Discourses of rap for pleasure (i.e., before a downfall into commodification) and improvisation denote in KRS-One's address both the "real hip-hop" and genuine skill. In short, the generic progression in "MCs Act Like They Don't Know" allows KRS-One to ground his performance in a certain historically-cued notion of authenticity (reinforced by the "live" suggestions of hand-clapping), while subsequently allowing him to update his style to the present.

If attributing such significance to rhythmic style seems far-fetched, then it is worth recalling that "MCs Act Like They Don't Know" is a song in the "toasting" tradition. Toasting might be designated a "free-floating" topic at home in any genre; it involves boasting about the MC's own verbal skills (sometimes with put-downs of a real, or imaginary, opponent). Even those only remotely familiar with rap

---

[19] Rap music consumers are capable of being extremely time-conscious. Thus, the historical disjunction between the sung and speech-effusive flows would not be lost on many such consumers.

music would probably recognize toasting as basic to just about any MC's repertory. But the fact that a toast does not identify a specific genre does not necessarily occlude its significance to the generic context of party rap. KRS-One's toasting marks the "party" genre's authenticity; and the boast about his skills is reinforced by a popular and oft-lamented memory (however selective) of a time when hip-hop was supposedly about skills and fun.

The brief examination of KRS-One shows that genre is not just a matter of topics (which, indeed, like the toast, may not necessarily be genre-bound), or simply of musico-poetics – though it clearly may be described, as here, in terms of both – but rather may simply be its own sets of strategies for "authenticity" and selected points of historical contact. Historicity and verisimilitude may, then, be taken as constituents of all rap genres, in fashions that will become clear in the discussions that follow.

Mack rap

Just another such genre is that of the "mack" (or "pimp"), and the historical resonances of this one are at least as rich and complex as those of the "party" genre. A "mack" is not necessarily a literal pimp, although that possibility is not precluded, and rap about "the life" has a significant presence in hip-hop culture.[20] Rather, a mack may simply be a man whose confidence, prolificness, and (claimed) success with women mark him as a "player." In any case, as is widely recognized, the sexual and/or criminal transgression sometimes implied by the term bears profoundly ambiguous status, both in terms of its literal implications and in terms of the tension invoked between lurid attraction and moral scandal.

The history of mack poetry and prose fiction is long, distinguished, and well documented.[21] That it therefore should survive as a rap genre should not, then, be surprising, and indeed, its presence is of long standing (by rap standards, of course). From Big Daddy Kane to Sir Mix-A-Lot to Ice-T, Too $hort, and Smoothe Da Hustler, the mack genre has just about never lacked a significant presence in rap music. Its contribution to rap's reputation as misogynist music is undeniable, and it is indeed difficult to listen much to some of the harder-core

---

[20] Too $hort provides a prominent example, as does some of Ice-T's music, as well as that of some more "popularized"-style artists such as Sir Mix-A-Lot.

[21] Of course, Iceberg Slim provides the best-known example. Among those who discuss the legacy in more general terms are Wepman et al. (1976), Smitherman (1977), and Jackson (1974); Cross (1993, pp. 24, 183) discusses Iceberg Slim's influence on mack rap, including Ice-T. His continued presence is signaled by Ice Cube's recently announced intention to create and star in a biography of Slim.

mack rappers like Too $hort without being tempted to some of the more moralizing modes of reception typical of public demonizations of the music. At the same time, like any genre, mack rap has spawned its share of parody and intelligently slanted approaches, and at its best, some of those slightly bent efforts can throw the genre itself into a critical perspective. Songs such as Aceyalone's "Annalillia?" from *All Balls Don't Bounce* (1995) show that, in fact, it is perfectly possible to inhabit some features of the mack genre without surrendering entirely to exploitation, even engaging critical perspectives.

It is also worth noting that the mode of address in this genre can vary greatly. The mack-to-man address, so to speak, tends most to resemble older traditions of toasting and other oral poetry: the speaking persona addresses a third person, boasting of his experiences with women, his power over women, his sexual prowess, or, in perhaps more modest cases, his desire for women or sex.[22] On the other hand, a mack-to-woman address (i.e., in which the woman is addressed in the second person), while certainly also finding analogues in some toasts, allows for more approximation to the venerable love-song tradition in popular musics. This, in turn, seems to allow greater possibilities for appreciation by both sexes and mass commercial appeal; the enduring success of LL Cool J, for example, and his (by rap standards) high proportion of female fans show that the mack genre by no means precludes the possibility of widespread appreciation by both sexes.[23] Even a blatantly gender-regressive song (and video) like "Doin' It" (from LL Cool J 1995) does not seem to affect adversely LL Cool J's appeal across gender lines.

Whatever form of address a mack-genre song might take, the musical poetics are often surprisingly narrow in their range. R&B styles are probably the most commonly found, with live instrumentation far more common than in other genres.[24] In fact, a full-fledged R&B band, consisting of, say, a drum kit, bass, (often multiple) keyboards, guitars, and sometimes horns, is far from rare in mack rap. Although sometimes looped, the music played in this

---

[22] The language here is purposefully gender-specific, as the mack genre, more than the others, has historically resisted adoption by women. Recently, however, some artists such as Li'l Kim and Foxy Brown have in fact met with sizeable commercial success at times deploying the genre. Nevertheless, macks remain, by and large, men in the public imagination.

[23] The implications here for gender interpellation form a question worthy of a separate study, deserving far more careful thought than moral panic or simple condemnation. Likewise, the softer macking styles of much hip-hop R&B, for instance by KC and Jo-Jo, are clearly implicated in the process.

[24] When I say "R&B," I am talking about the post-disco "smoother," keyboard-heavier (and radio-friendlier) style of, say, R. Kelly or, closer to Top 40 R&B styles, Mariah Carey.

instrumentation is just as often recorded through. Consequently, the layering techniques, if indeed there is any significant layering at all, are not nearly as stark, intricate, or uneven as those in many other genres. In fact, it is often the case that a mack-rap song ends up sounding like an R&B song with a rap track added.[25] It is not uncommon for mack rap to feature sung choruses, quite often sung by a woman. The Notorious B.I.G.'s final hit, "Hypnotize," would thus fall into this generic description, although the song approaches a kind of recent hybrid, the don subgenre – a phenomenon to be discussed presently. There is also a substantial subgenre of mack-rap/R&B style that features dance beats, into which "Hypnotize" might fall, and certainly songs such as Little Shawn's "Dom Perignon" (from the *New York Undercover* soundtrack 1995). As the title of the last-named song might be taken to imply, images of wealth are extremely prevalent in mack rap along with the boasts of sexual prowess and/or attempts at seduction. All such topics, of course, form a continuity with the practice of toasting.

The generic separation of mack rap from the denigrated "commercial rap" is often ambiguous or perhaps sometimes cannot be said to exist at all. The ambiguity of the line has been increased in recent years by the tendency of the more mainstream-targeted rap music to flaunt (both lyrically and in video images) exaggerated wealth and female bodies. On top of this, R&B (especially dance) styles are precisely those that tend to predominate in the most "commercial" hip-hop. Sean "Puff Daddy" Combs provides a ready-made example in "Mo Money, Mo Problems," and "All About The Benjamins" (from Puff Daddy 1997), among others; both songs focus on wealth and only secondarily women. In fact, more generally, one might observe a trend in "commercial" rap to rebalance the classic mack formula, the latter having traditionally emphasized sexual domination over "go for the money" talk. In the mainstream formulas, by contrast, the money is often very much more foregrounded (as in the music of Ma$e). Still, it can by no means be said that the symbolic domination and possession of women disappears.

The money-flaunting, R&B-flavored song has become something of a genre of its own, at the same time reminiscent of mack style and palpably different from it. The ostentatious wealth display has even spawned a term to describe it, "Big Willy-ism." It is not by accident that it was one of the rap groups most prized by "connoisseur" rap

---

[25] The mack genre's musical styles can also themselves become the focus for reflexive representation and critique, as in Ice Cube's "Who's The Mack," from Ice Cube (1990a).

fans, the Roots, who produced a video parodying "Big Willy"-style videos ("What They Do," from the Roots 1996); scene after scene in the video imitates the style in comically exaggerated form, with subtitles and some slapstick events underlining the purported ridiculousness of the genre. Thus, much of the imagery (and in the case of "What They Do," musical style, too) of mack rap can be deployed critically, as parody. And such a strategy can, in turn, become a marker of some other genre (in the case of the Roots, jazz/ bohemian). Mainstream artists, or artists reaching out for mainstream appeal, adopt the Big Willy/mack formula to such an extent that often an R&B-style song in itself is enough to bring on accusations of "commercialism" and "selling out." The opening cut ("Intro") of the second CD from Wu-Tang Clan's second album, *Wu-Tang Forever* (1997), is an address from group-member RZA to the listener, asserting that some artists had recently been trying to turn rap into R&B – which he translates as "Rap and Bullshit" – and funk. In contrast, the RZA promises rap "in the purest form." Never mind that the liner notes include advertisements for the clothing line bearing the group's name, along with ordering information and web-site addresses; the gist of the "little announcement," as he calls it, is to position the group against a presumably commercializing aspect of musical style. The popularity of R&B-style rap (mainly, though not exclusively, in the mack or mack-related "Big Willy" genre) and its association with dance music, then, renders it a common target for those who wish (or project the desire) to protect rap against the pressures of commodification.

Jazz/bohemian

The title of this genre may vary a great deal, and it is probably less well-defined than the two already discussed. In terms of its topics, it is also a permeable genre, often extending into the closely-related "science" sub-genre of reality rap to be discussed next. Nevertheless, jazz/bohemian's devotees are often fans who scorn all other genres, thus forming a "connoisseurs'" culture. And it is not coincidental that those who wish to disdain it often refer to it as "college-boy" rap, probably referring less to any official demographic than to a perceived projection of artistic arrogance among some of this genre's devotees.

Groups whose music would largely be included in this generic classification include A Tribe Called Quest, Freestyle Fellowship, De La Soul, the Jungle Brothers, Black Sheep, Organized Konfusion, Black-Eyed Peas, and the Roots, among others. As the name of the genre implies, the use of jazz, both sampled and live, is a frequent mark of this style, although it is by no means a *sine qua non*.[26] Also widely to be found, especially in De La Soul and the Jungle Brothers, are substantial and relatively complete samples of soul and pop musics from the 1950s through the 1980s.[27]

Musical style

Most generally, musical styles are more difficult to characterize here, even in the sense of a "mainstream," than in the party or mack genres. Now, this diversity in itself speaks to significant aspects of the genre, especially when one keeps in mind the "college-boy" characterization. That epithet would seem to refer to the development, in jazz/ bohemian hip-hop, of an "art music" genre.[28] For the eclecticism of musical styles, and especially the frequent "playfulness" of the sampling, together foreground both irony and cultural mastery. A prominent example of this would be De La Soul, whose sampled music often remains intact enough to create the "groove," but is framed in such a way as to remain, so to speak, in quotes. Similarly, an ethos of playful irony is suggested by the tendency in the genre for artists to sing in places, including but not limited to refrains and choruses. Such singing often takes on a conspicuously informal manner (as in the gleefully out-of-tune singing in De La Soul's "I Can't Call It," from the *High School High* [1996] soundtrack). Such playful and careless mastery mesh well with the specific prominence of jazz, since representations of jazz, both within and outside hip-hop culture, often invoke a validation related to a presumed status as

---

[26] The "bohemian" part of the title would seem to stem largely from A Tribe Called Quest's first (1990) album (as evidenced, for example, in Abdul-Lateef 1998, pp. 78, 80). It is perhaps an exercise in idealism to speculate whether to include in the genre some of the more outright exercises in "fusion," such as Buckshot Lefonque (1993) or Guru's *Jazzmatazz* (1995). On the one hand, the authenticity ethos which many fans would attach to the genre would be difficult for many of them to grant to Buckshot Lefonque, with their more mainstream image and the anchor figure of Branford Marsalis. All the more strange, perhaps, that the same fans would probably classify the Roots as squarely jazz/bohemian, even though their first full-length US release, *Do You Want More?!* (1995), was a stylistically very similar exercise in combining rap with live jazz performance.

[27] By "relatively complete," I mean that the sample from the quoted music is lifted more or less whole, and/or combined with very few new tracks (perhaps a drum machine and extra bass, for example).

[28] It seems worth considering that, in fact, recorded rap may have become a certain kind of "art music" genre. This would mean that a fan culture exists with a profoundly historicized aesthetic consciousness (by no means including *all* rap listeners, of course). Applying that label to the jazz/bohemian genre, then, would suggest a difference of quantity, rather than of kind.

black "classical music," or some related musical (and American) modernism.[29]

Flow

In terms of the rhythmic delivery of the MC, the label "eclectic" applies fully as much as it does to the musical tracks. The widespread practice of informal singing has already been noted; beyond that, it can perhaps be said that the rhythmic styles tend to fall somewhat between sung and effusive. Q-Tip exemplifies jazz/bohemian MCing nicely, with frequent end-rhymes and rhythms stylized to musical motion, both suggesting a sung rhythmic style not far removed from party rap. But on the other hand, even when delivering sung rhythms, Q-Tip not infrequently uses timbre and attack to emphasize offbeats, and to create polyrhythms with the musical tracks and surrounding lines. In other words, he frequently veers into percussion-effusive style. Overall, Q-Tip deploys a variety of rhythmic strategies from both sung and percussion-effusive styles to create a sort of meta-polyrhythm, a widespread characteristic of jazz/bohemian MCing. His delivery in the song "Keeping It Moving," from A Tribe Called Quest (1996), may be taken as emblematic.

In addition to the infusion of sung with percussion-effusive style, those sung rhythms which are used are mixed up considerably, so that while one might know that *some* sung rhythm is probably about to be performed, which *particular* one will be performed is rarely knowable (on first hearing, of course).[30] Thus, his MCing can be said to engage, on a certain level, the rhythms of singing or instrumental playing, while on a broader level, the rhythmic patterns are constantly shifting.[31] Often, he walks a fine line between rapping and singing, and pitch is seldom far in the background. Q-Tip's versatility and eclecticism, as well as the moderate pace of his delivery (as opposed

[29] The Buckshot Lefonque song "Music Evolution" (from the 1997 album of the same name) provides a vivid case of validating rap as a contemporary equivalent of jazz. Of course, Guru's *Jazzmatazz* (1993 and 1995) projects bear crucially on this phenomenon. More overtly experimental or "crossover" artists like Digable Planets and Buckshot Lefonque often bear an interesting relationship to jazz/bohemian rap. They are clearly related at certain stylistic and ideological levels; but they extend some parts of the eclectic stylistic mix to a point where audience reception often places them outside, or at the fringes, of rap music altogether.

[30] The point here is not to privilege a first hearing as somehow providing the most meaningful response to music, as in some so-called "phenomenological" theories of music. Rather, the point is to say that the patterning of Q-Tip's MCing is regular only in the very short run.

[31] All of this is to leave aside the issue of Q-Tip's timbre, which is readily recognizable and widely remarked.

to the more rapid pace of many "reality" rappers), suggest the broad aesthetic navigation of jazz/bohemian rap music. This is consistent with the earlier suggestion that it has become, within rap music, something of an "art music" genre, foregrounding its own eclecticism and appealing to notions of wide-ranging artistic invention.

Topics

The topics addressed in jazz/bohemian songs tend to explain the frequent claims of its being a "conscious" genre, in contrast to the purported limited political vision of other rap genres. [32] On the more didactic side, jazz/bohemian rap emphasizes the value of gaining knowledge, criticizes the assumed "negativity" of some other rap genres, or perhaps promotes Afrocentric values and artistic traditions. When overlapping other genres topically, a jazz/bohemian song might narrate a story to or address a man or women being romanced, or it might toast about an MC's skills (a humorous example of the former being A Tribe Called Quest's "Bonita Appelbaum," from A Tribe Called Quest 1990). Jazz/bohemian has also provided some of rap's more searing parodies, along with alternative portraits of black life capable of exposing what we will call reality rap's "ghettocentricity" and "hardness" as so much dreary posing (which is not to suggest that reality rap is somehow *essentially* that).

De La Soul, for example, has for a long time had the reputation as one of the most savvy critics of so-called "gangsta rap," and their songs about it display the mastery and irony discussed here. The song "Pease Porridge," from *De La Soul Is Dead* (1991), both critiques "hardcore" images in hip-hop culture and challenges those fans who would deny "hardcore" status to artists advocating peace. Their advocacy of "peace," their heavy borrowings from 1960s popular musics (especially on the first, and unexpectedly successful album, *Three Feet High and Rising* 1989), and their albums' and videos' visual style all have lent the group a popular association with hippies (as they acknowledge on the lead song from *De La Soul Is Dead* [1991], "Oodles of O's"). The popular image of hippies – principally, middle-class whites – may seem surprising, especially given the long survival (and consistent popularity) of De La Soul in class- and race-conscious hip-hop culture. Add to this the group's well-known origins in middle-class Amityville, Long Island, and it becomes clear that

---

[32] On the other hand, it might also be fair to speculate that such a label belies one of the great untold stories of hip-hop culture, namely its virtually unrelenting stylistic and historical self-consciousness. Such properties might help to explain Jeffrey Louis Decker's (1993) suggestion that hip-hop black nationalists are precisely Gramsci's "organic intellectuals."

"keeping it real" in this genre is not necessarily a ghettocentric affair. One lesson here, then, is that popular equations of hip-hop culture with an exclusive focus on the ghetto, while certainly containing some truth, tend to focus on generically narrow portions of rap music. Furthermore, the middle-class origins and image of De La Soul could go to reinforce the ideas of some commentators that battles for and against gangsta rap are largely class-driven. De La Soul's critiques of gangsta rap may seem to imply that jazz/bohemian rap can be preachy, and I have heard more than one fan complain along those lines. But in fact, quite a few African-American oral traditions have had primarily didactic functions, as Gates (1988, pp. 75–88) reminds us, and the traditional locus of teaching in poetry is not lost on all rap listeners. Much of that didactic function is visible in rap music, and its continuation may help to explain why what seems to some audiences heavy-handed morality could seem to other audiences a comfortable function of verbal art.[33]

Not only the topics of the jazz/bohemian genre, but also the techniques of tropological signification mark it off from other genres. Artists working within it are known for the complexity and abstraction of their lyrics, with De La Soul in particular often being singled out as, at times, close to incomprehensible. Now, certainly verbal complexity, word games, far-flung similes and metaphors, and more generally, linguistic mastery are valued in all genres, as one might expect from rap's lineage in toasting, sounding, and Signifyin'. And indeed, it would be impossible to establish definitively a yardstick by which jazz/bohemian lyrics may be pronounced "more complex," or "more abstract" than those of other rap genres. But at the same time, the very fact of jazz/bohemian's *reputation* among fans and in the popular media as a more thoughtful, verbally complex form of art contributes to the reputation of certain groups and individuals as thinking person's artists.[34] Black Thought's delivery on the Roots album *Do You Want More?!* (1995) often seems to suggest something as close to beat-poetry as rapping, and the association with

[33] Coolio's "C U When U Get There" (from Coolio 1997), Xzibit's "Paparazzi" (from Xzibit 1996), and Ice Cube's "Doin' Dumb Shit" (from Ice Cube 1991) are all examples of songs about which I have heard such varied reactions. More generally, what might seem like a disingenuous practice, in songs like "Doin' Dumb Shit," of narrating lurid stories of violence followed by a brief moralistic assessment might be taken as less cynical if one keeps in mind the didactic traditions of some African-American oral poetry. Ice Cube (hooks 1994, pp. 125–42), for instance, claims this as one of the motivations behind his gangsta tales. Still, such claims rarely seem to reach popular media coverage of his music.

[34] Mahmoud Abdul-Lateef's (1998) view is not atypical in his discussion of A Tribe Called Quest: "Deconstruction of their lyrics and intricate production is a rite of passage within some circles" (p. 77).

poetic tradition, in turn, may carry with it intimations of "art."[35] It is certainly true that there are artists outside the jazz/bohemian genre whose technical prowess and intellectual abstraction are widely cited: Ras Kass, for example, falls closer to the reality genre, while Common (formerly Common Sense) often seems somewhere on a cusp between the latter and jazz/bohemian.

Reality rap

This last genre brings us to the most culturally charged (and most lucrative) area of the rap music industry, since it includes so-called "gangsta" rap. The latter category of music is called "reality rap" by many of its practitioners, and that is why I am using the term here. "Reality rap," however, refers to a broader field than the narrow term "gangsta rap," if by the latter one understands rap music that describes gang life, or more generally, life in the ghetto from the perspective of a criminal (or liminal, transgressive) figure. Instead, the "reality" may designate any rap that undertakes the project of realism, in the classical sense, which in this context would amount to an epistemological/ontological project to map the realities of (usually black) inner-city life. Those realities might range from the rather fanciful and mystical rhetorical flights of fancy of the Gravediggaz to the more popularly "realistic" portraits of the ghetto proffered by the likes of 2Pac and Mobb Deep. The ideological tendency to naturalize the highly coded construction of that "reality" does not, of course, separate it from classical literary realism (the latter being, after all, one of the great proving grounds of semiotic de-naturalization). Nor does mapping the poetics of that "reality" in any way suggest that there is no reality out there to be reflected. Rather, it stresses the mediation and (above all) the historicity of reality rap's particular means of representation. And, in fact, recognizing that historicity underlines the point that the realism of reality rap cannot ultimately be held simply as some sort of current-day equivalent of literary realism (or, for that matter, the very different photorealism to which the latter is often compared). For even if we may posit some formal equivalence and even some overlap in social mission (such as social betterment via the revelation of some effects of capital), reality rap departs radically from both literary realism and film documentary in its historical situation, and in its situation within the social totality.

The well-known public controversies surrounding so-called "gangsta rap" have such unfortunate prominence in North America

---

[35] The very name of this MC suggests an aura of intellectualism underscored by many aspects of the Roots' music.

(and not without significant racist force, as hooks 1994 has argued), that some context needs to be established. First, reality rap may often share the didactic function normally attributed to the jazz/bohemian genre, but with a different audience.[36] One must certainly allow the most cynical interpretations of reality rap, especially gangsta rap, namely that it is a ploy by record companies to sell records to infatuated teenagers, a modern kind of minstrelsy. And it may indeed be true, as has been widely rumored, that record companies have largely been responsible for pressuring artists to adopt gangsta personae. But at the same time, if there is to be projected some portrait of the lives lived in dangerous and marginal situations by people our society has consigned to ghettos, one must ask whether to expect anything other than a highly mediated representation, embodied in the most lurid commodity form possible. One must also ask whether that representation would thus better be obscured or obliterated.

But the concern here is not so much to question the sincerity of some "authenticity," as if our mission were to find an expression of some internalized characteristic within artists or music. Rather, it is to examine *how* it is (i.e., via the poetics) that the genre is demarcated for whatever social function it might serve. If such an investigation may risk the closure of aesthetic analysis, as the first chapter argued, then the question of broader social function is here only narrowed, not canceled. The following discussions will then allow the poetics described here to take their rightful place in the more general processes of cultural representation.

Musical style

Musical tracks in reality rap have greatly changed over the years, and it is within the genre that one may trace a good many innovations and trends in sampling and (when applicable) instrumental techniques. For example, with Public Enemy and their production team, the Bomb Squad, some of the most extremely complex layering and sampling techniques came, in the late 1980s, to mark out a new musical meaning of rap "hardcore." It is by no historical accident, but rather by fine cultural (and commercial) judgment that Ice Cube chose the Bomb Squad to produce his first solo album after leaving NWA, *AmeriKKKa's Most Wanted* (1990a). And so generalized did that highly diffentiated and densely layered musical texture become, that several years later as far away as Montreal and Eindhoven (the Netherlands), groups like Zero Tolerance and 24K, respectively, deployed the

---

[36] Ice Cube, for instance, claims as much in hooks (1994), pp. 125–43.

musical/production style in their own localized version of hardcore authenticity.

But there have been many different musical styles in reality rap, largely because of its being the locus of so much development and innovation. Indeed, some of rap's most famous producers, from the Bomb Squad through DJ Premier, through the RZA and (to the extent that he works in the genre) Sean "Puffy" Combs (better known as the MC Puff Daddy), have offered their contributions in the reality genre. I would like to suggest, though, that there has been at least one relatively stable ethos in reality rap, even in the midst of all the changes: each successive style of musical tracks marks out, in its specific historical period, something which, in the genre system of its time, connoted "hardness."[37] Now, what could possibly connote such a thing would have to vary with the predominant genre system of the time. Since the present description is of a late 1990s genre system, we would have to specify that the current indices of such hardness include a (pitch-wise) unfocused but dominating bass (both in terms of balance and in terms of predominance in the mix); radically dissonant pitch combinations; and samples that foreground their own deformation and/or degrees of reproduction. The indices of deformation and degrees of reproduction may include pitch instability (as in "Everyday Struggle," from The Notorious B.I.G. 1994), surface (especially vinyl) noise (as in "Take It in Blood," from Nas 1996), timbral distortions, and/or distance in the mix (the last two both figuring prominently in the mix of "Love Comes and Goes," from Ed O. G. and Da Bulldogs 1993).

A record review from *The Source* (the most widely circulating hip-hop magazine) will demonstrate the extent to which audiences are expected by the record industry to invest in the poetics of "hardness":

[Coolio's album] *My Soul* encompasses more of a soulful atmosphere than a [hardcore] hip-hop one with the grooves provided by live musicians. This leads to the loss of the gritty aura often associated with hip-hop releases ... the sound may be too challenging for the modern rap fan. [The album features] far from hardcore beats. (Baker 1997)

Notable here are the association of live instrumentation with an R&B style (described in the earlier discussion here of the mack genre); the contrast of that style to "hardcore" beats; and the reviewer's insinuation that the distance from "hardcore" beats may even prove a

---

[37] Hence my hesitation to admit Puff Daddy's production entirely to this genre, since in many cases, his style has been described as "smooth." One need only listen first to The Notorious B.I.G.'s first album, *Ready to Die* (1994), and then his (largely Puff Daddy-produced) second album, *Life After Death* (1997), to realize that Puff Daddy's production often departs from much of what is taken as "hardcore."

formidable obstacle to the enjoyment of "the modern rap fan" (in itself an interesting collapse of the reality genre onto the world of rap itself).

The "hardness" to be invested in here provides an important link between strictly musico-poetic features (specifically, the assemblage of musical tracks) and more general aesthetic attitudes invested with social and representational value. Chapter 4 will show how this happens in detail; but much more broadly, one may observe in hip-hop culture the centrality of "hardness." The links of that concept, in turn, to ghettocentricity and masculinity have always posed difficulties to women in rap music and hip-hop culture, as has its centrality in constituting hip-hop music, fashion, slang, and identity.[38] What can be added to that well-known picture, then, is that the musical strategies described here (and in the next chapter) are central to constituting "hardness" in fans' musical experiences and investments, and thus to a highly gendered process. In the present genre system, a crucial component of "hardness" may be called the "hip-hop sublime."[39] The hip-hop sublime is a product of dense combinations of musical layers.[40] All of them reinforce the four-beat meter, but in the domain of pitch they comprise a sharply dissonant combination, even by the standards of jazz, or soul, harmony. In fact, layers tend not even to be "in tune," so to speak: they are separated by intervals that can only be measured in terms of fractions of well-tempered semitones. The result is that no pitch combination may form conventionally representable relationships with the others; musical layers pile up, defying aural representability for Western musical listeners.[41] The "detuning" of musical layers just described is a widely used technique of rap musical production, as is dissonant harmonic combination, even within compatibly tuned layers. Another (inseparable) aspect of the hip-hop sublime is timbral: the layers tend to be marked by clashing timbral qualities, often associated with

---

[38] Rose (1994) provides the most comprehensive discussion of the problems of women in hip-hop culture. Another perspective is provided by Sister Souljah (1996).

[39] The phrase "hip-hop" is used rather than "rap" because it is used in other closely related genres, such as hip-hop R&B. For present purposes, though, its principal import is in the context of rap music.

[40] Rose (1994), p. 74, mentions "layering" as one of the fundamental musical procedures in rap music.

[41] The unrepresentable combination of layers should be separated from the African-American musical tradition of expressive pitch-bending. Pitch-bending assumes a fairly constant and unified referential tuning, from which departures are then expressively marked elements. In the present case, each layer is unified in the same way within itself; but the layers remain statically at their own separate pitch levels, never allowing for a referential tuning.

73

varying sound sources (e.g., sampled from a loud vinyl surface, or dubbed from a highly-processed "live" source). The incompatible timbral properties both contribute to the sound sources' aural separation and also form their own sublime counterpart to the incompatible pitch combinations. Both pitch and timbral domains, then, defeat conceptual boundaries and unifying descriptions.

The hip-hop sublime may help to account for the widespread impression that rap music soundscapes sound menacing and aggressive, quite apart from the lyrical content. In such perceptions one can see in the present a return of some classic descriptions of the sublime, especially that of Edmund Burke, which underline that it involves the simultaneous response of fear and pleasure. Fredric Jameson (1991), in a project that updates Burke for an articulation of postmodern culture, describes how the sublime "takes its object as the pretext and the occasion for the intuition through it and beyond it of sheer unfigurable force itself, sheer power, that which stuns the imagination in the most literal sense" (p. 34). Burke's and Jameson's characterizations of the sublime are, I would like to posit, important indicators of how the incommensurate layering in rap production comes to imply "hardness" and "realness." For if the consumption of such production techniques involves both an "unfigurable force" of layering combination and a pleasure of stunned musical imagination, then we are dealing with a specifically musical sublime. Adding in the fact that this production style has become an important indicator of the "reality" in reality rap, one can see how intimately the musical poetics in this music converses with semantic and representational issues.

As will turn out to be the case with MCing styles, West Coast rap deserves special mention in any discussion of reality rap's musical strategies. For one of the great commercial presences in the history of rap music has been G-funk, a style of generally West Coast rap whose musical tracks tend to deploy live instrumentation, heavy on bass and keyboards, with minimal (sometimes no) sampling and often highly conventional harmonic progressions and harmonies. Dre's *The Chronic* (1992) serves as a milestone in G-funk, as well as releases from Snoop Doggy Dogg and the Dogg Pound, some Ice Cube releases like Ice Cube (1993), and a good many others. Given the description just offered of the consistent hardness ethos in reality rap, G-funk can clearly be seen as anomalous. Now, one could argue at this point that the anomaly is simply a result of the limitations of my description in the first place, so why not simply add characteristics of G-funk to the list of musical hardness-indicators, and have done with the issue? My objection would be that outside of the context of G-funk many of its musical characteristics are in fact *not* indices of hardness, but rather of something else, whether it be the distinct style/genre of mack rap (e.g., Too $hort), or the dubiously and shiftingly constituted category of "commercial" rap (e.g., Salt 'n' Pepa, or Puff Daddy). The record review (of Coolio's *My Soul*) quoted on p. 72 above, for example, leaves little doubt how close some characteristics of G-funk might come to invoking a judgment of "not hardcore" – for G-funk, of course, a potentially deadly judgment. The seeming inconsistency between G-funk's musical sound and its realness value underlines that geography constitutes at all times a tremendously powerful force in rap music. Its force crisscrosses musical styles in uneven ways, sometimes reinforcing it, and sometimes carving out its own parameters. In this case, the location of "West Coast" would serve to license the sounds of G-funk as appropriately hardcore. Let G-funk, then, be noted as a strong reminder, in this discussion of style and genre, of the dangers of taking those two categories as somehow internally determined and autonomous. Rather, just when we may be feeling the seduction of turning discussions of genre, style, and musical poetics into closed systems, the localized real social deployment is sure to return and disrupt our will to systematize too locally. And in this case, what a powerful reappearance it is – G-funk has been, for many years, one of the great driving forces, in commercial terms, in the rap music industry.

Flow

The flows of reality rap have provided the most elaborate MCing rhythms in the entire field of rap music. If there is a flow (or are flows) endemic to the genre, at least since 1993 or so, then it is most certainly speech-effusive. That having been specified, it is worth noting that the other effusive style, percussion-effusive, tends not to mark out any particular genre, but rather to cross-cut rap genres and mark out the ideologically central category of "personal style." So, Treach of Naughty by Nature (generically somewhere between party and reality genres), KRS-One (reality genre), and Ice-T (mack genre) are all marked by percussive deliveries which lend their voices almost instrumental properties. Thus, one could not single out (for example) reality rap as particularly characterized by percussion-effusive MCing. The definitions work in the other direction: reality rap is indeed characterized by effusive MCing, whether percussive-, speech-, or both.

Some of the most stunning virtuosic verbal performances, from AZ to Ras Kass to the RZA, have arisen as "faster cadences" and "new rhyme patterns" (as Marriott 1997 put it) have become emblematic of reality rap. Some oral traditions in hip-hop history trace the speech-effusive style back to KRS-One, whose LP (with Boogie Down Productions) *Criminal Minded* (1987) is, perhaps not coincidentally, also frequently cited as the first gangsta-rap album. Also frequently mentioned is the Freestyle Fellowship, or, interestingly, even some Southern artists and traditions. In any case, it probably makes little sense to identify it as an individual effort rather than a broader change in rap's aesthetic strategies. One can see speech-effusive styles not only in the work of artists who have always been squarely in the reality genre, but also in the stylistic mutations of more venerable artists whose careers have stretched across genres. In fact, the spread of speech-effusive flow across generic divides may serve to indicate the cultural and commercial strength of reality rap within the overall rap genre system, not to mention hip-hop culture overall.[42] Veteran MCs such as Parrish Smith (of the recently re-formed EPMD), Queen Latifah, Guru (of Gangstarr) and MC Lyte, among others, could all provide ample illustration of the extent to which speech-effusive technique has come to mark out a significant space of rap poetics; for their own flows have developed noticeably in that direction over the years.

So far, the discussion has focused on speech-effusive style; but a certain extreme of *percussion*-effusive delivery also may mark out *geographic* stylistic differences.[43] Geography will be the focus of Chapter 4, but it needs to be raised briefly here. For there are certain regions of the United States whose best-known MCs rap in a manner rhythmically both rigid and internally highly varied, alternating among clusters of even quarter-, eighth-, and sixteenth-, and other duply-divided note values. Often, the quickest note values will arrive in a group on the downbeat. The result of such a technique is a sound somewhat approaching a rapidly tapped-out drum patterning, or, alternately, a manic and rhythmically unpredictable singing style. Perhaps the best-known example of this is the highly commercially successful Cleveland group Bone Thugs 'N' Harmony. Their MCing is, in fact, mainly pitched, but in melodic patterns whose pitches themselves change slowly and move in tight ranges, especially compared to the lightning-fast and highly varied rhythm of the note attacks.[44] The group's MCing demonstrates what was observed

---

[42] This is not prematurely to totalize either the market or a closed hip-hop culture as the sole motivators of musical poetics. Indeed, it may well be the case that the artists discussed here find themselves quite willingly adopting new styles and challenges for a variety of reasons. Still, one might consider conceiving the market as a conduit for musical poetics.

[43] Those differences, otherwise conceived, might be deemed sub-genres; but for the focus of this book, it will be more useful to concentrate on geography.

[44] The group now live and record in Los Angeles, and in fact, while their MCing style

earlier, namely that percussion-effusive styles may, in fact, achieve something of an *opposite* effect to speech-effusive styles in a certain respect: it may *distance* the MCing from any resemblance to speech. In terms of the semantic topics the group addresses, Bone Thugs 'N' Harmony fall squarely into the reality genre, perhaps even gangsta rap. And yet the flow, especially the rapid pitched delivery, marks the group out geographically from both New York and Los Angeles reality rap. Other places also seem marked by reality rappers with special percussion-effusive deliveries. Chicago, for example, has produced Crucial Conflict, while New Orleans has produced Mystikal, and Atlanta has produced Outkast. In all these cases, the MC(s) rap rhythmic patterns that, if spoken American (including Ebonic) English is taken as "natural," could only be called, by contrast, "stylized" or "musical." The rhythms are rapid, often producing constant alternations between, on the one hand, groups of quick and even attacks, and on the other hand, slower and more differentiated rhythmic values, sometimes leading to outright singing. The artists and places just named, taken together, might seem to suggest that the extreme end of percussion-effusive styles is not particularly demarcated geographically. But in fact, that is not true, in an important respect. For New York, the mythical cradle of hip-hop culture, is remarkably free (at least in commercial terms) of such extreme percussion-effusive MCs. Insofar as New York MCs are effusive in any way, it is the speech-effusive style that characterizes that city (for example, in the rapping of Nas, Big Pun, Jay-Z, AZ, and various members of the Wu-Tang Clan).[45] So certain over-the-top percussion-effusive styles could indeed be said to mark out an MC geographically, albeit negatively as "not-New York." Chapter 4 will argue that this, in itself, is a significant category in the rap music industry. Overarching the geographic markings, though, for the purposes of genre classification, *some* sort of effusive MCing style, whether percussion- or speech-, tends to mark out the genre of reality rap.

On the topic of geographic marking, and further to the topic of MCing styles in reality rap, West Coast, and particularly Los Angeles, reality rap deserves special mention (as in the case of musical style). For the speech-effusive styles of reality rap are not necessarily endemic to West Coast artists. In fact, the more generalized cultural

may carry connotations of their origins, the musical tracks to their work, much of it produced by the late West Coast producer (and former NWA member) Eazy-E, foreground their adopted city. Still, the group retain representations of their native city's locality, sometimes calling their style the "Cleveland sound."

[45] Certainly, the converse would not be true: there are speech-effusive MCs from outside New York.

representations of California as "laid-back" are figured symbolically in the generally slower and more sung MCing rhythms. Mack 10 (in songs like "Backyard Boogie") can be cited, for example, as an artist with a high proportion of end-rhymes arriving in couplets, a relatively slow delivery, and "sung" rhythms. Thus, the aesthetic ethos of "laid-back" West Coast rap (often discussed in such terms in the rap media and by fans) finds its embodiment in MCing styles, including those of reality rap.[46] Furthermore, the well-known car culture of Los Angeles, and the representations thereof, cannot be separated from both the idea of life-pace and the slow funk groves of West Coast G-funk.

Topics

Topics of reality rap do vary greatly, but few of them are inconsistent with Robin D. G. Kelley's (1994) assertion of rap music's "ghettocentricity." But while Kelley's term is applied to rap music in general, I would argue that it is particularly relevant to this genre. While the swaggering, toasting, confrontational lyrics describing gang/criminal life are perhaps the best-known variety, laments are not uncommon (such as the Geto Boys' "Ghetto Fantasy" from Geto Boys 1996, Ice Cube's "Dead Homiez" from Ice Cube 1990b, Scarface's "Smile" from Scarface 1997, or 2Pac Shakur's "Dear Mama" from Shakur 1995). Lust/macking songs abound, which nevertheless remain distinct from the mack genre, examples being Raekwon's "Ice Cream" and Ghostface Killa's "Camay." An entire sub-genre exists, as well, that often focuses on didactic, political functions, with Afrocentric and Five Percent Nation (and/or Nation of Islam) ideologies forming a background for lessons on both history and the present. Nostalgia is an emerging topic, especially now that hip-hop culture seems to have entered a period when the "old school" and the historicity of rap music in general are increasingly prominent. The nostalgia can be personal or collective, although it is rarely one or the other exclusively; Ice Cube's "Dumb Shit" might tend toward the former category, while the Alkaholiks' "Flashback" presents a more resolutely collective image of hip-hop origins.

Semantic topics in reality rap tend, more than in other genres, to determine the style of the musical tracks. The hip-hop sublime most often accompanies "hardcore" topics (i.e., those dealing with "street life," gang life, and the threatening aspects of inner-city existence). Thus, "Can It Be All So Simple (Remix)," from Raekwon's *Only Built 4 Cuban Linx* (1995), images the place being described with generically

---

[46] Ras Kass can be counted as an exception, his flow more resembling that of some of the more effusive New York MCs. So, to some extent, could the Luniz.

appropriate musical tracks. On the other hand, the lamentation topics (such as in 2Pac Shakur's "Life Goes On" in Shakur 1996, and Master P's "I Miss My Homies" in Master P 1997) may well invoke rock- or R&B-ballad styles, as might the more moralizing topics on ghetto life (such as Common's "Retrospect for Life" from Common Sense 1997 with its gospel-flavored soul musical tracks).

The mack topics within reality rap seem to take one of two directions. Either they will involve a funk/R&B style that raises the question of a temporary bridging into the mack genre itself (such as in The Notorious B.I.G.'s "Playa Hater" from Notorious B.I.G. 1997), or they will remain, in terms of musical tracks, closer to the mainstream musical strategies of reality rap (i.e., the "hip-hop sublime"), as in Ghostface Killa's "Camay" (from Ghostface Killa 1996) or Raekwon's "Ice Cream" (from Raekwon 1995).

Another sub-genre of reality rap, though, is generally demarcated not by musical style, but rather simply by its semantic aspects, and that is one we might call "knowledge" rap. Its distinctive aspects are confined to its focus on political or historical tales, religious lessons, or other didactic modes of information. Thus, semantically this sub-genre has a great deal in common with much jazz/bohemian rap, but with musical tracks and flow more in keeping with reality rap.[47] It is in this sub-genre, as well, that the influence of the Nation of Islam has been remarked.[48] Generally overlooked, though, is the at least equally prominent presence of the Five Percent Nation religion.[49] Signaling that presence, in many cases, are lyrics rife with numerology, references to racial evolutionary theories, and references to black men as "god." Much of the music of the Gravediggaz (e.g., "Fairytalez" from their 1997 second album) would serve to illustrate, as would a good deal of music by the RZA (from the Wu-Tang Clan).

As with jazz/bohemian rap, knowledge rap may usefully be related

---

[47] It might seem that the inclusion of knowledge rap in the reality rap genre indicates a preference of musical tracks and flow over semantic reference, in my articulation of generic categories. In fact, however, my setting of knowledge as a sub-genre of reality rap is more based on the artists whose repertory includes both and very few, if any, other, genres. Such artists' repertory thus forms something of a practical linkage of knowledge rap to other forms of reality rap. Some examples are (early) Ice Cube, Killah Priest, and Ras Kass.

[48] Decker (1994), for example, discusses this.

[49] A Five Percent Nation website (http://sunsite.unc.edu/nge) claims a remarkable number of well-known artists as either affiliates or at least sympathetic. Brand Nubian is best known for propagating Five Percent Nation ideology, as are artists like the Poor Righteous Teachers and the X-Clan. But even less overtly religious artists like the Wu-Tang Clan and Ras Kass are not without manifestations of at least Five-Percent-Nation rhetoric. Although the website's list is perhaps to some extent wishful, in many cases the artists' own lyrics confirm the claim to some extent.

to traditional didactic functions of African-American oral traditions, but it may also be related to more contemporary and commercial forces. In particular, there is a certain subset of rap fans for whom the music bears a mission of spiritual/cultural elevation. That phenomenon itself is inseparable from an end-of-the-twentieth-century development of Afrocentric thought, including a serious investment in the possibilities of rap music for communication and social transformation.

The rap genre system, history, and representation

The above outline lays out a field for discussion of musical representation in rap music. It should be clear by now that the phrase "in rap music" does *not* mean "embedded right there in the sounds," but rather means "mediated by sounds and their socially situated interpretations." And indeed, the genre system just outlined forms a crucial aspect of the social situation by which rap music becomes social action; other aspects will be discussed, in the course of this book, in more particular contexts.

The phrase "genre system" just invoked, though, raises the question of a systematic relation among the genres enumerated. And indeed, one enabling premise of this whole discussion has been the notion of the genre system itself, defined as a field of production and consumption in which relations among genres are defined, maintained, and often transformed. Those relations, in turn, enable the constructions of identity which are more properly the objects of much work in cultural studies. So it is worthwhile to outline the parameters implied in the phrase "genre system."

Fredric Jameson (1990) invokes a relevant context in a discussion of classic Hollywood film, in which he explores some analyses of representation either in individual films or in the broader genre of classic Hollywood realism. Responding to such projects, he asserts:

It is only at the level of [genre] systems that the ultimate relationship between genre and representation (or the illusion of reality) can be grasped ... [Jameson's] presupposition is that the ideological conception of "reality" or the "literal," let alone of verisimilitude, is not particularly operative within any of the individual genres taken by itself ... What the project of a genre system implies rather is that the reality socially constructed by Hollywood "realism" is a map whose coordinates are parcelled out among the specific genres, to whose distinct registers are then assigned its various dimensions or specialized segments. The "world" is then not what is represented in romantic comedy or *film noir*: but it is what is somehow governed by all of them together ... and governed also, something more difficult to think, by their implicit generic relationships to each other. The unreal – the not-said, the repressed – is then what falls outside the system as a whole and finds no place in it ...   (pp. 175–6)

Jameson is correct about the difficulty of thinking through the implicit relationships of genre in classic Hollywood film; and the difficulty may be said to be even more extreme in the case of rap music. In the latter, very little scholarly attention has been paid to its genres, let alone its genre system. The word "scholarly" is surely operative, here, since genre works crucially on an everyday basis in fans' pronouncements that one artist or another is a "gangsta" rapper, or that some MC is too "commercial" and "dance-oriented" for that fan's taste. Such remarks are not simply about musical style or visual imagery. On the contrary, they much more broadly refer to a field in which somehow Puff Daddy and Ma$e are grouped as similar, while Ras Kass and AZ are also grouped as similar. Aesthetic, moral, and representational values are mobilized to mark their similarity-categories as carrying some very specific cultural weight.

I would like to posit here that the concept of a rap genre system will be needed to tell just such kinds of stories about the music's history and its present, and thus, that a genre system is needed to understand representation in the present. The *differentiality* of judgments about genre underlines that the individual genres just described do not work in isolation from each other; instead, they operate by sets of contrasts to each other. Those contrasts are not in any respect static, but they are at any given point well known to artists, record companies, and audiences. As a concrete illustration, it should suffice to consider the fates of classic gangsta and mack rap since the former's major commercial advent in 1989, the year that NWA's *Straight Outta Compton* (1989) was released.[50] First, let us consider the situation until roughly 1993. Representations of gang/street life in gangsta rap circulated among well-defined semantic parameters: there were boasts about physical/violent/gun prowess, boasts about the "hardness" of a particular location (e.g., Compton, Houston, or some borough of New York), narratives about criminal life, satires of "mainstream" society through gangsta eyes (e.g., Ice Cube's "A Gangsta's Fairytale" from *AmeriKKKa's Most Wanted* [1990a]), bonding gestures with a particular posse, and other formats that projected a "realistic" image of the hand-to-mouth (and "gat"-in-hand) socially marginal, transgressive (generally male) gangsta.[51] In addition, there was frequently explicitly political commentary on institutions (such as

[50] There are legitimate claims by, for example, Schoolly D to be the first true gangsta rapper, while others cite KRS-One (for Boogie Down Productions' [1987] *Criminal Minded*) or Ice-T. But surely, NWA's first album marked the genre's explosion onto the commercial scene, and that is the important consideration here.

[51] Kelley (1997, pp. 15–42) provides an important historicizing critique of the black

81

the police, the various levels of government, and racism itself) which had failed inner-city African-Americans. In the realm of musical tracks, generically appropriate "hard" beats were characterized by increasingly dissonant and stark combinations of tracks, along with slower tempi. Flows were marked by their effusiveness, first percussion-effusion and then increasingly speech-effusion.

In the meantime, the mack genre combined the sexual politics of exploitation and scopo(phono?)philia with the pleasures of transgressive conspicuous (often exaggerated) commodity consumption. Thus, MCs such as Too $hort and Sir Mix-A-Lot rarely boasted much about their localities or a posse. Instead, they inclined toward the image of the lone hustler, with endless sexual prowess and desire, control over large numbers of women, and at least the external trappings of wealth with which both to manifest and to perpetuate the whole package. Explicit social commentary was rare, as the figure of the sexually and financially powerful individual seemed to preclude too sharp a focus on community and political contexts.[52] Musical tracks tended toward funk, live instrumentation, lush textures (by rap standards, anyway), and consonant combinations. And flow was markedly sung, even resolutely so.

The relations between representation in the two genres may then be said to have consisted of certain basic contrasts. In gangsta rap, one confronted the social unit of the posse, images of violence, oblique or direct social engagement, "hard" beats, and effusive flows.[53] In mack rap, on the other hand, one would find the social unit of the individual (super-)powerful male, the flaunting of wealth and sexuality, minimal social engagement, "smooth" funk and R&B musical styles, and sung flows. Of course, as with any such system of contrasts, there were mixed and ambiguous cases; but such cases nevertheless (often self-consciously) referred to just such remarkably stable sets of contrasts.

The "implicit generic relationships," then, to use Jameson's formulations, were drawn, on both semantic and musico-poetic levels, rather sharply.[54] But somewhere in the early- to mid-1990s (say,

---

gangsta figure and a genealogy of its prominence in the (especially) American imagination.

[52] Thus, much of the mainstream media (and intelligentsia) may be said to have missed the boat in targeting gangsta rap as nihilistic, when, in fact, mack rap would have been a much more reasonable target for such critiques.

[53] Significantly, the posse itself, rather than the often socially devastated surrounding community, comes to stand metonymically for the locality. The formation of an inner-city gang as a substitute family and community has been too often reiterated in social science and popular representations to call for elaboration here. Suffice it to say that in classic gangsta rap the symbolic substitution was often complete.

[54] Jameson means, of course, more than that by "implicit generic relationships," since

around 1993 or so, although too clean a periodization would miscast the gradualness of the development) that relationship started to shift. Its shifting illustrates the *systematicity* itself of generic relations in commercial rap music. For around that time, a new genre started to emerge which combined elements of both gangsta and mack raps, and which can be called, for lack of a current popular term, don rap (as in a Mafia Don).[55] This new genre combines, on the semantic and imagistic levels, the dominating imagery and toasting of the older gangsta genre with the wealth, individuality, and personal "smoothness" of the older mack genre.[56] The persona of the crime boss provides the perfect nexus of transgressive domination and conspicuous consumption, and hence both the frequency and the popularity of crime-boss images. One could adduce as examples figures such as the Wu-Tang's "Wu-Gambino" personae (Johnny Blaze, Tony Starks, etc.) on Raekwon's (1995) album, and on the Wu-Tang's second (double) album, *Wu-Tang Forever* (1997); The Notorious B.I.G., especially in *Life After Death* (1997), but also as early as "Juicy" from *Ready to Die* (1994); Puff Daddy and Ma$e; the Firm (Foxy Brown, Nas, and AZ, including their solo work); the Dogg Pound; some work of Dr. Dre and Snoop Doggy Dogg (including the latter's tellingly titled *Tha Doggfather* 1996); Jay-Z; the (also tellingly named) Junior M.A.F.I.A. (including solo work by Lil' Kim); Master P (e.g., in Master P 1998); recent Ice Cube; and quite a few others. And this is only to name the more commercially successful examples. In all these cases and more, one cannot claim simply the older flaunting of commodified life that characterized the pimp figure, though most certainly that element is present. Rather, purely on the semantic level, at least two factors separate don rap markedly from, say, the older narratives of Ice-T, Too $hort, or, for that matter, Iceberg Slim. For one thing, don rap, like gangsta rap, may foreground criminal activity, violence, and domination (as in the lyrics and video of the Firm's "Firm Biz" 1998). But unlike the case of gangsta rap, such imagery is framed more and more as fantasized and spectacular. It is the fantasy-framing of don rap, with its anti-verisimilitude and often-playful jumble of popular-culture references, that separates it both from mack

the context for his discussion is modalities of representation. That more abstract level of generic relationship will come into sharper focus in later chapters, as aspects of identity formation.

[55] The title of Master P's (1998) album *MP Da Last Don* is only one of the more explicit references to the existence of this new genre.

[56] The existence and commercial presence of the new genre is signaled in a historicizing remark by Styles of The Lox, when he says "Back then, to be hardcore, you had to come with an army suit or sweatshirt. Now you can be hardcore – fly, a lady's man – and still sell records" (Simpson 1998, p. 98).

rap and from the earlier gangsta rap. In fact, the ambiguous propriety of calling don rap "reality rap," as apologists for gangsta rap often did to the genre they were defending, illustrates a profound shift in the mode of representation. That shift, in turn, suggests that although don rappers are often still called "gangsta rappers," something has taken place that undermines such a designation.[57] "Incarcerated Scarfaces" from Raekwon's *Only Built 4 Cuban Linx* (1995) could be invoked as an illustration, its title alone indicating a vein of film-inspired fantasy that runs through the album and helps to establish the don ethos. Its last verse offers quick references to "Lou Ferigno on coke," "Arabs . . . coolin' like Kahluas in rocks," "bitches who fuck dreds on Sudafeds," and a crowning claim that "I seen it, like a 27-inch Zenith – believe it!" Remarkable here is not only the sublime, hyper-quick collage of popular-cultural references, but also the final line, in which the bottom epistemological line emerges: the truth there is gauged by its appearance on a large (and, of course, expensive) television set. We are not in "reality rap" anymore.

But the semantic level is not the only one on which the generic hybridization occurs. The possibilities for musical tracks have shifted from the earlier genres of gangsta and mack raps, along with the characters, images, and poetics of representation. As was discussed above, before the advent of don rap, the genres of gangsta and mack rap maintained fairly discrete normative practices, and the musical style of one would be anomalous in the other. But with the emergence of don rap, the possibilities for the musical tracks expand. Along with the more fantastic modes of semantic representation, a flexibility develops in the musical styles, forming a counterpart to the flexibility in the variety and forms of social representation in don rap. If the standard of adequacy to the life of "real" gangstas or "real" street hustlers no longer applies, then the corresponding limits on the musical styles have similarly loosened; or, to put things more concretely, if an acceptable figure for "hardcore" rap may be AZ as a crime-boss figure (as in much of AZ 1995), then the lavish semantic imagery may call for lavish musical tracks (as in the album's single "Sugar Hill").[58] So it is that musical tracks in don rap not only

---

[57] That the shift has not been total is illustrated by the fact that gangsta rap, in the older sense, does still exist and even constitutes a substantial commercial presence. The No-Limit family (e.g., Master P) and Mobb Deep suffice to illustrate this (although the former do often seem to verge over into the newer don formation, including, of course, Master P 1998).

[58] There are many aspects of musical tracks that are not foregrounded in this kind of discussion. For instance, the well-known competitiveness among DJs to find obscure and interesting older tracks to sample forms an aspect of track-building that often criss-crosses generic designation in complex, unpredictable ways. In addition, some producers may have certain "signature" sounds that override generic dynamics. The

embrace all the possibilities of the earlier gangsta and mack genres; they also allow (among other things) for much of the recycling of 1970s and 1980s Top 40 (and not particularly black-identified) hits which have been so remarked in recent rap music.

The fantastic commercial success of Puff Daddy, for instance, including as a producer for artists generally deemed "gangsta" rappers like The Notorious B.I.G., indicates that overtly dance-oriented musical tracks, as well as "smooth" hip-hop R&B tracks, formerly taboo to the authenticity of "reality rap," can, in fact, be widely accepted in don rap.[59] It is not difficult to believe that the R&B tracks common in the mack genre in some way paved the way for this, especially since the dance-oriented tracks on *Life After Death* (1997) alternate with songs whose musical tracks suggest strongly the gangsta genre (such as "Ten Crack Commandments," significantly produced by prominent reality-rap producer DJ Premier). But musical tracks are not the only musical poetics going on, and Biggie Small's flow, rhythmic style (effusive), and semantic topics all preclude the possibility that he is "going pimp." Rather, taken together, the music tracks and the flow force us to consider that we are encountering a new genre to which elements of the older gangsta and mack genres are not at all foreign but to which neither is adequate.

Sometimes don rap may avoid dance style but nevertheless mark itself through (pimp-style) R&B tracks. AZ's "Sugar Hill" (from the 1995 album *Doe or Die*) foregrounds what could have long been apparent in mack rap, namely how lush musical textures, R&B harmonies, and a slow tempo may connote the object-world of luxury. In fact, such a well-established connotation – also noticeable in *Ready to Die*, not to mention the music of many of the don MCs just listed – is probably a key to understanding how readily don rap has expanded the musical-track possibilities over the earlier "hardcore" reality rap. "Sugar Hill" also serves well to illustrate another notable aspect of musical form in don rap, namely the vastly greater prevalence, compared to earlier genres, of (generally woman-sung) R&B-style choruses. The popularity of such choruses is all the more remarkable when one recalls how just a few short years before the

RZA is one such producer (along with some of his production disciples), and the Wu-Tang family is generally exempted from the opening-up of musical-track possibilities being discussed here.

[59] Chapter 3 elaborates on the gangsta taboo against dance-oriented tracks, in the context of Ice Cube's establishing of a specific identity. By "dance-oriented," I am referring to musical tracks with relatively triadic harmony, few layers, little variability in the layering, and, perhaps most important, a faster tempo than in most rap music. As in the case of persona, Styles of The Lox historicizes the new hardcore acceptance of R&B: "A few years ago in Hip-Hop, you was dissin' R&B. Now the hottest thing you can do is go in the studio and get with an R&B person" (Simpson 1998, p. 98).

advent of don rap, singing, not to mention a substantial female presence of any sort, had been the mark of "softer" styles. That mark, of course, had served to threaten the masculine-identified reality rap authenticity.[60]

Flows in don rap are generally speech-effusive, and this can be seen as a major point of input from gangsta rap style. The complex rhythmic relationships and uneven proportions of speech-effusive flows, in fact, come, in the new genre, to bear more variable relationships to the rest of the musical activity, since the musical tracks have themselves become so much more varied compared to gangsta rap. In dance-oriented songs like The Notorious B.I.G.'s "Hypnotize" from *Ready to Die*, or in R&B-laced songs like "Sugar Hill," the speech-effusive rhythmic "edginess" is significantly undercut for a radio-friendly effect (and, indeed, the former, especially, was extremely successful as a single).[61] In songs that take over more of the musical strategies of reality rap, like Raekwon's aforementioned "Wu-Gambinos," the speech-effusive deliveries will find their counterpart in a more generalized sublime already familiar from post-NWA gangsta rap.

The exposition just offered of don rap suggests that the rap genre system is capable of major transformations, as genre systems, of course, generally are. Nevertheless, it should be underlined that the emergence of a new genre does not necessarily suggest the death of earlier genres. Rather, a new *dominant* may be emerging in the larger genre system.[62] Mobb Deep and the No-Limit "family" of artists have already been mentioned as continuing representatives of gangsta rap, to which may be added some of 2Pac Shakur's thriving artistic afterlife. G-funk gangsta style remains audible in some music of Snoop Doggy Dogg, the Dogg Pound, Dr. Dre, and Mack 10, among others. All this is not to mention the work of artists already discussed that remain at times in the gangsta genre, such as The Notorious B.I.G.

---

[60] Indeed, woman-sung choruses in reality rap before, say, the epitome of G-funk's fame, were relatively rare. When they did appear, furthermore, they were often in the mode of parody, such as in Ice Cube's "Giving Up the Nappy Dugout," from *Death Certificate* (1991).

[61] The video for "Hypnotize" illustrates, in an exemplary manner, the new kinds of representation already identified in don rap. The gangsta imagery, far from a ghetto situation, is imbricated in imagery of transgressive wealth (a yacht, a Mercedes), while the fantastic car-chase scenario emphasizes a regime of verisimilitude quite distanced from that of reality rap.

[62] Raymond Williams (1977) suggests viewing cultural change as a matter of the rise and decline of various "dominants." Such culturally powerful tendencies may be compared to "residual" (i.e., still present, having earlier been dominant) and "emergent" (i.e., nascent) social relations. A good brief explanation of the concepts can be found in Williams (1981), pp. 203–5.

in the "Ten Crack Commandments," which appears on the same (double) album (1997) as "Hypnotize."

The last observation brings us to a point that cannot be overemphasized, namely that like many popular albums, rap LPs only very rarely instantiate one genre. Rather, full-length albums tend to mix genres. This is particularly true of "hardcore" artists, whose albums may alternate several of the genres discussed here. It would not be accurate, though, to suggest that rap albums thereby form microcosms of the rap genre system. For in virtually all cases, there is a predominant genre which helps to classify the artist and/or the album overall. Hence the ridiculousness, for example, of a hypothetical attempt to identify Lil' Kim as a jazz/bohemian MC, or dub Busta Rhymes a mack MC, although each has some individual songs arguably in those genres. The rap genre system, then, should not be described as relating artists as monads to other artists as monads. Rather, the system could be said to relate either individual songs to each other, those songs themselves having fairly stable, if hybrid, generic identifications, or the predominant generic identities of artists to each other. In fact, both views of genre – as registers of songs and as registers of predominant tendencies of artists – would seem to have their moments of truth. Their particular truths come into focus when we recall and adapt Jameson's view that the genre system in classic Hollywood film parcels out the field of representation – i.e., parcels out whatever is being presented as "reality." By inference, any individual genre signifies (among other things) in *relation* to the others, and in terms of a larger dynamic that is always functional (if generally as any unitary term). Given that as a context, what is significant in any particular rap album may be the genres that are excluded, the parts that are left out of the implicit system of reference. Thus, for example, A Tribe Called Quest's *Beats, Rhymes, and Life* (1996) can be cited as excluding the reality genre (or, by my own arguments, also the don genre) and the mack genre, as well. The party and jazz/bohemian genres, then, predominate. It is therefore perhaps not surprising that fans of that group tend to lament (what they see as) the dominance of gangsta rap in hip-hop culture, as well as the misogyny and preoccupation with wealth of much rap music. The group's lyrics and public remarks reinforce such views of hip-hop culture and rap music. An ethos is thus created by which entertainment (the party genre) and education (the jazz/bohemian genre) become the authentic mission of rap music and hip-hop culture, from which reality rap may be cast as a commercialized and denigrated deviation. In other words, the album's position within rap's genre system enables a positionality of fandom, embracing a selective portion of the total field of representation available in the broader genre system. Of course, it enables a positionality of fandom not so much by "convincing" fans as by appealing to a certain self-selecting group of fans. But then, the music also reinforces fans' views of rap authenticity.[63] Similarly, A Tribe Called Quest, as artists, are consistent with respect to genre systems. Their public personae (or, as Goodwin 1992, pp. 98–130, would put it, their "star texts") may more generally be referred to a certain part of the generic constellation.

From this scenario, it may be inferred that generic positioning also implies regimes of authenticity. This should not be surprising, if indeed we take as a premise the notions about representation of reality borrowed from Jameson. And indeed, we may even speculate that the link to some purported authenticity is one of the things that kept the musical tracks in reality rap within certain parameters for quite a while, excluding, for example, the R&B styles that were deemed too "soft" for the genre. The change with respect to acceptable musical style had to wait for the advent of don rap and the changes of generic parameters. So, while it may be true that genres carry within them their own regimes of authenticity and representation, it may also be said that those regimes, in turn, remain *relational* to the genre system as a whole. The system, in turn, partitions formal and semantic aspects of rap music, which may then be redistributed in certain strategic ways by artists, record companies, and consumers.

A change somewhere in the genre system of rap music will fan its effects out across the system, leaving nothing ultimately untouched. Queen Latifah may be offered as an example. Her 1998 album *Order in the Court* (e.g., the song "Bananas") amply illustrates how her technique has changed since her earlier music, and how much more her rhythmic technique has come to resemble that of more reality-identified artists and their speech-effusive flows. But her status as a "reality" MC – at least, as implied in her flow – conflicts to some extent both with her earlier "star text" and with the semantic reference of her lyrics. By the latter's measure, and by her historical association with the so-called Native Tongues movement and groups like A Tribe Called Quest and De La Soul, she would seem more categorizable as a jazz/bohemian artist. Her generic conflictedness, though, may well illustrate precisely the effects of a genre system. The generic location of most of her best-known earlier work is one we might call Afrocentric positivity within the jazz/bohemian genre (and very much the spirit of the Native Tongues movement itself). Such a

---

[63] The dynamic being described here bears some relation to Thornton's (1996) description of subcultural capital, and its relation to notions of authenticity and commerciality. Her insistence on media complicity can also be maintained in the present context.

generic location barely existed by 1998 in its earlier form (insofar as it remained, having been absorbed into the broader jazz/bohemian genre). Her former sung delivery, her heavily didactic, somewhat feminist (or, at least, woman power) topics and her clear, percussion-heavy textures had outlined, during her greatest popularity in the late 1980s and early 1990s, a socially conscious and engaged stance. She stood in exemplary opposition to the subjugation of women in hip-hop culture and society in general, and as a model of a certain Afrocentrism. But such a stance having lost its generic home, the 1998 Queen Latifah found herself in the throes of a new genre system, with a new public identity to build musically. Her new and more speech-effusive style marked that new situation.

If the rap genre system distributes regimes of authenticity, then it will be recalled from earlier in this chapter that the distribution occurs in several parameters, among them geography. Since a good deal of this book is concerned with illustrating that point, I will only add here that the genre system being discussed almost always finds its local inflection. Only in the homogenization of mass-distributed rap music could such a thing as a clear genre system be found in a "pure" form. But precisely because of the music industry's mass status, such a system will form something of a culturally acquired background to local interpretations, inflections, and, indeed, deflections. This is quite a different matter from saying that it is imposed from above without any degree of receptive/creative alteration; on the contrary, some such alterations will be outlined in later discussions of rap music in Edmonton and Amsterdam.

Afternote on genre

It has been much remarked, in popular music scholarship and else-where, that genres are constantly shifting entities, guidelines at best. They are not universally shared and yet they remain indispensable for approaching the uses of music. Furthermore, the scholar proposing to outline a set of related genres encounters the problem posed by the very positing of something like an overarching abstract principle. On the level of methodology, what has been more thoroughly and power-fully critiqued in the humanities in the last twenty years or so than the notion of a signifying system, presumably a relic of the days of structuralism, at best? On the other hand, it has equally been remarked that we cannot simply dismiss categories as if it were possible to purge language and thought of their contradictions and aporias by fiat. Thus, abstract principles and categories continue to be used by scholars on all parts of the methodological spectrum, with the signal difference from earlier practice that the categories are somehow *bracketed*, be it as "discourse," as "provisional," and so on. My own positing of genres and styles in rap music thus carries with it some extra baggage: the study of style, in particular, but perhaps of genre as well, may well invoke in musicologically oriented scholars a skeptical response for its generalizing and internalizing enterprise. Even more troubling, the scholars most likely to interrogate my invocations of those terms may well be precisely those most open intellectually to many arguments in this book.[64] For what does it mean to focus on musical style, if not aggressively to contain the study of music history within the category of "intrinsic" criticism and thus to bracket music as a social force?[65] Even in the cases when "style" refers not to an individual manner but rather to a common poetic procedure of an artistic community or tradition, it may quickly (and justifiably) become suspect for its implication of aesthetic autonomy. Indeed, this would be a legitimate concern, as the intrinsically oriented music history which many music scholars confront as part of their training often relies heavily on a certain conception of musical "style." In that conception, the music itself becomes a self-perpetuating and internally developing force.

Indeed, as discussed in Chapter 1, much of what is practiced as "music theory" relies on closely related notions of musical autonomy. But such a notion of musical autonomy has not been replicated here, and the ideas of "style" and "genre" just elaborated have designated those two as levels of musical signification, which is to say, as social *acts*. Instead, style may be constructed as highly visible and readily observable aspects of the production and consumption of rap. Style here appears as it is discussed both by audiences' behavior and in artistic/commercial communities, in other words, as *everyday music theory structuring social interaction*. When rap consumers talk about "hard beats," about "old-school flows," about "West Coast style production," or about "smooth beats," a certain poetics of rap is being constructed and perpetuated, even if it is never called that.[66] The terms are quotidian categories, invoked to generalize about specific aspects of the music. Record companies and distributors take note and

---

[64] On the other hand, some of the most distinguished progressive work in musicology, such as Kallberg (1996), Kramer (1990), and McClary (1991), relies on arguments from some assumption of style.

[65] A classic example would be Crocker (1986).

[66] Terms such as those just referred to will quickly arise in most discussions with devoted rap fans. Those looking for written instances may consult the letters to the editor, interviews, and recording reviews of such magazines as *The Source*, *Rap Pages*, or *Vibe*. Also significant are song lyrics and conversations in fan communities. Online sources such as rec.music.hip-hop or various rap/hip-hop websites are also available, although it is important to keep in mind that factors such as computer access may shape the audience sample.

advantage of popular notions of rap style; promotional material, advertisements, and artist appearances all appeal to style simultaneously with (and inseparably from) genre systems. An advertisement or CD cover featuring, along with the artist, expensive clothing, jewelry, and furnishings, for example, may promise musical tracks that are heavy with R&B styles, with thick, keyboard-laden textures and frequently sung choruses. The topics there may deal with the hustler's life, seduction, sex, and money. The cover design may also separate out a certain segment of the rap music market as target consumers. Such a deployment of style, leading from the visual to the aural, is less abstract than, but not far removed from, any attempt we might make to deploy "genre" in a narrative of historical development. What I am saying here parallels to some extent Frith's (1996) discussion of genre, looking everywhere to embed the generic and stylistic categories in social action. For those coming from musicological backgrounds, my conception of genre can be taken as a strategic response to musicology's (and music theory's) frequent deployment of style and genre as props for a narrative of music's developmental autonomy. I would like, in other words, to reconceive genre as frankly worldly activity. "Style," then, need not connote a conception of musical autonomy, but rather may refer to the most material possible aspects of music, namely the ways in which people position themselves to buy and enjoy music, as well as the ways in which companies position themselves to produce and sell it. Of course, this book will eventually open style to further uses, since one of the principal theses being advanced here is that style is also used to create *identities*, a function which overlaps only partially with marketing and consumption. But the marketing aspect alone should suggest strongly that *some* conception of musical style is necessary for understanding rap music culturally. The argument that style is further necessary for understanding rap's role in creating identities will be left to Chapters 4 and 5.

Concepts of genre are, of course, subject to the similar charges of essentialism and (in cases where Marxist methodologies are being refused) totalization. But in the case of rap music, the status of genre is in many respects even easier to support than that of style, provided that one maintain an analogous perspective. That is, genres are outlined at least as much in social discourses around the music as in the "music itself" – or more precisely, in music only as mediated by discourses. For rap music audiences are among the most self-conscious and fierce of all audiences in policing the boundaries of aesthetic and generic (and, often equivalently, political) validation. And the validation often falls along coordinates of individual genres, or groups of genres. Thus, one will find audiences for whom "commercial" rap and "gangsta" rap alike are politically unacceptable and unpalatable, and for whom thus only more "conscious" forms are acceptable. Conversely, one may find others for whom only "hardcore" rap properly reflects hip-hop culture's social significance, while more "political" forms misrepresent or ignore some purported reality. While these terms often differ and may be unpredictable in their admixture, they describe an often surprisingly well-defined genre system in the world of North American rap. I might even speculate that its outlines and definitions often seem better set than in many popular musics, though such a notion would probably be impossible to prove. And the genres of North American rap music, while not globally uniform, have global consequences, as we will see in Chapters 4 and 5. Furthermore, the commercially projected rap genre system may even be used didactically, as one informant explained to me while narrating his early development as an MC: "[When beginning to rap] I guess in terms of a style, I didn't have one, and I didn't know how to look for one" (Krims 1997). The notion that there is a field of stylistic possibility "out there" from which to choose indicates that a rap genre system is not simply a high-level abstraction. Rather, it may play a concrete role in musical *production*. In this way (as well as many others), a genre system may be performative, feeding back into production and thus crossing the line between audience and artist, consumer and producer.

Of course, as with any discussion of genre, the customary warning must be signaled that they are reference points, and that any individual case (song, artist, video, album) may easily fall between any genres, incorporate any number of them, or change their mutual articulations. Genres may be blended by any artist, album, or song (as in the case of Naughty by Nature, which occupies generic spaces between what have been described as party and reality genres, sometimes blending them in one song, sometimes alternating). Similarly, salient aspects of rap style may float freely among genres and even be endemic to most or all of them. Thus, a generic system can only determine certain limited aspects of representation. Nevertheless, some far-reaching claims have been made here about the genre systems of North American rap. From here we can expand into more specific cases and watch them operate and transform.

3

The musical poetics of a "revolutionary" identity

This chapter is an attempt to examine a song and theorize some ways in which it may project (and help form) notions of a certain community and an identity; it will make use of the notions of musical poetics developed so far, at the greatest level of detail of any chapter in the book. "Identity" here does not necessarily mean "resistant identity"; thus, while the project here may resemble in some respects those for which music may be validated as radical practice or resistance to domination, the only operative assumption is that *somehow* the identities being discussed are formed symbolically – not necessarily that they overturn the discursive structures lined up against them. Thus, what was earlier referred to, following Jody Berland (1998), as the "optimism of cultural studies" is here replaced by something that might even, at one point in intellectual history, have been deemed "semiotic," an attempt at a description of how signification works. A further judgment about political function, it seems to me, requires a closer look at how acts of discourse circulate, and their distant, sometimes surprisingly contorted future in the throes of capital and its own far-flung social effects.

Unlike the more generalized discussion on the genre system in Chapter 2, the present discussion takes some of its cues from notions of culture developed by James Clifford (1988).[1] Clifford argues that there has been an increasing sense, in the twentieth century, that the older "culture concept" no longer applies to the (post-) modern world; instead, there is a widespread "feeling of lost authenticity, of 'modernity' ruining some essence or source" (p. 4). Although this sense is often presented as a nostalgia for earlier "purity," Clifford

---

[1] All further references to Clifford in this discussion refer to Clifford (1988) and will specify only the page number. At the same time, this analysis is not consistent with many of the critiques that Clifford poses for the issue of ethnographic authority (especially pp. 21–54). Instead, I would emphasize Clifford's recognition that "a purely dialogical authority [which he tends to favor] would repress the inescapable fact of textualization" (p. 43). Still, I would not pretend that this aspect of my analysis is consistent with Clifford's work. It is probably closer in spirit to Spivak (1988), in the sense that it considers the problem of subaltern self-representation.

"does not see the world as populated by endangered authenticities – pure products always going crazy" (p. 5). Rather, the situation, as he sees it, prompts the question, "What are the essential elements and boundaries of a culture?" (p. 8). He concludes that contemporary cultural identity can be understood "not as an archaic survival but as an ongoing process, politically contested and historically unfinished ... a form of personal and collective self-fashioning" (p. 9). Accordingly, "cultural identity" is not a tie with some pure and distant past, so much as it is a matter of continual appropriation, revision, and creation in the present, with an eye toward the future. This creation, in turn, is necessarily imbricated in the intersections among what used to be considered "cultures":

Because discourse in global power systems is elaborated vis-à-vis, a sense of difference or distinctness can never be located solely in the continuity of a culture or tradition.   (p. 11)[2]

Cultural identity, then, is dialogic, or polylogic; it brings to the fore a "need to stage authenticity *in opposition to* external, often dominating alternatives" (p. 12; emphasis Clifford's). In the process, "[T]he roots of tradition are cut and retied, collective symbols appropriated from external influences" (p. 15); thus, "[t]wentieth-century identities no longer presuppose continuous cultures or traditions" (p. 14). In the specific case of art, the consequences are enormous:

If authenticity is relational, there can be no essence except as a political, cultural invention, a local tactic ... A whole structure of expectations about authenticity in culture and in art is thrown in doubt.   (pp. 12–14)

The analysis presented here will illustrate one such "local tactic," in the specific context of music. If "culture" is constructed in a series of local acts of definition, music may carry the significance that Martin Stokes elaborates in his admirable introduction to *Ethnicity, Identity, and Music* (1994). There, noting the role that music often plays in building "notions of difference and social boundaries" (Stokes, 1994: p. 3), he asserts that "[m]usic does not ... simply provide a marker in a prestructured social space, but the means by which this space can be transformed" (Stokes 1994, p. 4).

Music can play a special role in establishing cultural identity, according to Stokes, because of its alliance with the construction of pleasures in a society: "It is perhaps this that distinguishes [musical] ethnicity ... from the 'everyday' practices of boundary construction and maintenance with which much social anthropological writing on

---

[2] This particular observation will be crucial, when it turns out that Ice Cube's fashioning of a black revolutionary identity is contingent on representations by the hegemonic culture he rejects.

ethnicity is concerned" (Stokes 1994, p. 13). Most important for present purposes, Stokes points out a musical practice that bears directly on rap contexts:

Subcultures borrow from the dominant culture, inflecting and inverting its signs to create a bricolage in which the signs of the dominant culture are "there" and just recognizable as such, but constituting a quite different, subversive whole. (Stokes 1994, p. 19)

Here, Stokes's description approaches what has been widely re-marked in rap music, namely the process of "signifyin'" that Gates (1988) identifies as a central aspect of black cultural production. It will be seen in the analysis that follows that borrowing, "inflecting and inverting" signs of the (Eurocentric) culture constitute much of the "signifyin'" with which Ice Cube establishes a specific ethnicity.

Such a scenario should immediately raise the question, "Establishes an identity for whom?" Here issues of persona arise, issues that can only be contextualized in broader questions of early "gangsta" rap, and which are further magnified in the case of Ice Cube, one of the original public rappers in the genre. For one of the principal authenticating strategies of early gangsta rap has precisely been the symbolic collapsing of the MC onto the artist – the projection that the MC himself (with the gender-specific pronoun purposefully unmodified) *is* the persona – a voice from the "streets," speaking from authentic experience. Ice Cube's entire early persona, straight down to the ubiquitous scowl, depends on the collapsing of the angry, aggressive, and politically charged figure onto the historical figure of O'Shea Jackson (Ice Cube's given name); thus, while the identity formed in the song "The Nigga Ya Love to Hate" is as virtual, in a sense, as that of any singing or rapping voice in a song, the production of that identity serves a dual purpose. "The Nigga Ya Love to Hate" here is both persona and artist, the formation of the necessary collapse of the two which one may see as synonymous with "keeping it real." The effectiveness of the collapsing strategy, including the effectiveness of the present song, may be measured, if not in any other way, in the more recent reproaches of Ice Cube among rap fans as having lost his edge, as having "sold out," precisely because he no longer performs songs that project the same persona. In a sense, the identity formed in "The Nigga Ya Love to Hate" continues to haunt Ice Cube's career, defining, in popular imagination, a persona now remembered as simply "the real Ice Cube"; the collapsing of persona and artist was all too effective.

The song, from Ice Cube's (1990a) first solo album (*AmeriKKKa's Most Wanted*) since leaving Niggas With Attitudes (NWA), was, like the other songs on the album, produced by The Bomb Squad.³ This is significant for two major reasons. First, The Bomb Squad were (and now again are) the producers for Public Enemy; as was mentioned in Chapter 2, Public Enemy's production style generated a new model of hardness, complexity, and authenticity in rap music and ended up widely imitated. Thus, by engaging The Bomb Squad, Ice Cube was availing himself of a then-new sound, and furthermore – and importantly – a sound associated with politically engaged rap music, radical in a way closely associated with black nationalism. Second, Public Enemy is a New York group, thus establishing themselves as a geographic rival to Los Angeles artists like Ice Cube; and while the notorious and widely-hyped "East Coast/West Coast" rivalry was then only nascent (and largely because of the commercial success of NWA), the geographic contrast was already highly significant, and in fact, there were fans at the time that criticized Ice Cube for "selling out" to East Coast dominance.

But the commercial success of the album – and its survival in popular memory as one of the great all-time rap albums – eventually overshadowed those criticisms, and Ice Cube's collaboration with The Bomb Squad is often imaged, in fan reception, as an apex of political engagement and responsibility from which he has gradually declined. Thus, even now, something like a full decade after the release of the album, it looms as a highly significant presence in rap music and hip-hop culture; hence its meriting a detailed discussion.

In light of Clifford's discussion, the present analysis will seek out how Ice Cube establishes, in the musical poetics of the song, a certain vision of black ethnicity. Or rather, I should say, a specific position *within* an ethnicity, for with this song, Ice Cube defines a political stance within his community, not only against the hegemonic culture, but also against fellow blacks that he sees as helping to perpetuate that culture's injustices. Therefore, "The Nigga Ya Love to Hate" fashions what I will call "black revolutionary identity," i.e., an identity constructed for revolutionary black politics. With it, Ice Cube stakes out, for himself and, equivalently, the rapping persona, not only a boundary of blackness, but also a boundary of the "five percent nation."⁴

³ Thus, an imperfection of the present discussion is my use of the phrase "Ice Cube" to describe a persona jointly formed by the efforts of Ice Cube and The Bomb Squad. While it could be argued that Ice Cube's oversight of the projects alone justifies discussing him as an active agent of the song, I would prefer to leave it that the phrase "Ice Cube" here is simply a relatively less awkward way to refer to what is, in reality, a collective agency (all of which is beside the greater question of music-industrial mediation).

⁴ "Five percent nation" refers to the idea, widespread in the Nation of Islam, that at any

Some detailed discussion will be needed to show how this works, and this is where the "close reading" comes in. Stokes, in common with the other authors mentioned above, provides an indication that some attention to aesthetic detail is needed for the discussion of ethnicity in music:

[It] is important that music and dance ... not just [be] seen as static symbolic objects which have to be understood in a context, but are themselves a patterned context within which other things happen ... Complex aesthetic vocabularies, or single terms covering a complex semantic terrain point to minute and shifting subtleties of rhythm and texture which make or break the event ... Without these qualities, however they are conceived in a particular society, the ritual event is powerless to make the expected and desired connections and transformations. (Stokes 1994, p. 5)

What follows is an attempt to observe just such a "patterned context" in action, creating Ice Cube's black revolutionary identity. Some terminology will be presented in order to show how this works, since much of the methodology of traditional music theory would be inadequate to the music at hand. Thus, our discussion will become technical; the level of detail, however, will remain engaged in the task of examining the song as a cultural production.

Figure 3.1 gives the lyrics to Ice Cube's "The Nigga Ya Love to Hate," from the album *AmeriKKKa's Most Wanted*. Each line is set by one measure in time. The lines (and measures) are numbered for later reference. The beginning of each line corresponds either to the downbeat or the first rapped section after the downbeat, while the rest of the line falls within the four-beat measure following that downbeat.

Crucial here is the technique of layering already described in Chapter 2. As a procedure, layering is basic to this and many other rap (and often more generally, hip-hop) songs. Its significance to the present song should not be at all surprising, given the then-novel complexity and ambitiousness of the Bomb Squad's production techniques. Indeed, as will become clear, it is largely the interactions of layering with Ice Cube's MCing that form notions of a black revolutionary identity in the song.

Figure 3.2 gives what I call a *layering graph*.[5] The graph runs in

given time, only 5 percent of people in any population are politically aware enough to be influential. That 5 percent presumably determines the destiny of the other 95 percent of the population. It should not be confused with the Five Percent Nation religion, which takes its name from such an idea but has developed separately.

[5] The use of layering graphs, rather than staff notation, is preferable here for several reasons. First, in textures such as those examined here, it can become difficult to project the separate activity of more than three or four sound sources at once, without an unwieldy number of staves; and the activity of separated layers will turn out to be crucial. Second, layering graphs allow easier and quicker reference to the exact

eighty-eight numbered columns, which represent the successive measures of time, eighty-eight of them in all. The top two rows in each column count the measures, the first by tens and the second by ones. The third row, labeled "configs," shows *configurations* – this is what I call combinations of tracks which remain more or less stable over an extended period of the song. A vertical line indicates the beginning of a new configuration, while solid horizontal lines indicate a continuation of the last-numbered configuration; each new one is numbered just to the right of the vertical line. If a horizontal line restarts with no vertical line, the last-numbered configuration is restarting. A diagonal slash ("/") indicates a half-measure continuation.

The fourth row shows *upbeats*, that is, one-measure combinations of tracks that directly precede points of formal articulation in the song (e.g., beginnings of verses, beginnings of refrains, and so on). They are all indicated by one-measure horizontal lines and numbered below the lines. The fifth row shows what I call *adjuncts*, which are one or more tracks superimposed either to configurations or to refrains. They, too, are indicated by horizontal lines and numbered below the lines. To preserve proportions, the two-digit labels for adjuncts 10 through 20 are written vertically. No vertical lines separate each from the next, since all but adjunct 20 last one measure; adjunct 20 lasts two measures. The sixth row shows *refrains*, of which there are two in the song; both are seven-measure events featuring the shout "Fuck you, Ice Cube" and various responses. Both are numbered below the lines. Each of the last four rows just described will be referred to as a *layer*; thus there is a configuration layer, an upbeat layer, an adjunct layer, and a refrain layer. At the bottom of Figure 3.2, the three verses are represented by the numbers 1, 2, and 3. Verse 1 extends from line 1 through line 24; verse 2 extends from line 33 through line 56; and verse 3 extends from line 65 through line 86.

The song divides easily into four-measure groups from the very beginning; the groups are marked by breaks (rhythmic and semantic) in the rapping, and often by new musical events as well. These musical events tend to begin either at the commencement of each four-measure group or on the last measure of a four-measure group.

---

metrical position of each event than traditional staff notation. Third, layering graphs arguably allow simpler projection of musical events and easier visual accessibility, without sacrificing information. Fourth, most of the events discussed here are either non-pitched (by traditional Western calibrations of pitch) or ambiguously pitched; thus, placement on staff lines designed primarily to represent pitch would be superfluous and potentially distracting, if not misleading. And finally, layering graphs do not rely to any substantial extent on musical "literacy"; thus, they remain accessible to some scholars who may otherwise be excluded from my discussion.

In the former case, the event is labeled either a refrain (if it involves "Fuck you, Ice Cube" and responses thereto) or a configuration; in the latter case, it is labeled as a refrain. One exception is configuration 2, which arrives at measure 33, in the middle of a four-measure group; this will be discussed shortly. Adjuncts may arrive anywhere in the song; they are always accompanied by a configuration or a refrain, except in the last two measures of the song.

Each event is represented on the graph by a solid, continuous line. Below the beginning of each such line is an ordinal number; this number simply counts the different patterns within each type. For example, the "1" in the configuration row, measure 1, indicates "configuration 1," while the "2" in the configuration row, measure 33, indicates "configuration 2," and so on. When a vertical line interrupts a horizontal line and is followed by a new ordinal, there is a change in the pattern. A repeated ordinal reflects a repeated pattern; thus, the music of configuration 1', extending over measures 65–9, is repeated in measures 73–6. As a generic term, all numbered patterns within each layer will be four cells in the upbeat layer, twenty cells in the adjunct layer, and two cells in the refrain layer.

All layers have only one cell present at any one time, with one exception: adjuncts 12 and 1 occur together in measure 80 (symbolized in the figure by the subposition of "1" to "12" in the adjunct layer). As the figure shows, there is sometimes only one cell occurring overall at a given time, sometimes more than one.

Figure 3.3 gives further information about the cells. Each cell labeled in Figure 3.2 is listed in the left-hand column of Figure 3.3; in the right-hand column, each one is cued to the relevant text being rapped (except adjuncts 19 and 20, which occur after the end of the rapping). The cells are listed in their order of occurrence within the song. In the left-hand column are rows indicating the instruments present.[6] The central columns of the figure number beat-classes (BCs) 1 through 4, 1 being the downbeat of each measure and 4 being the pickup.[7] Each beat is divided into four equal-length subparts, marked by the letters x, y, and z. Thus, the first quarter beat of each measure extends from 1 to 1x, the second quarter-beat from 1x to 1y, the third from 1y to 1z, and the fourth from 1z to 2. And so forth, for each of the four higher-level beats. Thus, in total, sixteen BCs or subdivisions are being counted in each measure. Only one sound in the song is placed

---

[6] For the entirety of this chapter, all musical data, like the lyrics, is gathered according to my hearing of the song. Thus, I must accept any responsibility for any misinterpretations.

[7] Unlike in earlier chapters, I do not assign a BC 0. This is because the focus here will not be on modular rhythm. I have elected to use numbers that accord more closely with how musicians count the beats.

between these BCs: the cow-bell in configs 1 and 1' is attacked half-way between BCs 1z and 2.

Filled triangles on Figure 3.3 indicate attacks by non-pitched percussion. Note names that are not underlined indicate attacks of pitches; when underlined (as during the upbeat 2 cell), they indicate chords of which the notes are the roots. Dotted lines (as in the refrain 1 cell) indicate that the sound preceding them is being sustained. In some places, information about a sound is provided in parentheses after the name of the instrument, in which case the symbol marking its attack may be neither a note-name nor a filled-in triangle. For instance, in config 1, for synth(esizer) 3, the notes D♭, B♭, A♭, F are specified as a chord. The attack of that chord is then indicated on BC 1z by a circled x. The arrows modifying the 's in refrain 1 indicate slight upwards and downwards variations in pitch; a cedilla attached to a note-name (as in upbeat 1) indicates a slight and quick upwards-sweeping grace note. In config 1', the parenthesized 1's and 2's after the rock and bass guitar labels indicate that the following music occurs during each first and second iteration of the cell, respectively. And the As in adjunct 19 are in parentheses to indicate that those notes sound much more softly than the simultaneous Cs.

All of this having been explained, we may turn now to Figures 3.1 through 3.3 in order to begin observing how the song stakes out a certain black revolutionary identity for the MC as a persona, and thus for Ice Cube as a public figure. It is perhaps easiest to begin with semantic aspects of the text, using Figure 3.1 as a guide.

Figure 3.1: The lyrics of Ice Cube's "The Nigga Ya Love to Hate"

I heard

1 Pay back the muthafuckin' nigga, that's
2 Why I'm sick of gettin' treated like a goddamn
3 Step-child, fuck a punk 'cause I ain't him
4 You gotta deal with a nine-double-m,
5 The damn scum that you all hate, just
6 Think, if niggas decide to retaliate
7 And try to keep you from runnin' up, I never
8 Tell you to get down, it's all about comin' up,
9 So why did you go and ban the AK? The
10 Shit wasn't registered any fuckin' way,
11 So you better duck away, run, and hide out
12 When I'm runnin' real slow and the light's out,
13 'Cause I'm about to fuck up the program,
14 Shootin' out the window of a drop-top Brougham,
15 Well, I'm shootin', let's see who drops, the
16 Police, the media, or suckas that went pop,
17 The muthafuckas that say they too black,

18 Put 'em overseas, they be beggin' to come back,
19 And sayin' peep about gangs and drugs, you
20 Wanna sweep a nigga like me up under the
21 Rug, kickin' shit called Street Knowledge,
22 Why are more niggas in the pen than in college?
23 Because of that line, I might be your
24 Cell-mate, from the nigga you love to hate!

25 [group, shouting:] Fuck you, Ice Cube! [Ice Cube, rapping:] Yeah!
    Ha, ha!
26 It's the nigga you love to hate!
27 [group, shouting:] Fuck you, Ice Cube! [sample:] Anyway, yo'
    mutha
28 Warned ya about me. [Ice Cube, rapping:] It's the nigga you love
    to hate!
29 [sample, black man:] Yo, you ain't doin' nuthin' positive, you
    ain't – you ain't doin'
30 Nuthin' positive about it! What you got to say for ya-
31 Self? [Ice Cube, rapping, voice heavily processed:] You don't like
    how I'm living? Muthafuck you!
32 [Ice Cube, rapping, voice as before:] Once again, it's

33 All in the muthafuckin' cycle: 'Ice
34 Cube you bitch killa, cop killa,'
35 Yo! Runnin' through the lies like bruthas, no
36 Pot to piss in, I blew my piston,
37 Now who do you love to hate?
38 'Cause I talk shit and down the eight-ball,
39 'Cause I don't break, you beg and I fall off,
40 You cross color, might as well cut them balls off,
41 You git'cha ass ready for the lynching,
42 Da Mob is droppin' common sense in
43 We'll take and up here we'll shake any
44 Tom, Dick, and Hank, and git'cha ass
45 Thinkin' not about how right and wrong ya live, but how
46 Long ya live, I ain't with the bullshit,
47 I meet mo' bitches, mo' hoes,
48 Don't wanna sleep, so I keep poppin No-Doz,
49 And tellin' young people what they gotta know,
50 'Cause I hate it when niggas gotta lay low and
51 If you're locked up, I gotta get my style in
52 From San Quentin to Riker's Island,
53 We got 'em afraid of the funky shit
54 I like to clown, so pump up the sound in your
55 Jeep, make the ol' ladies say, "Oh my
56 God, hey, it's the nigga you love to hate!"

57 [group, shouting:] Fuck you, Ice Cube! [Ice Cube, rapping:] Yeah,
    c'mon,
58 Fool! It's the nigga you love to hate!

59 [group, shouting:] Fuck you, Ice Cube! [Ice Cube, rapping:] Yeah, what up,
60 Punk? It's the nigga you love to hate!
61 [Woman, shouting:] Yo, what the fuck you think you are, callin' us bitches?
62 We ain't all that! That's all I hear, "bitch, bitch"!
63 I ain't nobody's bitch! [Ice Cube, rapping:] A bitch is a
64 [group shout:] HOE! [spoken voice:] train [Ice Cube, rapping:] Soul

65 Train done lost they soul, just
66 Call it "Train" 'cause the bitches look like hoes,
67 I see a lot of others, damn!
68 It all hurts, look like a Bandstand,
69 You ask me, do I like Arsenio?
70 About as much as the Bicentennial,
71 I don't give a fuck about dissin' these
72 Fools, 'cause they all scared of the Ice Cube,
73 And what I say, what I betray, and
74 All that, and they ain't even seen a gat,
75 I don't want to see no dancin', I'm
76 Sick of that shit – listen to the hit! 'Cause
77 Y'all ever look and see another brotha on the
78 Video, tryin' to outdance each other?
79 I'm-a tell T-Bone to pass the bottle,
80 And don't give me that shit about "role model"
81 It ain't wise to chastise and preach,
82 Just open the eyes of each, 'cause
83 Laws are made to be broken up, what
84 Niggas need to do is start lookin' up, and
85 Build, mold, and fold themselves into
86 Shape, of the nigga you love to hate!

[two measures of music follow]

The song stages, among other things, Ice Cube's role in political and cultural resistance to the dominant white culture. (Many of his songs, especially from his early career, address this to some extent.) Verses in which Ice Cube raps alternate with refrains, in which Ice Cube confronts verbal attacks and responds to them. The first two verses, lines 1–24 and 33–56, elaborate what Ice Cube regards as politically motivated attempts to silence him, and his success at communicating despite them. The final verse, lines 65–86, criticizes other blacks in the entertainment industry for reinforcing existing power structures. At the end of the final verse, Ice Cube instructs listeners to emulate him, despite (and because of) his failure to conform to traditional images of "role models" that he obviously rejects.

The description he gives of other black performers in the final verse is a good place to begin observing how a black revolutionary identity arises in the song. He first identifies *Soul Train* (the 1960s–70s television show) as having "lost they soul" (ll. 64–5)[8] stating that the "bitches look like hoes" (ll. 65–6). (The misogyny of this statement will be discussed later.) It is compared to *American Band Stand* (a 1950s–70s television show designed primarily for white audiences). Next Arsenio is mentioned negatively, though a reason is not given (except for his being "scared of the Ice Cube") (ll. 69–72). Ice Cube then registers a general objection: "I don't wanna see no dancin', I'm / sick of that shit" (ll. 75–6). Then this objection is visualized: " 'Cause / Y'all ever look and see another brotha on the / video, tryin' to outdance each other" (ll. 76–8). Ice Cube juxtaposes himself to this defiantly: "I'm-a tell T-Bone to pass the bottle, / And don't give me that shit about 'role model' " (ll. 79–80).

In this way, a connection is made between dancing and Ice Cube's rejection of some other black performers. In fact, in much of Ice Cube's music, and in some of his interviews, he has made clear that his music is only secondarily for entertainment; he thinks of his role as primarily that of an educator about life in the ghetto.[9] The use of rap music for dancing is, to him, a betrayal of that purpose.[10] He makes this point early in the song, in fact, when he says "I never / tell you to get down, it's all about comin' up" (ll. 7–8).[11] It is no coincidence, then, that one of the targets of his metaphorical drive-by attack is the "suckas that went pop" (l. 16).[12] References to his self-designated role

---

[8] Henceforth, "l." or "ll." in parentheses followed by a number or numbers will refer to line numbers from Figure 3.1.

[9] Ice Cube is explicit about this in hooks (1994) (pp. 129–30, 133–4). Ice Cube's claim of educational value is related both to the notion of "nation-conscious hip-hop" (i.e., rap music that helps to define a black political identity), and to the hip-hop cultural concept of "representin'." The latter is a complex term involving many strands of meaning, among which is the idea that rap should clearly project its geographic and social contexts, if it is to remain "genuine." Krims (1998c) explores some of the implications of the term.

[10] In a duet that Ice Cube does with Scarface on the latter's album *The Diary* (1994), Scarface refers to rap as "our only way of communicatin' with our people."

[11] Here, "get down" is used in the 1970s slang sense of enjoying the music in a visceral way – dancing, feeling the beat, and so on. "Comin' up" means growing up. Thus, Ice Cube is saying that he encourages his listeners to treat the music not as an occasion for dance, but rather as an occasion for learning.

[12] That this image is metaphorical is obvious from the prospective targets: "the / police, the media, or suckas that went pop" (ll. 15–16). One could argue that the police may be the target of a literal drive-by shooting (despite the fact that in reality, it is other gangs that are normally targeted); but the addition of "the media" (a large, amorphous mass of individuals) and "suckas that went pop" (also a large number of people unlikely to be standing together somewhere) makes clear that it is not a literal drive-by that is being fantasized. Rather, Ice Cube's rapping and social instruction is the instrument of attack. The confusion of violent metaphors with the advocacy of literal violence is, in my view, one of the sources for much popular criticism of hard-core rap music, especially among those who are not familiar with it.

Figure 3.2: Layering graph of "The Nigga Ya Love to Hate"

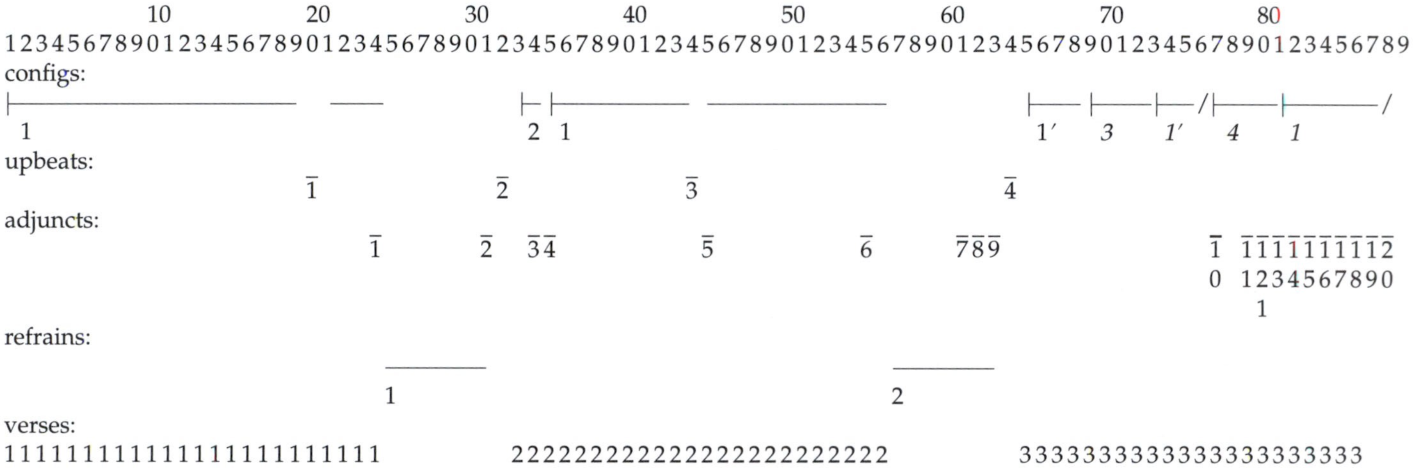

```
         10        20        30        40        50        60        70        80
1234567890123456789012345678901234567890123456789012345678901234567890123456789
configs:
 |———————————|     |———————|   |———————————|                    |———|  |—|—/|——|
 1                  2  1                                          1'   3   1'  4  1

upbeats:
              1̄        2̄        3̄        5̄         6̄       7̄8̄9̄                   1̄ 1̄1̄1̄1̄1̄1̄1̄1̄2̄
                                                                                0 1234567890
                                         4̄                                                 1

adjuncts:
              1̄        2̄        3̄4̄                                    4̄

refrains:
                  1                                      2

verses:
1111111111111111111111111   222222222222222222222222222      333333333333333333333333
```

as an educator occur frequently in the song (as in ll. 7–8, 19–22, 38, 42, 45–6, 49–50, 71–3, and 81–8).

Thus, a central dichotomy between Ice Cube and other black performers in the song is that of education versus entertainment, respectively. This is quite well established on the semantic level; our task will now be to trace it on other levels. We will begin with a look at the cells.

Figure 3.2 – the layering graph – shows that at all times during the song except the last two measures, one can hear either a configuration or a refrain; the exceptions are the upbeats and the last two measures, which will be discussed later. Figure 3.2 also shows that configuration 1 is present during most of the first fifty-six measures in the song. It is interrupted only by upbeat 1 in measure 20; refrain 1 in measures 25–31; upbeat 2 in measure 32; configuration 2 in measures 33–4; and upbeat 3 in measure 35.

Figure 3.4 isolates and collates the configurations and refrains from Figure 3.3, placing them in order of their appearance. These two categories of cells merit particular attention, since they are the longest-lasting cells in the song and thus are implicated in long-range musical processes. Among many parameters that could be used to characterize these cells, we will here concern ourselves with two: textural density, and amount of pitched (versus non-pitched, percussive) material.[13] By following patterns of textural density and pitch content, we will provide some context for discussing the identities that Ice Cube projects for his persona (and thus, for himself).

Configuration 1, the music that dominates the first fifty-six measures, despite engaging three high-pitched synthesizers, consists mainly of a bass guitar, a bass synthesizer, and three percussion instruments. The high-pitched synthesizers attack only once each per measure (though synthesizer 3 plays a four-note chord). The bass synthesizer is only active during the last one-and-a-half beats of each measure, with three attacks. Thus, the bass guitar and percussion instruments provide most of the activity.

Figure 3.3: Details of cells

	1	x	y	z	2	x	y	z	3	x	y	z	4	x	y	z	"Payback"
config 1																	
synth 1 (cow bell)		C															
synth 2										F#							
synth 3 (Db/Bb/Ab/F)				⊗													
bass synth												Ç		Bb	G		
bass guitar		Bb				Bb		Ab			Ab			Ab			

---

[13] The isolation of these parameters should not, of course, be taken to imply that they are the only relevant ones. They are chosen here to illustrate our purposes, rather than to give a comprehensive analysis.

synth whoosh	▲	▲
snare	▲	▲
bass drum	▲	▲ ▲

---

upbeat 1	1 x y z 2 x y z 3 x y z 4 x y z	"Wanna sweep"
bass synth	Ç B♭ G	
synth whoosh	▲ ▲	
snare	▲ ▲	

| adjunct 1 | 1 x y z 2 x y z 3 x y z 4 x y z | 'Cell-mate, from" |
| high synth | Ç B♭ C | |

---

refrain 1	1 x y z 2 x y z 3 x y z 4 x y z	"Fuck you, Ice Cube"
synth 1	D -	
synth 2 (B,F,C?)	- -	
bass synth	Ḍ Ḋ Ḋ Ḋ Ḍ Ḋ Ḋ Ḋ	
cymbals	▲ ▲ ▲ ▲	
snare	▲ ▲	
bass drum	▲ ▲ ▲ ▲	

| adjunct 2 | 1 x y z 2 x y z 3 x y z 4 x y z | "You don't like" |
| E♭ voice-press | ▲ ▲ ▲ ▲ ▲ ▲ ▲ ▲ | |

---

upbeat 2	1 x y z 2 x y z 3 x y z 4 x y z	"Once again, it's"
synth (high)	F -	
guitar – bar chords	B♭ B♭ B♭ D♭ E♭ F	
bass synth	B♭ D♭ E♭ F	
bass guitar	B♭ D♭ E♭ F	
cymbal	▲ ▲ ▲	
snare	▲ ▲	
tambourine	▲ ▲ ▲ ▲	
bass drum	▲ ▲ ▲	

---

config 2	1 x y z 2 x y z 3 x y z 4 x y z	"all in the mutha-"
siren	- - - - - - - - - - - - - - -	
bass guitar	E♭ E♭ B♭ D♭ D♭E♭	
cymbal	▲	
snare	▲ ▲	
bass drum	▲ ▲ ▲ ▲	

| adjunct 3 | 1 x y z 2 x y z 3 x y z 4 x y z | "Cube the bitch killa" |
| electric scratching | ▲ ▲ ▲ ▲ ▲ ▲ ▲ ▲ ▲ | |

| adjunct 4 | 1 x y z 2 x y z 3 x y z 4 x y z | "Yo, runnin' through" |
| bass guitar | E♭ | |

---

upbeat 3	1 x y z 2 x y z 3 x y z 4 x y z	"Tom, Dick, and Hank"
electric cymbal	▲ ▲ ▲ ▲	
electric scratching	▲ ▲ ▲ ▲	
bass guitar	Ç B♭ G	

The musical poetics of a "revolutionary" identity

```
adjunct 5          1 x y z 2 x y z 3 x y z 4 x y z   "Thinkin' not about"
electric cymbal    ▲

adjunct 6          1 x y z 2 x y z 3 x y z 4 x y z   "Jeep, make the old"
synth (high)               C - - -

refrain 2          1 x y z 2 x y z 3 x y z 4 x y z   "Fuck you, Ice Cube"
horns + bass guitar  Gb Ab    Gb Cb Db Gb Ab   Gb Cb Db Gb Ab    Gb
bass synth           Ab Ab                     Ab Ab    Ab    Ab
snare                          ▲                         ▲
high hat             ▲  ▲                 ▲   ▲
bass drum            ▲                         ▲

adjunct 7          1 x y z 2 x y z 3 x y z 4 x y z   "Yo, what the fuck"
electric scratching              ▲
shout "Bitch!"                           !

adjunct 8          1 x y z 2 x y z 3 x y z 4 x y z   "We ain't all that!'
electric scratching        ▲   ▲   ▲
shout "Bitch!"                           !

adjunct 9          1 x y z 2 x y z 3 x y z 4 x y z   "I ain't nobody's"
stuttered "ah"         a a        a a a a

upbeat 4           1 x y z 2 x y z 3 x y z 4 x y z   "HO! (train)"
synth brass (vc 1)   Eb - - - - - - - - - - - - - - - - - - -
synth brass (vc 2)          Ab - - - - - - - - - - - - - - - -
synth brass (vc 3)                   C - - - - - - - - - - - -
bass synth           Ab                        Bb

config 1'          1 x y z 2 x y z 3 x y z 4 x y z   "Train done lost"
rock guitar (1)      Eb  F         Eb  F         Eb  F
rock guitar (1)      C   Db        C   Db        C   Db
rock guitar (2)      Eb  F         Eb  F
rock guitar (2)      C   Db        C   Db
synth brass              Bb  Ab        Bb  Ab
synth (cow bell)         C
bass guitar (1)      Bb      Bb  Ab        C    C Bb Ab
bass guitar (2)      Bb      Bb  Ab        Ab       Ab
high hat                 ▲              ▲
snare                    ▲              ▲
bass drum            ▲                  ▲   ▲

config 3           1 x y z 2 x y z 3 x y z 4 x y z   "You ask me, do I'
bass guitar          Bb      Bb Bb   Ab Ab
cymbal crash         ▲  ▲  ▲      ▲
snare                    ▲              ▲
bass drum            ▲      ▲      ▲▲       ▲   ▲ ▲ ▲

config 4           1 x y z 2 x y z 3 x y z 4 x y z   "Y'all ever look"
snare                    ▲
```

	1	x	y	z	2	x	y	z	3	x	y	z	4	x	y	z	
tom-tom									▲								
bass drum	▲		▲			▲	▲		▲		▲		▲				
adjunct 10	1	x	y	z	2	x	y	z	3	x	y	z	4	x	y	z	"Y'all ever look"
cymbal	▲		▲		▲		▲		▲								
adjunct 11	1	x	y	z	2	x	y	z	3	x	y	z	4	x	y	z	"I'm-a tell T-Bone"
wah-wah guitar											B♭						
											G						
phase-shifted drum									▲								
cymbal	▲		▲		▲		▲		▲				▲				
adjunct 12(w/adj11)	1	x	y	z	2	x	y	z	3	x	y	z	4	x	y	z	"And don't give me"
wah-wah guitar	B♭				B♭				B♭		B♭		B♭		B♭		
	G				G				G		G		G		G		
phase-shifted drum									▲								
adjunct 13	1	x	y	z	2	x	y	z	3	x	y	z	4	x	y	z	"It ain't wise to"
synth portamento	B♭				F				D♭		E♭	D♭E♭		E♭	D♭E♭		
(imitating scratch,																	
pitches approximate)																	
adjunct 14	1	x	y	z	2	x	y	z	3	x	y	z	4	x	y	z	"Just open the minds"
synth portamento	B♭				F					D♭E♭	D♭E♭	D♭E♭					
(imitating scratch,																	
pitches approximate)																	
adjunct 15	1	x	y	z	2	x	y	z	3	x	y	z	4	x	y	z	"'Cause laws are made"
synth (becoming	D♭				E♭				▲		▲						
less pitched)																	
adjunct 16	1	x	y	z	2	x	y	z	3	x	y	z	4	x	y	z	"Niggas got to do is"
synth	▲				▲				▲				▲	▲	▲	▲ ▲	
adjunct 17	1	x	y	z	2	x	y	z	3	x	y	z	4	x	y	z	"Build, mold, and fold"
synth	▲				▲		▲	▲			▲	▲		▲		▲ ▲	
adjunct 18	1	x	y	z	2	x	y	z	3	x	y	z	4	x	y	z	"Shape of the nigga"
synth	▲ -	-	-	-	-	-	-	-	▲		▲		▲		▲		
adjunct 19	1	x	y	z	2	x	y	z	3	x	y	z	4	x	y	z	
synth									C		C						
									(A)		(A)						
wah-wah guitar	C		A														
cymbal	▲		▲		▲		▲		▲		▲		▲		▲		
adjunct 20	1	x	y	z	2	x	y	z	3	x	y	z	4	x	y	z	
synth					▲												
wah-wah guitar	C		A														
electric needle							▲										
scratch																	
cymbal	▲		▲		▲												

Figure 3.4: Configurations and refrains in the song

```
config 1                1  x  y  z  2  x  y  z  3  x  y  z  4  x  y  z   "Payback"
synth 1 (cow bell)                   C
synth 2                                          F#
synth 3 (D♭/B♭/A♭/F)           ⊗
bass synth                                       Ç     B♭    G
bass guitar             B♭       B♭       A♭          A♭          A♭
synth whoosh            ▲              ▲                 ▲
snare                            ▲                          ▲
bass drum               ▲                                  ▲     ▲

refrain 1               1  x  y  z  2  x  y  z  3  x  y  z  4  x  y  z   "Fuck you, Ice Cube"
synth 1                 D - - - - - - - - - - - - - - - - - - - - - - - - -
synth 2 (B,F,C?)          - - - - - - - - - - - - - - - - - - - - - - - - -
bass synth              Ḍ     Ḋ          Ḋ Ḋ Ḍ    Ḋ           Ḋ Ḋ
cymbals                 ▲              ▲  ▲                 ▲
snare                            ▲                          ▲
bass drum               ▲        ▲              ▲          ▲

config 2                1  x  y  z  2  x  y  z  3  x  y  z  4  x  y  z   "all in the mutha-"
siren                                   - - - - - - - - - - - - - - -
bass guitar             E♭       E♭ B♭   D♭             D♭ E♭
cymbal                           ▲
snare                            ▲                       ▲
bass drum               ▲                 ▲  ▲     ▲

refrain 2               1  x  y  z  2  x  y  z  3  x  y  z  4  x  y  z   "Fuck you, Ice Cube"
horns + bass guitar     G♭ A♭     G♭ C♭ D♭ G♭ A♭    G♭ C♭ D♭ G♭ A♭    G♭
bass synth              A♭ A♭                       A♭ A♭     A♭    A♭
snare                            ▲                          ▲
high hat                ▲     ▲                 ▲     ▲
bass drum               ▲                    ▲

config 1'               1  x  y  z  2  x  y  z  3  x  y  z  4  x  y  z   "Train done lost"
rock guitar (1)         E♭    F          E♭    F          E♭    F
rock guitar (1)         C     D♭         C     D♭         C     D♭
rock guitar (2)         E♭    F          E♭    F
rock guitar (2)         C     D♭         C     D♭
synth brass                      B♭    A♭          B♭    A♭
synth (cow bell)                 C
bass guitar (1)         B♭       B♭       A♭          C     C B♭ A♭
bass guitar (2)         B♭       B♭       A♭          A♭          A♭
high hat                         ▲                       ▲
snare                            ▲                       ▲
bass drum               ▲                                ▲     ▲

config 3                1  x  y  z  2  x  y  z  3  x  y  z  4  x  y  z   "You ask me, do I"
bass guitar             B♭       B♭ B♭    A♭ A♭
cymbal crash            ▲     ▲     ▲           ▲
```

snare			▲			▲		
bass drum	▲	▲		▲ ▲		▲	▲ ▲ ▲	

config 4   1 x y z 2 x y z 3 x y z 4 x y z "Y'all ever look"

snare			▲					
tom-tom						▲		
bass drum	▲	▲		▲ ▲		▲	▲	▲

Refrain 1 thickens the texture considerably. Synthesizers 1 and 2 play loudly and are held continuously throughout each bar.[14] The bass synthesizer has eight attacks and plays throughout the measure (as opposed to three attacks at the end of the measure in configuration 1). The percussion is more active than in configuration 1, with ten attacks rather than seven. Configuration 2, by contrast – arriving after refrain 1 – thins the texture to relatively inactive percussion (seven attacks, as in configuration 1), a bass guitar solo, and a siren. After only two measures configuration 1 returns, and, except for upbeat 3 in measure 44, stays until the end of measure 56.

Refrain 2, like refrain 1, thickens the musical texture and introduces prominent pitched elements, but it does so to an even more dramatic extent. Instead of refrain 1's sustained synthesizer notes, it features a loud and busy (synthesized) brass ostinato (thirteen attacks), six bass synthesizer attacks, and eight percussion attacks.

With configuration 1', the increasing textural density climaxes. Not only does a rock guitar enter prominently for the first time (in an apparent illustration of *Soul Train* musical style), but it also receives a (synthesized) brass response, with a bass guitar part busier than that of the original configuration 1 (six or seven attacks, rather than five). Thus, configuration 1' may be marked out aurally as a highpoint of textural density.

Such an impression is only reinforced by the fact that after configuration 1', the texture thins quickly and dramatically. Configuration 3 retains only bass guitar among the pitched instruments, and far less prominently than in earlier cells (in part because of its low tessitura, in part because of its five attacks and only two different pitches). The percussion, on the other hand, features more attacks than in any previous cell (fourteen). And finally, configuration 4 continues the process by having no pitched instruments at all, so that the percussion plays alone. The percussion texture is actually less dense than that of configuration 3 – nine attacks instead of fourteen.

---

[14] The synthesizers in each cell are numbered for reference only within that cell; so, for example, a "synth 1" in one cell may or may not be the same instrument as a "synth 1" in another cell.

Some patterns may be abstracted from the configurations and refrains just described. There is a steady increase in both (overall attack) density and pitched material from the beginning of the song, climaxing in configuration 1'; the pitched material then drops off sharply at configuration 3 (measures 69–72). At this same time, the density of percussion increases suddenly and dramatically, only thinning slightly into configuration 4 (measures 77–80), where the pitched material finally drops out altogether. When configuration 1 returns at measure 81, the initial state of relatively low pitch and percussive density is restored.

Although relatively uncomplicated, the process just discussed leaves something out – configuration 2. Although only two measures long (measures 33–4), that configuration stands out because it does not fit into the process: it is less dense in attacks than configuration 1. Measures 33–4, then, are exceptional; we will shortly have reason to return to this point.

The process itself merits such detailed discussion because of the way it projects previously discussed semantic aspects of the lyrics. The initial density increase coincides with the bravado of the first two verses – detailing attempts to silence Ice Cube and how he overcomes them – and with the confrontations of the first two refrains. The process climaxes (measure 65) just as Ice Cube mentions the first of the black television entertainment media that he dislikes (*Soul Train*). The first quick decrease in density, focusing on percussion (measure 69), coincides with the second disdained black television program – Arsenio Hall's television show (at the time of the song's release among the most visible black presences on television, particularly for hip-hop fans and rap music listeners). And the final focus on percussion (measure 77) coincides with the final negative reference to black television entertainment (a more generalized image of blacks trying to "outdance each other").

Some might wish to ascribe these events to something akin to "word painting": configuration 1'''s rock guitar and brass may "paint" the 1960s and 1970s dance style of *Soul Train*; and the subsequent focus on percussion may "paint" the image of dancing. I have no problem with this interpretation, but it would not account for the specificity of the gestures (e.g., why just percussion for generalized reference to dancing, rather than, say, funk guitar?). Nor would it address larger developments in the song of which these late events form a part.

A return to the semantic register of the lyrics will help specify further. The dance aspect of music there is presented negatively, as are the people who sponsor their televised images. Thus, the isolation of a percussive dance beat is not a neutral illustration; rather, it is an ironic quotation. In this sense, the textural climax and the gradual isolation of percussion become an occasion for a two-sided projection of black musical identity. On the one hand, the musical elements gradually acquire rhythmic force and the percussion becomes prominent in the manner generally characteristic of break beats; this would normally be the occasion for an appreciation of the rhythmic drive that often helps propel rap music. But, on the other hand, this appreciation, and a common response – dance – are being stigmatized as contrary to the song's purpose. A pleasure is created at the same time as it is stigmatized.

This pleasure in rhythm is far from socially neutral in a society for which both pleasure and rhythm have historically been loaded with racialized discourses. The simple basic rhythms and complex counter-rhythms of rap music are closely related to (and often make explicit reference to) similar traits in other Afro-diasporic musics.[15] As such, the foregrounding of rhythm may invoke and reinforce old racist stereotypes about African-Americans. Thus, what is being stigmatized is not just a certain musical practice, but a whole complex of social representations of African-Americans, produced (for example, on television) for society as a whole.

The result of all this is what Gates (1988) would call a "motivated Signifyin'": an element of cultural production is quoted and troped for the purpose of critique. The consciousness that Ice Cube shows here about popular images of black people and black music would seem to indicate clear gestures toward establishing a counter-identity, for a certain aspect of hip-hop culture generally and for Ice Cube in particular.

Simultaneous with the intensification and isolation of rhythm, there is a more subtle process, but one that intersects some prominent gestures in the song. That process engages alternations and conflicts between duple and triple rhythms throughout the song. Figure 3.4 once again illustrates. Configuration 1 contains a combination of triple and duple rhythmic intervals. The percussion is steadily duple, with attacks always on the beat or on the "y" of some beat (with the exception of the final bass drum attack). The bass guitar, however, begins the measure with triplet intervals and then turns to duple intervals: its attacks occur at 1, 1z, 2y (thus so far in triplets), 3y, and 4y (these last two producing duple whole beats).[16] In this way, the bass guitar marks the first half of the measure in triplets and the second half in duplets.

---

[15] Rose (1994) makes this point, pp. 64–74.

[16] This is a fairly common rhythmic pattern for the bass in funk and dance styles. Walser (1995, p. 202) identifies it in a loop from a Public Enemy song, remarking that the pattern occurs often in African and Afrodiasporic musics.

The rhythmic dichotomy continues throughout the song in different contexts, sometimes between cells and sometimes within them. However, the conflict in rhythmic values builds slowly. Most of the cells in measures 1–65 have very few triplet rhythms and a great number of duple rhythms. There is one notable exception: in upbeat 3 (measure 45) an electric cymbal plays a triplet (attacks on 1, 1z, and 2y). Two factors underline this triplet: first, the cymbal is simultaneous with each of the rapped names in the line "Tom, Dick, and Hank"; second, it is the only instrumental sound at that point in the song. After this initial figure, the rest of the measure returns to a duple rhythm. We will return to this moment shortly.

The departure of configuration 1 at measure 57 discontinues the duple/triple rhythmic conflict temporarily. But the entry of configuration 1' in measure 65 reintroduces it, bringing the same superimposition of duple and triple values that had characterized configuration 1. The rock guitar, synthesized brass, and percussion all project duple rhythmic values; but the bass guitar again projects the initial triplets followed by the duplets that characterized configuration 1. (The bass guitar here also combines the bass guitar and bass synthesizer parts from configuration 1.)

After configuration 1', there are no significant triplets until adjunct 12; there, the wah-wah guitar attacks on 1, 1z, and 2y, after that reverting (like configurations 1 and 1') to duple rhythm. This instance is significant for two reasons. First, it is the first case of triplets in an adjunct; adjuncts, until this point, had reinforced duple rhythm. And second, it is the first of seven adjuncts which will now accompany every line remaining in the song; until this point, adjuncts had been distributed far more sparsely (as reference back to Figure 3.2 will show). Thus, these triplets commence a major mutation in the texture of the music and its rate of change.

The mutation has permanent effects: after adjunct 12, these triplets become common. They appear in adjunct 13's (measure 81) synthesizer part between BCs 1, 1z, and 2y; in adjunct 14's synthesizer part (perhaps trivially) between BCs 1 and 1z; in adjunct 15's synthesizer part between BCs 1, 1z, and 2y; in adjunct 16's synthesizer part between BCs 1, 1z, 2y, and 3x (thus extending one triplet farther than earlier cells); in adjunct 17's synthesizer part between BCs 1 and 1z and then 2y and 3x (with a duple value in between); in adjunct 19's wah-wah guitar and synthesizer parts between BCs 1 and 1z, and 3y and 4x, respectively (thus engaging those last two BCs for the first time as triplets); and in adjunct 20's wah-wah guitar part between BCs 1 and 1z. Thus, every adjunct after the twelfth engages triplets, except adjunct 18 (which, in fact, is very squarely duple).

It is important, also, that this concentration of triplets overlaps the

end of configuration 4 and the final return of configuration 1. In that
sense, it provides a link from one to the other. (This is especially
notable, given the otherwise strong division between measures 80 and
81 by rhythm, rhyme scheme, configuration change, and break in
syntax.) What, then, can be said about this linkage, given the
concentration of rhythm already observed, and the associated
semantics aspects of the lyrics?

Adjunct 17 (measure 85) may be a good place to begin an answer,
because it stands out in a way analogous to upbeat 3. It will be
recalled that upbeat 3 (measure 44) was a place where one instrument
(an electric cymbal) played alone, where that instrument played a
triplet, and where that triplet coincided with the rhythm of Ice Cube's
rapping ("*Tom*, *Dick*, and *Hank*"). The relevant instrument in
adjunct 17 is not isolated in the same way, since it sounds along
with configuration 1. But the latter is a stable element, while
the synthesizer is constantly changing; and the synthesizer is foregrounded in the mix. Adjunct 17's synthesizer, then, is foregrounded
in a similar way to upbeat 3's electric cymbal. More important, it
performs an analogous function: for here is the only other place where
an instrumental part coincides with the rap's rhythm during four
consecutive attacks. Specifically, the synthesizer's attacks on 1, 1z, 2x,
and 2y coincide with the attacks of the words, "Build, mold, and
fold."

Another relationship between upbeat 3 and adjunct 17 highlights
their similarity. In measure 44, the syllables "Tom, Dick, and Hank"
fall on BCs 1, 1z, 2x, and 2y, respectively; and upbeat 3's electric
cymbal attacks on BCs 1, 1z, and 2y. One result is that the electric
cymbal ends up reinforcing the proper nouns "Tom" "Dick" and
"Hank" while leaving "and" unaccompanied; another result is that
the electric cymbal, unlike the voice, ends up projecting two
consecutive triplets. In measure 85, the words "Build, mold, and
fold," like "Tom, Dick, and Hank," fall on BCs 1, 1z, 2x, and 2y,
respectively. But adjunct 17's synthesizer attacks not only on BCs 1,
1z, and 2y, as had upbeat 3's electric cymbal; it also attacks on BC 2x.

So where upbeat 3 had failed to reinforce the word "and," adjunct
17 in fact does so. On the other hand, this extra attack interrupts the
two consecutive triplets that had made upbeat 3 so distinctive. More
informally, we might say that adjunct 17 supports the rapped words
more fully, while upbeat 3 supports the rhythmic figure of a triplet
more fully.

Semantically, adjunct 17 marks an important moment in the song.
Its importance comes not only from setting the beginning of the final
couplet; rather, the last six lines of the song are the most explicitly
didactic: "It ain't wise to chastise and preach, / Just open the eyes of

114

each, 'cause / Laws are made to be broken up, what / Niggas need to do is start lookin' up, and / Build, mold, and fold themselves into / Shape, of the nigga ya love to hate!" Not only does Ice Cube's political advocacy become most explicit here; the passage also recontextualizes the line "the nigga ya love to hate." Since that line is the refrain ending each section (and the title of the song), the recontextualization is dramatic. Although in earlier instances, the "nigga ya love to hate" is used sardonically – reflecting on those who think that way, rather than the "nigga" himself – the final couplet constitutes the only time that the phrase actually describes a desirable goal. Thus, when adjunct 17 presents the verbs "build, mold, and fold," it begins the transformation of one of the song's principal images: the "nigga ya love to hate" becomes an explicitly positive value.

Upbeat 3, on the other hand, supports different semantic value. "Tom, Dick, and Hank," in Ice Cube's music, refers metonymically to "white" people in general (appearing elsewhere on the album, as well). Since Eurocentric culture is painted in this song as an Other against which Ice Cube defines himself, "Tom, Dick, and Hank" is framed as a negative value.[17]

How, then, can we resolve the conflict between, on the one hand, the triplet figure's unfavorable semantic value in upbeat 3, and on the other hand, its favorable semantic value in adjunct 17? Perhaps it is an issue not so much of resolution as of mutation: the figure changes its value as the song progresses. This possibility allows us to reintroduce the general plethora of triplets already noted from measure 80 to the end of the song. It was noted above that from adjunct 12 (measure 80) to the end of the song, triplets appear in great numbers. This stretch of music coincides with the turn to didacticism (lines 80–6); the metaphors and exemplars of conflict and resistance that characterized most of the song fall away to explicit prescriptions for social change. The semantic transition would seem to indicate that Ice Cube involves triplets in his projection of a black revolutionary identity.

But this interpretation leaves two important loose ends. One is the projection of "Tom, Dick, and Hank" just discussed. The other is adjunct 18. That cell is a curious case, since it is the only one after adjunct 12 that does not present a triple rhythm. The anomaly is highlighted by the fact that adjunct 18 sets the final rapped lines of the song (line 86: "Shape, of the nigga ya love to hate").

We end up, then, with two symmetrical problems. On the one hand, one instance of triplets (an instance prominent for its isolation in an

---

[17] It is possible to hear, in the "Dick," a suggestion of Dick Clark, host of *American Bandstand*. My thanks to David Lewin for pointing this out to me.

otherwise duple context) projects a "white" Other. On the other hand, one instance of exclusively duple meter (analogously prominent for its isolation in an otherwise triplet-heavy context) projects the black revolutionary figure being advocated. What these two instances have in common, however, is that each projects *a contested identity*.[18] In one case, the contest involves resistance to "Tom, Dick, and Hank"; in other words, Ice Cube uses this image to establish one term ("white" Eurocentric) of a binary value from which to differentiate himself – a solidly alien target of struggle. In the other case, "the nigga ya love to hate" emerges victoriously in the final rapped line: in the course of the song, Ice Cube has changed that phrase from a derogatory reference to a model of black resistance. In the latter context, it is significant that Ice Cube speaks of "build[ing], mold[ing], and fold[ing]" oneself into shape; the conscious effort to create an identity is explicit, as is its ongoing and dynamic nature.

Rhythmic variance from a local uniformity, then, appears to support a contest of identity. On this hearing, the saturation of triple rhythms in the final measures provides a context in which "the nigga ya love to hate" can itself emerge with an energetic resistance to the local rhythmic formations. It is perhaps not surprising that the final rapped line should be set apart in this way; for at the end of the song, the path for black resistance is made more explicit and the final (and summary) statement is made. This final statement invokes the same refrain that ends each verse (and which provides the title of the song). And it is precisely that phrase – "the nigga ya love to hate" – which is not only reiterated but also *recontextualized* in the course of the song. It begins, in the first verse, as an object of fear and animosity; in the second verse, the phrase is presented somewhat comically, as an utterance of the "ol' ladies," with Ice Cube encouraging his listeners to solicit the response; and in the third and final verse, the "nigga ya love to hate" is something to emulate as a strategy of political resistance.

If both "Tom, Dick, and Hank" and "the nigga ya love to hate" are projected by the strategy of local rhythmic anomaly, in another respect they are mirror images of each other. The former is a highly foregrounded triple rhythm in a duple context, while the latter is an isolated moment of duple rhythm. Thus, although the two are united in being contested identities, they are also opposed to each other in a binary configuration (as one might expect).

---

[18] There is a vast literature dealing with ethnic identity as an object of public contest. The writings of Bakhtin are certainly seminal in this regard; Gardiner (1992) gives an excellent overview of Bakhtin's contributions to this issue. Said (1978) and Spivak (1987) demonstrate other approaches, specifically concerning marginalized ethnicities (and gender). Clifford (1988, pp. 177–246) provides an example of contested cultural identity in an unusual context.

Once we have opened up this field of struggle and identity, many other aspects of the song can be seen in a similar light. We have already seen how Ice Cube identifies his particular strategy of political resistance late in the song with a decrease in pitched material and an increase in unpitched percussion. The identification was secured in the semantic field by his derogating "getting down" and images of blacks dancing on television. In the present context, it is crucial to notice that the negated images here are not "white," Eurocentric figures, but rather representations of other blacks. Thus, one of the broader musical and semantic processes in the song involves not the binary black/white, but rather a binary between a black identity that Ice Cube wishes to claim, and a different black identity that he wishes to reject. Importantly, this differentiation becomes most insistent and explicit, both semantically and musically, in the final verse (especially ll. 65–80), as Ice Cube prepares his closing prescription for black political action (ll. 81–6). And one of the technical aspects of this process – the gradual de-pitching of the synthesizer over adjuncts 13–20 – dovetails with the duple/triple rhythmic process in an interesting way: for it is precisely the now de-pitched synthesizer that in adjunct 17 supports the rhythm of "build, mold, and fold." Thus, although discussed separately, those two long-term productions of black identity intersect not only in the semantic field of the song, but also at a crucial moment in the musical development.

All this having been said, there is an issue that was mentioned earlier and whose discussion was promised: within the pattern of increasing, then decreasing, attack density that runs through the song, configuration 2 was noted as an anomaly. Although short-lived – lasting only two measures – it remains prominent, not only because it interrupts the broader pattern, but also because it marks the beginning of the second verse. Configuration 2 is also notable for supporting musically the most explicit reference so far to representation: "[Once again, it's/] All in the muthafuckin' cycle: Ice / Cube the bitch killa, cop killa." Although this "cycle" is not mentioned elsewhere in the song, it is clear what the cycle is perpetuating: a cultural image of Ice Cube as brutalizer and murderer of police and women (which is, of course, more broadly an image many have of rap musicians). Thus, this exceptional moment in the song highlights in its own way the issue of representation. This is especially so, since configuration 1 takes over from configuration 2 at just the point where discussion of representation (at least temporarily) ends, namely line 35.

Configuration 2 thus occupies an ironic position in the song. On the one hand, it interrupts a musical process involving representation – the gradual build in texture that culminates in configuration 1' and Ice

Cube's assertion of a particular black identity; on the other hand, it introduces its own representation. The difference is, of course, that the image projected during configuration 2 is strictly one that Ice Cube is opposing, while configuration 1′ (and the other cells it surrounds) supports both opposed and favored representations. One could find a certain sense, then, in configuration 2′s interrupting a larger process of constructing a positive representation; in itself, it projects a negative representation, a moment of slippage in a goal-oriented musical process.

But even that may be an oversimplification; because although configuration 2 is being painted here as exceptional, there is a sense in which its disruptive effects reach into other parts of the song. For contained within the lines it projects (ll. 33–4) are the ultimate objects of resistance in the song – not so much "white," Eurocentric culture per se, but rather the representations of black culture which the "nigga ya love to hate" both reinforces and challenges.

Further, there are senses in which cycles become more prominent at the same time that, ironically, Ice Cube's black revolutionary identity is being most strongly established (i.e., toward the end of the song). The first sense involves the length of the configurations; this can best be seen by reference back to Figure 3.2. In the first verse (ll. 1–24), there is no change in configuration (and furthermore, there are no adjuncts); there is no sense of transformation, much less cycle. In the second verse (measures 33–56), there is an odd proportion between the two configurations, 2 and 1; the former lasts two lines, while the latter lasts twenty-one lines (ll. 35–57, with upbeat 3 interrupting for one measure). Thus, although there is a change in the basic supporting music, there is no repeating proportional pattern. In the third verse, however, there is a pattern of 4:4:4:4:8 lines for configurations 1′, 3, 1′, 4, and 1, respectively.[19] In this sense, a cycle of four-line changes participates in Ice Cube's construction of a black revolutionary counter-identity (which is, after all, the project of the final verse). It may be heard as a counter-cycle: the explicitly mentioned "muthafuckin' cycle" of verse 2 (l. 33) is challenged and overturned by the musical cycle that ends the song.

The second sense in which cycles recur involves the use of adjuncts, also in the final verse. Again, reference back to Figure 3.2 will illustrate this. In the first three verses, adjuncts are scattered at irregular intervals: the first one occurs in line 24; the second one at line 31; the third and fourth ones at lines 34 and 35, respectively; the

[19] The pattern is not perfect, however: this count includes the half-measure interruption of silence (l. 76) as part of the second configuration 1′. Interestingly, this gap itself supports the words "Listen to the hit!," thus engaging the construction of a revolutionary black identity, as discussed earlier.

118

fifth one at line 45; the sixth one at line 55; and the seventh, eighth, and ninth ones at lines 61, 62, and 63, respectively. (These last three mentioned adjuncts will be discussed shortly.) In the third verse, however, the adjuncts take on an aspect of regularity. After an initial isolated adjunct 10 in line 77, the other adjuncts arrive, starting in line 79, at a rate of one per line. The pattern continues even beyond the rapped portion of the song, into the short instrumental postlude.

The third and final cycle engages a process discussed earlier. It will be recalled that in lines 7–8 and 75–80 Ice Cube stigmatizes the pleasures of rhythm and dancing. Adjuncts 14 through 18, however, gradually transform a constantly-present synthesizer from pitched to unpitched material. Thus, the concentration of rhythm makes a return, just after having been explicitly posed in opposition to Ice Cube's black revolutionary identity. The result is a more abstract "cycle" than the other two, but in a sense, a more important one. That "cycle" engages a process crucial to the song – the appropriation and transformation of a cultural seme. The focus on percussion in configuration 4 is marked as a negative value by the rapped text (ll. 75–81); but its return in the synthesizer then supports the final prescriptive statement of the song (ll. 81–6). Rather than simply being the return of a repressed value, the distillation of music into rhythmic activity involves a claim and a reinterpretation of a culturally loaded musical parameter.

Once this transformation is recognized, other aspects of the song can be seen in a similar light. The prominent descending minor thirds in the guitar during adjuncts 19 and 20, for example, are played with the same wah-wah timbre as the funk guitar in configuration 1'. But we could hardly accord them the same social value, after the activities of appropriation that separates them; the reclaiming of black music for Ice Cube's political purposes, starting with the explicit rejection of *Soul Train*, asserts that the wah-wah guitar cannot survive untouched in anything except an acoustic sense. (It is also worth noting, given the earlier discussion, that the notes here are triplets, unlike the wah-wah guitar notes in configuration 1'.)

The acts of adoption and revision just discussed lend perspective to the violent imagery of the song. The drive-by shootings of the "Police, the media, or suckas that went pop" (l. 16) are in fact revisions of their own constructions of black identity; the song itself accomplishes this. Likewise, Ice Cube advises the listener to "git'cha ass ready for the lynching" because "Da Mob [i.e., Da Lench Mob, Ice Cube's 'crew'] is droppin' common sense in" (ll. 41–2); if it had not already been clear from these lines alone that the lynching is metaphorical and involves education, then it should be abundantly clear by the end of the song.

The appropriations and revisions already discussed create a black revolutionary identity with no explicit gender. Still, some aspects of the imagery seem to implicate a male identity. And at one point, the song does integrate a gendered perspective to its identity, via a confrontation in one of its refrains.[20] Further, the confrontation is disturbing for its apparent misogyny. In lines 61–4, Ice Cube stages an encounter with a female critic.

She upbraids him for his referring to women as "bitches" (as indeed he does in quite a few songs), to which Ice Cube offers his response in line 63 with "A bitch is a ... " Line 64 then brings a group shout (that is, with Ice Cube and some unidentified members of Da Lench Mob): "HOE!"[21] At that point, the response ("A bitch is a hoe!") seems redundant and therefore non-responsive. The failure to respond, in context, is abusive; the interrogating woman is treated as unworthy of substantive response, and one slur is reinforced by another.

But in the subsequent continuation, Ice Cube recontextualizes the event. This begins at the end of line 64, when, as the shout "HOE!" is still sustained, Ice Cube's voice is superimposed on BC 4, uttering only the syllable "train." That syllable is both rhythmically isolated from any other rapped material and less prominent in the mix; it therefore takes on the character of an aside, or a superimposition. Nevertheless, it provides an essential pivot to the next verse. The response to the interrogating woman is now, "A bitch is a HOE train." The utterance loses its ambiguity (even incomprehensibility) in the following verse, when Ice Cube says (ll. 65–6) "Soul Train done lost they soul, just / Call it 'Train,' 'cause the bitches look like hoes." It is this couplet that links the term "bitch" with the broader process of creating a black revolutionary identity. More specifically, the "bitches"' looking like "hoes" is a feature of *Soul Train* that indicates that the latter has "lost its soul"; being a "hoe," then, as the verse goes on to make clear, involves succumbing to the "selling out" of black identity which *Soul Train* (or images of dancing blacks in general) represents for Ice Cube.

Is Ice Cube saying, then, that his use of the word "bitch" in his music refers exclusively to black women who have betrayed his notion of black identity, i.e., to "hoes"? Is his use of "bitch," then, less simply misogynist then one might otherwise assume? Unfortunately,

---

[20] Although this discussion has not focused on the refrains and their representations of conflict, they nevertheless hold a great deal of potential interest here, because they present the images Ice Cube is contesting not virtually (as in most of the song), but explicitly.

[21] "Hoe" is a word from hip-hop slang. Although it stems from a pronunciation of "whore," it is often used as a derogatory term for all women, or large groups of women. In that sense, it is in some ways analogous to "bitch."

such a conclusion would be overly hasty, and Ice Cube's use of the word "bitch" cannot be so easily rehabilitated. For one thing, a general survey of his music makes this interpretation difficult to sustain.[22] Also, his invocation of a word ("bitch") often used as a slur on women in general and inextricably tied into a history of misogyny cannot be considered entirely innocent. Then, too, if the "bitches look[ing] like hoes" is evidence that "Soul Train / Done lost they soul," then how could the term "bitch" be *equivalent* to the word "hoe"?

Perhaps here we have to recognize an ambivalence in the song toward its own misogyny. On the one hand, Ice Cube does create a female interrogator, and he does attempt to limit the term "bitch" only to certain kinds of women, based on their behavior (i.e., on their complicity with a black identity he wishes to reject). On the other hand, his own discourse, in this song and elsewhere, seems to reinscribe the misogyny.[23] If the project of "The Nigga Ya Love to Hate," as I have argued, is to create a black revolutionary identity, then that project must still be considered incomplete if it excludes or marginalizes half (or more) of the black population.

Two more items should be mentioned, here. First, the discussion here has focused largely on the "musical backdrop" for Ice Cube's rapping, as well as the interaction of that backdrop with semantic and social aspects of the words. Thus, the material aspects of his MCing – especially the rhythms, Ice Cube's "flow," placements within the overall mix – have been slighted at the expense of concentrating on other aspects of representation.[24] Second, the guitar triplets that appear in adjuncts 19 and 20 could hardly be ignored after the extended attention we have paid to the role of triple rhythms in the song. They appear after the end of the rapped section; they (along with the echo of the first one in adjunct 19) constitute the final rhythmically articulated events in the song (before the synthesizer fadeout); and they invoke not only the triple-rhythmic processes of

[22] For example, "Don't Trust Em" (from Ice Cube 1992) projects an extremely unflattering and disturbing attitude toward women. On the other hand, Ice Cube has at times allowed for dialogue with black women, as in "It's a Man's World" (from Ice Cube 1990), a duet with Yo-Yo, a female MC whose career Ice Cube has been instrumental in promoting. Rose (1994, pp. 146–82) discusses dialogics between female and male rappers.

[23] bell hooks's (1994) interview with Ice Cube underlines his ambiguous and often surprising attitudes toward his own apparent misogyny (pp. 125–43).

[24] For example, the relationship of the rapped rhythm to the music seems to become increasingly skewed and complex as the song progresses. This, of course, could be linked, in an even more extended discussion, to the increasingly explicit resistance that Ice Cube musters to representations of black life. Walser (1995) observes a similar process in a song by Public Enemy.

the song, but also the particular and significant timbre of the wah-wah guitar. Since the wah-wah sound had previously been linked to the denigrated images of dancing blacks, its final and prominent appearance here is troubling. Does the synthesizer scratch that interrupts it and ends the song argue for a rap musical process (the scratch) as the elimination of an earlier (and problematized) musical style? Or is the wah-wah sound itself now transformed, after it has been embodied in the process of creating an alternative identity? In other words: is this yet another instance, like that of the triplets themselves, in which Ice Cube has appropriated and revised a musical/social meaning? It is tempting to hear this moment as a triumphant *Aufhebung*; but at the same time, we are constrained to recognize that, like the issue of misogyny, the revision of "blackness" in this song may be an open and unfinished process. There seems to me little doubt that this late musical event cannot remain unaffected by what has gone on before it; but at the same time, the return of the repressed – the images that Ice Cube is out to conquer – cannot simply be overcome by mastery, and Ice Cube's project here remains part of a much larger and more ambiguous social discourse.

It is to be hoped, however, that the foregoing has at least shown that "close reading" of musical processes may hold some promise for those of us who are interested in how rap may help to constitute imagined communities. Since the song examined here is formed within a very particular style and social-historical moment, among the many styles and moments of rap music and hip-hop culture, the above analysis could perhaps be taken metonymically, rather than as exemplifying a possible "central" practice of rap analysis. It could be taken to indicate that attention to "the music itself," rather than reinscribing the ideology of the art-work, may open itself onto larger, "extra-musical" social realities.

4

Rap geography and soul food

The most commonly recounted story of hip-hop culture traces its origins to New York, specifically to the South Bronx; and regardless of whether one acknowledges New York as its birthplace – and there are, of course, perfectly good reasons to do so – the representation of New York as the cradle of hip-hop culture and music is extremely well established.[1] The names of Kool DJ Herc, Afrika Bambaataa, and other such legendary figures have come to be metonyms for the great creative force that congealed in that city in the early-to-mid 1970s and soon unleashed its overwhelming power on a disco-and-pop-weary world. Even after Los Angeles (or its imagined equivalent, Compton) had established its identity as the home to a new and stunningly profitable form of rap music – say, by 1989 – New York loomed large enough in the public's imagination for any other East Coast city to be dwarfed in its proximity, both in the imagination of the record-buying public and in the eyes of artists as well. Occasional exceptions, such as the Fresh Prince and DJ Jazzy Jeff from Philadelphia, were limited in their appeal to the "hardcore" audience, for whom New York (and its musical styles) held something of a monopoly on "representing."

The 1990s, and especially, say, the period from 1992 to (at least) the present, saw a proliferation of commercially successful acts from outside both New York and Los Angeles. The Geto Boys won recognition for Houston, the "Miami bass sound" spotlighted that city (as 2 Live Crew villainized it), Too $hort allowed Oakland some prominence, Naughty by Nature implied a possibility that rap credibility could be extended at least into New Jersey, and, for somewhat different audiences, Sir Mix-a-Lot, while not exactly reflecting glory on Seattle, certainly signaled that the pimp genre may rely less on geographic "representing" than some other genres. Others, such as Chicago's Tung Twista and Boston's Ed. O. G. and Da Bulldogs, might be cited as evidence that New York's hegemony in the popular hip-hop imagination was weakening.

---

[1] Toop (1984), Cross (1993), and Rose (1994) are just three among many for whom New York bears this seminal status.

But as with so many processes of cultural hegemony, New York's eclipsing was not a simple matter, and its presence was not so much lost as transformed. Here it is important to recall how consistently geographic and localized notions of "representing" generally are, and the extent to which establishing an identity may often become a process of negation. The presence of New York often becomes a matter of the effects of its absence: for artists who arose outside the New York/Los Angeles axis (to whatever extent that axis might always have been fantasized, rather than lived in an everyday sense) have long imprinted their own authenticity as local, geographically based, and specifically in oppositional relation to New York.[2] The local flavor of artists is signified in song lyrics, album art, interviews, and media publicity; what a non-New York (and non-Los Angeles) MC or group lacks in linkage to hip-hop's origins, it receives in the projection of local authenticity. Even the names of artists and groups can be seen to reflect the absent centrality of New York in rap geography: the majority of groups with geographic names (e.g., the Westside Connection, the Fifth Ward Boys) hail from outside New York, while the names of New York groups rarely refer to that city. In other words, it is as if being from New York is an "unmarked" property (in the semiotic sense), while those from other localities show a greater predilection for "marking" themselves as such.

That process will be theorized in connection with two particular locales in Chapter 5; the case of the Goodie MoB and a focus on their song and video "Soul Food," from the (1995) album of the same title, will illustrate how a poetics of locality and authenticity can work through sound, visual images, words, and media images together. The group (consisting of Cee-Lo, Big Gipp, Khujo, and T-Mo) originates in Atlanta, and that fact will turn out, in the pages that follow, to determine much of the poetics to be discussed. Or more precisely, the group's origins in Atlanta, *together with a more global system of representation*, combine to create a complex field of signification, some of whose workings it is the task of the following analyses to trace.

Despite having a long and well-established local rap scene, Atlanta has only since 1994 or so acquired national (and international) prominence in the production of rap music. As the adopted home of

---

[2] The picture being described here should be rounded out with the acknowledgment that New York artists also project, in an equally explicit fashion, their geographic claims; but here, the processes work somewhat differently. For while most non-New York artists "represent" principally the city of their origin (as, for example, Crucial Conflict with Chicago, or Mystikal with New Orleans), with perhaps some smaller geographic units mentioned in song lyrics and shout-outs, New York artists "represent" specific neighborhoods or boroughs, with little conception of New York as a city. Thus, for instance, Nas, AZ, or Mobb Deep "represent" specifically Queensbridge.

former Bay Area mack rapper Too $hort, Atlanta attracted some attention in the US media; but it was not until Outkast's successful 1994 debut album *Southernplayalisticadillacmuzik* that the city's presence was nationally recognized as a rap music center. Already, that album not only established some of the musical poetics to be discussed here, but it also features some members of the Goodie MoB on several of its tracks (and the two groups not only continue to collaborate in various ways but also share the same production team, Organized Noise – which, given the importance of production in reception of rap music, is extremely significant).

Specifically, Atlanta is allowed, in international rap imaginations, to stand as a metonym for "Southernness" (as even the title of Outkast's first album suggests). Given that other Southeast United States cities (with the special and largely forgotten exception of Miami) had not yet produced mass-market successes in rap music, Atlanta's ability to become emblematic of a region might not be surprising; but at the same time, other factors ranging from Atlanta's popular image as the "capital of the South" to its Big City image (as compared to, say, Memphis or Charlotte) cannot but have contributed to its potential for effective geographical symbolism. And the Southeast, in turn, offers the (well-rehearsed) potential to construct a (to hip-hop culture) new model of African-American rootedness. For it is not likely that Atlanta was a starting point for a great proportion of the African-American workers that left the Southeast for urban centers all over the United States in the 1930s through roughly the end of World War II; but if it may stand in for the "South" in general, then much of what the "South" means in African-American culture and communal memory may be transferred to that city.

In the case of the Goodie MoB, their media appearances and interviews leave no doubt that geography forms a crucial part of their self-presentation to rap music consumers. Some quotations from an article in the popular magazine *Rap Pages* will illustrate just how central Atlanta and "Southernness" are in representations of the group:

For T-Mo [a member of the group], *Soul Food* represents Southern comfort – straight, no chaser ... Sitting down to talk to Cee-Lo [another member of the group] is like sitting down to chat with a country preacher over lemonade after Sunday service ... He responds to questions with a soon-to-be-signature twang as thick as red beans and rice. (De Priest 1995, p. 57)

All these images – comfort (leaving aside for now the pun), the country, religion, lemonade, and the red beans and rice that many African-Americans would recognize as soul food – leave no doubt that evocations of the South run across several registers and perform multiple functions.

Cee-Lo participates actively in this construction, comparing each of the group's members to an article of soul food, according to presumed qualities of the artist (T-Mo being like bread since he is independent, while Cee-Lo is like vegetables since he provides balance, and so on). As the figure of soul food acquires layers of meaning in the course of this discussion, Cee-Lo's equations will gradually take on the character of a guarantee – a guarantee of authenticity through one of the more common signifiers of viscerality.

For now, it is also important to note that rural location (e.g., De Priest refers to the group's "majestic sound as lush as the natural green landscape of their surrounding" [p. 54]) and numerous references to religion suggest an image of communal existence echoed in quite a few aspects of the group's public life. The album *Soul Food*, in fact, opens with a prayer recited in unison by the group, a gesture often startling to first-time listeners but wholly consistent with the ways in which "Southernness" is presented as a positive value.[3]

The foregrounding of religion, particularly one whose rhetoric connotes specifically Christianity (as when the aforementioned opening prayer addresses the "Lord"), might be expected to alienate a large proportion of potential record buyers in the secular (or, if religious, Islamic or Five Percent Nation) world of rap. But the positive reception the group receives in the major hip-hop media and their vigorous sales suggest that religion acts metonymically for some more widely appealing value: the following discussion will suggest that the value in question is precisely communal existence, and that communal existence in the song and video *Soul Food* arises as the real referent of the many images of food.

The wide-ranging references in the article to different aspects of "Southernness" find a homologue in the song, among other things, through the mediation of musical style. The musical texture here (pointedly in the contrast to that of the Ice Cube song discussed in Chapter 3) is remarkably consistent. Though built (as is now standard in much rap music) from multiple tracks and thus timbrally complex, it rarely engages the additive and subtractive changes that we call "layering technique." The beat is slow by rap standards, and (perhaps for a lack of high-pitched activity) the bass range dominates the texture. And in the generic and geographic system of rap music (discussed in Chapter 2), slow, continuous, and bass-heavy textures are indices of "Southern" musical styles. Now, within the seme "Southern," there is further differentiation, such as the dance-inflected "Miami bass" sound, or a particular Houston funk sound

---

[3] The name of the group, as well, conveys the intent to lend positivity to Southernness; it shortens the phrase "the good die mostly over bullshit."

initially popularized by the Geto Boys. Atlanta, by this regional system, may be better known for more outright funk than that heard in the present song – labelmates (and frequent artistic collaborators) Outkast have been instrumental in establishing that association;[4] on the other hand, as will become clear in the course of this discussion, the linkage to notions of community and "spirituality" necessitates some departures from the "player"-style images often associated with Outkast.[5]

Specifically, the conspicuous absence of guitars and funk-style bass (given, that is, the otherwise "Southern" style) combines with the tempo to open the possibility of *redefining* "Southernness." In a sense, then, the remarks that follow can be taken to address the question: what is then inserted in this stylistic opening? The first, perhaps the most obvious, answer to this question must involve the memorable chorus, sung in unison by the entire group;[6] and its status as a "hook," and certainly one of the keys to the song's (relative) commercial success, by no means mitigates the fact that it is a *particular* hook, and a highly marked one in the world of rap music, at that.

The chorus is not marked for being sung; in fact, one of the (at times regrettable) recent trends in rap (especially since the decline of classic so-called "gangsta rap") is precisely the R&B chorus, common in laments (such as 2Pac's "I Ain't Mad At Ya" [from Shakur 1996]), love/seduction songs (such as Method Man and Mary J. Blige's "You're All I Need" [from Method Man 1994]), and "player"/"Big Willy" poses (such as AZ's "Sugar Hill" [from AZ 1995]). But "Soul Food"'s chorus is emphatically distinguished from hip-hop R&B and brought closer to earlier, more gospel-inflected soul by the homophonic group singing, the closely spaced harmonies, and the unmelismatic melodies. If, as has sometimes been suggested, rap music often acts as a nexus of African-American musical memory (as Rose 1994 sometimes suggests), then the song's chorus is a stylistically assertive reflection of a more distant past than the more standard hip-hop R&B chorus. So, if it is not marked for being sung, the chorus most certainly *is* marked for its introduction of what might, in other contexts, be thought of as a temporal disjunction – namely, the

---

[4] And indeed, it may even be argued that the slow, keyboard-thick funk textures supporting a lot of mack rap render the Southern soul/funk style automatically suggestive of the genre.

[5] The album opens, in fact, with one such departure, as the group recites a prayer in unison.

[6] In calling this a "chorus," as opposed to my earlier usage of "refrain," I am drawing the following distinction. A refrain tends to be one or two lines that end a verse (often followed by some bars without rapping); while a chorus tends to be more extended and detached from the verses.

emergence of soul music conspicuously closer to pre-War (and just post-War) practices than rap usage normally brings about. Indeed, the chorus marks out a linkage of soul music specifically to *gospel* music (and intentionally so, as an excerpt from an interview with a group member shortly will show).

That having been established, it is now important here to distinguish between the *modality* of presentation in "Soul Food"'s chorus and that of either sampling or more specific musical troping. If the chorus had relied on sampling (as, for example, Ed O. G. and Da Bulldogs do so effectively in "Love Comes and Goes" [from Ed O. G. and Da Bulldogs 1993]), then the timbral/spatial distancing of the sample may well have served to emphasize the *separation* of a posited narrative present from the prominently bracketed past. Likewise, a trope on a well-known earlier song – such as in Warren G's (from Warren G 1997) "I Shot the Sheriff," with its complex path from Bob Marley through Eric Clapton and both Western and gangsta genres – would have foregrounded the *historicity* of the particular soul style the Goodie MoB invokes (as the invocation of well-known work from the past inevitably does).[7] But the "live" singing of an original chorus, with no perceptibly ironic relation to the rest of the song, suggests that its musical style must constitute a "here and now" and impose its historical time with true ontic force.

This is, of course, another way of saying that the singing suggests *authenticity*, and that the older soul style serves as an index of identity that is strikingly unironic in the context of rap. Here, the symbolic logic of the "music itself" rejoins an earlier part of our discussion, and the music is opened onto the implications of soul music's South-eastern (and rural) origins (including, but not limited to, African-American religious traditions). For both the present song and the album of which it forms a part assert not just an authentic identity – something they certainly share with a great deal of hip-hop culture – but furthermore an identity that is *oppositionally collective*.[8]

---

[7] As a *Gedanken* experiment to demonstrate this, the reader might wish to imagine the group singing their own version of a Soul Stirrers or Golden Gate Quartet song as the refrain. The social situation of such an act substantially shifts the way we might think of the Goodie MoB's invocation of such an older style.

[8] This term is not necessarily to imply that the song somehow successfully opposes the capitalist system of which it most assuredly forms a part; it could well be proposed, for example, that at a minimum, a community of political action is required to define effective resistance – and even then, one must be careful to examine effects, rather than assuming that any discourse of marginalized citizens is necessarily oppositional. Rather, the term "oppositionally collective" here suggests that some aspects of the song are symbolically counterposed to a socially destructive force, opposing collectivity to a presumed present fragmentation. The task here, then, is to identify the poetic strategy of counterposition.

Now, the Southern identity being projected in "Soul Food" is not oppositional simply for implying the existence of a collectivity: after all, the urban identities of hip-hop artists and audiences (from "posses" and "crews" to buyers of Wu-Wear[9]) are also imagined constructions of a collectivity. Rather, "Southernness" is here unusual in rap contexts for opposing itself to the urban *tout court*, and for risking a break with the mark of "urban-ness" which normally guarantees some degree of authenticity in hip-hop culture. For it is "Southernness" and "ruralness" which stand as negations of an absent semiotic center, a semiotic center constituted in rap's own genre system; if any social identity can be said to hold for the vast majority of rap music, perhaps outweighing that of "blackness" (the latter, of course, not necessarily being confined to black artists), then that identity may well be "urban." If the discussion of the group in *Rap Pages*, quoted above, emphasizes the rural collectivity with images of the country preacher and the Sunday service, then, as we will soon see, the song also qualifies the rural identity in other respects and regrounds the group in urban contexts, in ways that could, depending on one's theoretical approach, be called either polysemous and complex or bet-hedging.

Before going on to aspects of the song which emphasize the urban, though, it is worth here recalling the relative lack of layering technique in the song – that is, the relatively small degree to which the layer-density changes. As was mentioned back in Chapter 2, a number of sublimities (e.g., rhythmic, pitched) may be implied or enhanced by layering; no such possibility arises here. If, then, one infers from generic "hardcore" connotations of dense layering technique that the technique itself has something to do with "ghettocentricity," and therefore a certain discourse of the urban, then the relatively slow, simple, and sparse layering of "Soul Food" may be said itself to refuse designating the song as "ghettocentric," or even urban, in character.

The rapping technique follows a related, though different, course. Figure 4.1 transcribes the complete lyrics for the song, with the MCs' names entered in square brackets before their verses. As in the case of "The Nigga You Love to Hate" from the previous chapter, each line corresponds to a complete measure; the first syllable of each line either arrives on the downbeat or is the first syllable after the downbeat.[10]

---

[9] Wu-Wear is a rather expensive label of T-shirts, sweatshirts, skullcaps, and other clothing owned by members of the Wu-Tang Clan and marketed in their recordings and public appearances.

[10] I have adopted and modified the lyrics transcribed in the liner notes for the album, retaining spellings that may seem idiosyncratic (but are in fact common in hip-hop-related writing).

Rap music and the poetics of identity

Figure 4.1: The lyrics to the Goodie MoB's "Soul Food"

[T-Mo:]
My old boy from the point, but I'm from Southwest, and
Every now and then, I get put to the test, but I
Can't be stopped, 'cause I gotta come true. Ain't
Got no gun, but I got my crew. Didn't
Come for no beef, 'cause I don't eat steak. I got a
Plate of soul food, chicken, rice and gravy, not
Covered in too much, drinking a cup of punch, tropi-
Cal every last Thursday of the month.

[Big Gipp:]
Daddy put the hot grits on my chest in tha morning, when I was sick
Mary had tha hot soup boiling. Didn't know why
But it felt so good, like some waffles in that
Morning headed back to the woods, now I'm full as a tick,
Got some soul on blast in tha cassette,
Food for my brain, I haven't stopped learning yet. Hot
Wings from Mo-Joes, got my forehead sweating, cele-
Ry and blue cheese on my menu next.

[Khujo:]
        Southern Fry won't allow my body
To lie still, tied face goons surround
Me like cancer drill, me with second-
Hand obstacles but only to make matters
Worse, plus I'm getting pimped by this temp lady Jackie,
From Optima staffing niggas, laughing, shut up
Clown, don't talk to me like that, looking stupid of
Course, living day by day, and you ain't hard
Trick, hell you say?

[Cee-Lo:]
        It's such a
Blessing when my eyes get to see the sun rise, I'm
Ready to begin, another chance to get further a-
Way from where I've been. But I'll never forget every-
Thang I went through, I appreciate the shit, because
If I hada went and took the easy way, wouldn't
Be the strong nigga that I am today, every
Thang that I did, different thangs I was told, just
Ended up being food for my soul.

[whole group, singing:]
        Come and get you
Soul food, well,
Well, good old-fashioned
Soul food, all
Right. Everythang

130

Rap geography and soul food

Is for free, as good as
It can be. Come and get some
Soul food.

[Khujo:]
Sunday morning where you eating at? I'm on
Thirteen-sixty-five Wichita Drive, ole' burd
Working the stove ride, churches dripping chicken in yester-
Day's grease, didn't go together with this quart of Mickey's,
Last night hanging over from a good time,
Yeah, beef is cheaper, but it's pumped with red
Dye between two pieces of bread, Shawty look
Good with them hairy legs, wish I could
Cut her up, but my stomach come before sex.
A house full of hoes, now what's ingredi-
Ent? Spaghetti plus her monthly flow.

[T-Mo:]
        They know
They making it hard on the yard, fuck Chris Darden!
Fuck Marsha Clark! Taking us when we're in
The spotlight for a joke. Changing by the
Day, I see it's getting bigga in my square,
Looking at the Lennox from the outside with a stare, no
Money to go inside. Tameka and Tiffany out-
Side tripping and skipping rope to the beats from my
Jeep, as I speak wuz up from the driver seat.

[Cee-Lo:]
A heaping helping of fried chicken, macaroni and
Cheese, and collard greens, too big for my jeans. Smoke
Steams from under the lid that's on the pot. Ain't
Never had a lot but thankful for the little that I got.
Why not be? Fast food got me feeling
Sick, them crackers think they slick, by trying to make
This bullshit affordable. I thank the
Lord that my voice was recordable.

[whole group, singing:]
        Come and get you
Soul food, well,
Well.

[Big Gipp:]
    Hold up C, it's what I write, and Miss
Lady, acting like we in jail, says she ain't
Got no extra hush puppies to sell. Bankhead
Seafood making me hit that door with a mindful of
Attitude. It was a line at tha beautiful
J. J.'s Ribshack was packed too, looking to

Be one of dem days when Momma ain't cooking.
Everybody's out hunting with the family,
Looking for a little soul food.

[whole group, singing:]
        Come and get you
Soul food, well,
Well, good old-fashioned
Soul food, all
Right. Everythang
Is for free, as good as
It can be. Come and get some
Soul food. [repeat, fading out the second time]

The first verse, delivered by T-Mo, instantiates a rhythmic style that, given the release date, would be marked to rap consumers as squarely sung. Figure 4.2 transcribes the rhythms of the first four measures (with the upbeat "My old") from the song, numbering beat-classes (BCs) 0 through 3 and their imbricated sixteenth-note values (also 0 through 3) from left to right; attacks on each successive syllable are then marked, with the successive lines moving downward on the graph. Thus, the format here is the same as was used in Chapter 2's discussion of MCing styles. Below the graph, the corresponding lyrics are reproduced for easy reference.

Figure 4.2: Rhythms of the opening lines of "Soul Food"

0				1				2				3			
0	1	2	3	0	1	2	3	0	1	2	3	0	1	2	3
												x	x		
x		x	x	x		x	x	x		x		x			x
x	x	x	x	x		x	x	x		x	x	x		x	x
x		x	x			x	x	x	x	x		x		x	
x		x	x			x	x	x		x	x				

Text
My old
Boy from the point, but I'm from Southwest, and
Every now and then, I get put to the test, but I
Can't be stopped, 'cause I gotta come true. Ain't
Got no gun, but I got my crew.

The figure reinforces an impression one might simply garner from listening, namely that the rhymes arrive here in couplets, and that the couplets arrive on BC 3; the one exception is the last line of the passage, in which "crew" arrives a sixteenth-note early. Furthermore, the passage establishes a consistent pattern of a weaker caesura on BC

1, or a sixteenth-note earlier, as well as a weaker caesura on BC 2, or a sixteenth-note earlier. The result of the regularities, both in the realm of rhyme placement and in the realm of rhythmic pause (and therefore, of course, attack), is a pattern of regularized repetition – in other words, a sung style.

The rhymes occur in couplets ("West"/"test," "true/crew"), and those couplets themselves feature rhythmic characteristics that pair them off. The first two lines, for example, repeat a prominent rhythmic motive, namely the pause (or: two-BC value) starting on BC 2, followed by the rhyming syllable ("-west," then "test") within, respectively, two, then three syllables; in both cases, the rhyming syllable arrives on BC 3. The net result of the rhyming couplet is a strikingly closed and formally balanced unit by contemporary rap music standards – a markedly sung-style couplet. The second couplet both reinforces and repeats the closure: first, it changes the rhyming syllable (to "true" and "crew"); and second, it forms an equally closed pair of end-rhymes. Though the arrival of the rhyming syllables in the second couplet is staggered by a sixteenth-note in the second couplet, the overall regularity is arguably greater, with the attack rhythm of the first two BCs identical. The second halves of the lines are less similar, although it should be kept in mind that one of the dissimilarities – the third line's attack on the third sixteenth of BC 3 versus the fourth line's pause at that point – in fact constitutes part of the formal closure of the entire two-couplet unit, since the fourth line's pause there (and therefore, its lack of upbeat into the following line) helps to constitute the two-couplet unit's rhythmic cohesiveness and establishes some degree of separation from the rest of the song.

Thus, the rhythmic regularity of the lines transcribed in Figure 4.2 instantiates all the features of sung style – the end-rhymes landing at the same (or extremely proximate) rhythmic place within their respective measures; rhythmic repetition; coincidence of rhythmic and grammatical/semantic groupings; and segregation of lines into even-numbered formal units. In addition, it should be remarked that the four lines already present a contrast to the dense packing of rhymes often associated with (1990s) (North-)East-coast "hardcore" rapping styles (e.g., Big Punisher). One might even risk calling these couplets "sing-songy," if by that term one still reserves the possibility of some ultimate validation. Indeed, it is crucial to reserve the possibility of validating the style of the couplets; for the "sung" style may work its own terms of validation, particularly given the geographic self-positioning of the Goodie MoB.

To approach more closely the language of cultural studies in which this technical discussion must ultimately be contained: the rhythmic technique of the opening couplet establishes the two simultaneous discourses of identity and difference. The music is mapped geographically and chronologically, against dominant geographic locales (especially: New York, the Northeast) and against the effusive (especially speech-effusive) rhythmic techniques that mark out contemporary style. Now, it has already been argued in Chapter 2 that the effusive styles are popularly recognized as predominant in contemporary hip-hop music. Furthermore, the effusive rhythmic styles (again, especially the speech-effusive one) may be identified with a certain representation of urban life.

The rhythmic counter-representation of "Soul Food," then, works negatively against the hip-hop sublime and the associated projection of post-industrial urban life. Now, whether the resulting suggestion is simply of rural life or of industrial-era urban life is perhaps too fine a line to be drawn simply from rhythmic poetics, but it is a fascinating decision not to be able to make. Certainly, the public representations of rural qualities projected in the media reports and interviews quoted above indicate the rural as the proper negation of the urban. But here, we must perhaps tread more carefully, since, ultimately, Atlanta also forms part of the larger context of the Goodie MoB, as other songs from the album, such as "O.M.N.I. [One Million Niggas Inside]," make abundantly clear. In fact, it is instructive to recall here that the geography invoked during the lines just described – the Point and Southwest – is explicitly that of Atlanta itself. For now, it will suffice to bear in mind the tensions that have built up so far in this discussion, between the rural and at least some sense of the urban – that is to say, Atlanta itself. Later, we will return to this tension with a proposal of, if not a resolution, at least a more comprehensive picture than simply "tension" would convey.

In the meantime, some poetics from the rest of the song, including its video, will help to develop the themes of community, the rural, and the urban. Or more specifically, looking at the rest of the song, and at the video in particular, will problematize the "rural," as the literality of that concept as well as the presence of the urban enter a productive tension.

One way into this process is to notice that as the song progresses, the rhythmic style tends toward the speech-effusive. As the MCing progresses from one member of the group to another, the rhythmic patterns become less mappable, and we finally start verging into the complex, sublime flow of the speech-effusive, as the final five lines from Khujo's verse will illustrate. Here, the graphing technique is the same as previously, except that because of the speed of Khujo's delivery, it is necessary to subdivide sixteenth-notes. Therefore, a larger "X" in the figure indicates an attack halfway through the indicated sixteenth-note.

Figure 4.3: The end of Khujo's first verse

```
0               1               2               3
0   1   2   3   0   1   2   3   0   1   2   3   0   1   2   3
_____
      x   x   x   x   x           x   x   x       x   x   x   x
  x   xX  x   x   x   x   x           x   x           x   x
  x           x   xX  xX  x                           x   x   x   X x
x             x   x   x   x   x               x   x   x       x
  x           x           x   x
```

Text

... plus I'm getting pimped by this temp lady Jackie,
From Optima staffing niggas, laughing, shut up
Clown, don't talk to me like that, looking stupid of
Course, living day by day, and you ain't hard
Trick, hell you say?

The distance here from the rhythmic style of the song's opening lines could hardly be more dramatic, with unpredictable caesuras, sudden flurries of syllables in varying metric locations, and no appreciable repetition. In addition, the passage features no rhymes until the final couplet ("day" and "say"), and the grammar of the passage is erratic, portraying (presumably) a heated exchange between two parties. In addition to the distinct change from the rhythmic style of the song's opening, a topical and geographical change is in evidence: a reference to a largely urban profession – that of "temp" – and furthermore one notoriously prominent in post-industrial cities.

The rhythmic flow continues along speech-effusive lines, not constantly, but by and large: since members of the group are entering at various points for the rest of the song, there are also imbricated several instances of the common practice (discussed in Chapter 2) of proceeding from an initial sung rhythm into increasingly effusive styles. But none of the verses in the remainder of the song replicate the initial verse's maintenance of the sung style. In fact, Cee-Lo's own first verse inverts the sung-to-effusive progression, beginning with a complex counter-rhythm to the continuous beat, while the last couplet of his verse (before the sung chorus; see Figure 4.4) returns suddenly to a sung style. Here, the end-rhymes and metrically repeated caesuras outline an arrival at sung style. The reversal of the song's (and rap style's) sung-to-effusive process is no mere curiosity, but rather a dramatic development in the song, for several reasons. For one thing (and not at all trivially), Cee-Lo is by far the most publicly recognized figure of the Goodie MoB; media stories and interviews, publicity photos, and other aspects of the star machinery all render him the principal personality of the group. But the force of the moment does not stop there.

Figure 4.4: The end of Cee-Lo's first verse

0				1				2				3			
0	1	2	3	0	1	2	3	0	1	2	3	0	1	2	3
x	x	x	x	x	x	x	x	x		x	x			x	x
x	x	x		x	x	x	x	x		x	x			x	x
x		x	x	x		x	x	x	x	x	x		x		
x	x	x		x	x	x		x		x			x		

Text
If I hada went and took the easy way, wouldn't
Be the strong nigga that I am today, every
Thang that I did, different thangs I was told, just
Ended up being food for my soul.

For it is these lines that contain the play of words that connects the two major sets of imagery in the song. The pun of "soul food" as both a communal cuisine and "food for [the] soul" – the sense of the latter being the personal development that Cee-Lo predicates on hardship – allows the otherwise somewhat disjunct topics of the song to coalesce, in a gesture whose significance permeates the representational strands of the song. Here, scenes of communal eating and scenes of personal and collective challenge are equated; and the fact of eating's always being to some extent communal in the song so far strengthens the association – one has, in the song, always been referring to community, as descriptions of food consumption always refer either to family nurturing, group gatherings, or semi-public places. If soul food turns out to have been standing for community in the song, then its equation in these lines to personal challenges would collectivize the ethos of the latter, as well. In other words, soul food is always shared, even when it seems to come in the course of an individual life.

Cee-Lo's final couplet is followed by the first chorus and allows its multiple determinations to become explicit: the "soul food" being sung about relates eating to the facing of difficulties, and to communal experience in general. To grasp this last aspect, it is important to recall not only what has already been discussed here about the chorus, but also that the eating invoked in the song takes place in group contexts. In fact, it may well be argued that soul food in itself already implicitly invokes communal contexts, as inextricably tied as it is to notions of an extended family. In that case, the metaphorical sense of "soul food," referring to "food for the soul," equates the trials of living with the health and nourishment of group life.

So, the arrival of the chorus, hard on the heels of Cee-Lo's final couplet, takes immediate advantage of the new play on words of "soul food" to project the lives described in the song as part of a communally contextualized growing process. But, at the same time, the merging (by word-play) of the literal and spiritual nourishment cannot be assumed to erase the initial and basic reference of "soul food," namely, as a traditional food of mainly rural African-Americans in the South; and for that reason, the nourishment of communal life cannot be separated, in the song's representation, from images of rural (and Southern regional) life in general.

Food as an act of communion and community cohesion complements, indeed homologizes, the *musical* linkage of sacred and secular scripts, namely the choruses, in which homophonous male singing suggests both gospel and soul traditions. So, when after the Cee-Lo quote above, the chorus appears for the first time, the religious and communitarian meanings of "soul food" are intact, then rejoined by the musical conjoining of those worlds.

But food and music are not simply analogous links of the daily to the sacred: because earlier in the song, in a formally far less prominent place, the representational linkage of music to food is made more explicit in a line from Big Gipp's verse: "Got some soul on blast in tha cassette, / Food for my brain, I haven't stopped learning yet." The couplet serves several different purposes simultaneously. First, it helps to locate the song in the genre of "knowledge rap," in which the didactic purpose of music is foregrounded – for here is music related directly to learning. Second, it makes explicit the homology of food and music, not only by referring to the music on the cassette as "[f]ood for the brain," but also by making that music explicitly *soul* music – the linguistic, if not exactly the historical, complement of soul food. And third, soul music does parallel the *geographic* identity of soul food – especially the style of soul music presented in the choruses to come. In short, the couplet makes explicit what the formal organization of Cee-Lo's verse, and the following first chorus, can only imply.

Now, it was mentioned earlier that the song's layering activity is relatively modest, with little textural variation; what now can be remarked is that the chorus in question here is followed by the first dramatic layering event in the song, namely the complete halt of all musical tracks except the sustained synthesizer. The event accompanies the entrance of the next MC, Khujo, specifically his initial question, "Sunday morning where you eating at?"

The return to full texture follows with his response on his own behalf, "I'm on / 1365 Wichita Drive," followed by a description of a meal at that address. The layering event, then, highly marked by the otherwise modest layering differentiation in the song, articulates a geographic challenge, one that by this point in the song, interweaves (in this case very local) geography with community, food, religion (including by the temporal locality of Sunday morning), and (on more than one level) music.

Following Khujo's ethical challenge (and his response on his own behalf), the song's rhythmic style shifts markedly from the sung to the speech-effusive. Cee-Lo's second verse, for example, begins (Figure 4.5) with a dramatic contrast to the end of his previous verse (transcribed above in Figure 4.4).

Figure 4.5: The beginning of Cee-Lo's second verse

```
0             1             2             3
0   1   2   3   0   1   2   3   0   1   2   3   0   1   2   3
─────────────────────────────────────────────────────────────
    x   x   x   x   x   x   x       x   x   x   x   x   x   x
x       x   x       x   x   x   x       x   x   x
```

Text
A heaping helping of fried chicken, macaroni and
Cheese, and collard greens, too big for my jeans.

The quickness, and lack of rhythmic repetition, marks an opening gesture of effusive style which characterizes the verse as a whole. The one exception to the transformed rapping style is the final couplet of this verse, in which Cee-Lo remarks that white people ("crackers") believe they succeed "by trying to make / This bullshit affordable. I thank the / Lord that my voice was recordable." This is only a momentary and localized exception to the increasingly effusive rhythmic style, but it works similarly to his earlier verse-ending couplet, by making explicit a notion that had previously only been implicit in the song. In this case, the image of the song as resistance is foregrounded.[11] Of course, just what is being resisted symbolically is in a sense the scenario that is being drawn.

The second chorus that immediately follows the couplet is in fact a truncated one, or perhaps better said, a false start, which completes only the first of the four measures. Its interruption is probably the most striking moment of the song formally. (When I play the song for people who have never heard it before, this is the point that tends to get the strongest visible reaction.) The reasons for its effect, I would argue, are not simply the precedent from the first verse that the chorus should last four measures, nor even that in general, choruses in rap (or popular musics in general) should bear some proportion to verse length.

A further reason for the jolt of the interruption, I would argue, has to do with the fact that it disrupts a developing relationship; for the

---

[11] Further than that, the image is made explicit in terms of technology, in a manner that can be seen to confirm Rose's (1994) assertion that hip-hop culture is to a great degree *about* the appropriation of technology.

"smooth" and rhythmically relaxed chorus had previously promised counterbalance to the increasingly effusive rhythmic style of the MCing. Indeed, the promise had not only been stylistic; if one keeps in mind the popular association of effusive rhythmic style with a "hardcore" urbanity (discussed in Chapter 2), as well as the more rural and communitarian suggestions of the soul choruses, then the stylistic balance offered by choruses also had offered something of a balance of social ethoi. The interruption of the chorus, then, begins to tip the scale not only toward the speech-effusive (and often percussion-effusive, as well) style, but also toward a specter of the urban (and associated social disruption) which the figure of "soul food" is supposed to counteract.

What is more, a second and final dramatic layering event accompanies, and thus marks, the event – the entrance of the Big Gipp's next verse – that prematurely ends the chorus. The layering event involves the complete disappearance of all musical tracks, leaving stranded the Big Gipp's voice enunciating, "Hold up Cee[-Lo], it's what I write." If, as has been maintained here, layering articulates the semantic level, then the song projects this moment as a dramatic one. A listen to the recording renders remarkable that the Big Gipp singles out Cee-Lo as the addressee, and as the one who will presumably stop the chorus to make place for more rapping. The entire group, after all, sings in the chorus, in addition to other guest vocalists.[12] But even more puzzling, Cee-Lo can be heard on the recording following up his final couplet by saying "soul food!" and laughing, throughout virtually the entire completed measure of the chorus. So, Cee-Lo's being asked to end the chorus emphatically positions him as the group's leader; it underlines, as well, the fact that it is his own verses that, so far, have led into the choruses.

Indeed, in publicity about the group, it is Cee-Lo who receives the most attention, and his public persona is in many ways inseparable from the nexus of food, geography, identity, and music being discussed here. In interview situations, Cee-Lo insists on the role of religion in the music, saying, for instance, "I would say my music is directed toward God" (Gordon 1997, p. 51). His frank and frequent references to his Christianity are, in at least one case, explicitly integrated to his discussion of the choruses in "Soul Food": "Well, the foundation of [the choruses in "Soul Food"] is gospel and blues" (Gordon 1997, p. 51). The two particular genres Cee-Lo names are key, here; rather than naming the contemporary genre to which many listeners might assign the choruses – indeed, to which I would assign

---

[12] Specifically, Sleepy Brown and 4.0 are credited, with the group, on "background vocals."

them, given the otherwise contemporary context – Cee-Lo names the two genres which, in popular imagination, form the bases for most African-American music. The historical locations of blues and gospel furthermore complement the representational strands already identified throughout this discussion of "Soul Food": the two musics not only invoke a certain historical continuity consistent with the traditionalism of soul food itself, but they also suggest the rurality, religion, community, and the Southeastern African-American existence. In other words, by locating the choruses of the song in those two genres specifically, Cee-Lo attaches meanings to the choruses consistent with what seems to be their discursive and formal function.

At the same time, he projects an interpretation of his religion that reopens it from the personalized system of beliefs – as when, for example, he says that "I don't want to force my interpretation of God on nobody" (Gordon 1997, p. 51) – back onto a project of social identity:

> To me God stands for: Gaining One's Definition.[13] I know there is a God, because he gave that interpretation to me ... I don't know why it's not taught in church, the nationalities of the people in the Biblical days. They was Black!
>
> (Gordon 1997, p. 51)

The Afrocentric project here is not as explicitly manifest in "Soul Food" as it is in other songs from the *Soul Food* album (e.g., in "O.M.N.I."), but the opening of religion onto the field of collective identity and definition-gaining is central to religion's role in the song "Soul Food." And in fact, the (quasi-literal) deification of identity-building reflected in Cee-Lo's words even suggests the possibility that religion itself is a figure in the song, or at least configured as an occasion for community-building.

The video for the song would reinforce this notion.[14] It adds a narrative frame to the song (as happens so often in music video), yet one (*unlike* much music video) closely related thematically to the lyrics of the song. The narrative alternates (also commonly for music video) with "performance" scenes of the group rapping on the street or in the studio, and it describes three scenes of eating. The first such scene presents the members of the group as workers in a fast-food hamburger restaurant and is coterminous with the first verse. One

---

[13] Evidently the interviewer, Allen S. Gordon, found these remarks significant enough to title the interview "Gaining One's Definition."

[14] Discussion of the video here is not necessarily to suggest that the video and the song, taken together, somehow may form an integrated "artwork"; rather, since the focus is on the various strands of public representation surrounding the song, the video, songs, interviews, album artwork – and so on – would all seem equally relevant. Thus, the category of authorship, though certainly relevant in some contexts, takes a back seat in the present discussion.

MC serves customers and is subject to abuse from them; and the other three are involved with food preparation, which affords an opportunity for a lingering shot of a wan, gray hamburger sizzling unappetizingly in grease. The cooks are also subject to verbal abuse from a (white, female) manager, with one of them (Khujo) retaliating by purposefully oversalting the french fries. When the group loses its patience with the work, they storm out of the restaurant, handing a hamburger, on their way out, to a down-and-out looking elderly black man sitting against an outside wall of the restaurant.

Two things can be remarked here. One is that the song explicitly, at three points, stigmatizes the eating of both beef and fast food, which act as negatively valued semiotic binaries to chicken and soul food, respectively.[15] So the scenes of the fast-food restaurant, with its unappetizing hamburger, tap explicitly into an already negatively weighted value for the song. Now, the crucial observation here is that the scenes also link the food, via the abuse of customers and (especially) the manager, to social domination. Therefore, the group's defiant exit from the restaurant describes some sort of imagined resistance to that domination.

The second point to be noted here is that the exit of the group from the restaurant coincides with the singing of the first chorus. Given the representational strands that have already been discussed concerning the choruses, one can see in that detail a solidifying of the significances of the fast-food restaurant.

The second scene of eating continues the close coordination of scene to song, as Khujo's "Sunday morning, where you eating at? I'm on / 1365 Wichita Drive" overlies the group's entrance to a soul-food restaurant. In addition to specifying the significance of the address, the scene portrays a calmer situation, with the group seated together at a round table, in modest surroundings. Brief shots of other patrons portray a black clientele, and the soul-food restaurant scene even displays a praying woman during the (as already discussed, both formally and semantically important) final line of Cee-Lo's verse ("I thank the / Lord that my voice was recordable").[16]

The progression from fast food to soul food, coinciding as it does with the song's articulations, already parallels the ethical and political dichotomies of the song. But the video has a third location of eating, namely a women's shelter, whose identity is established by a brief

---

[15] The song also stresses, at some points, the time required to cook soul food, thus suggesting that the stigma of fast food involves a resistance to the very temporal structure of modernity, to which the traditional passage of time is contrasted.

[16] Viewers of the video who own or have seen the album will recognize here the similarity to the album cover, in which a wide-angle photo shows the group seated at a smaller, rectangular restaurant table, huddled in communal prayer.

shot of a sign explicitly naming it as such. Oddly, the transition to that third location coincides with the naming of "J.J.'s Ribshack," leaving undecidable the issue of its correspondence (if indeed there is any) of the scene to that moment of the lyrics. What is clearly visible, however, is that the women's shelter returns the group to the role of serving food, in contrast to the soul food restaurant, at which they were simply consumers. Here, the group is once again dressed in food service clothing, but in this case, they serve trays of modest food and drink to long rows of tables populated mainly by women and children.

The scene allows the notion of "service" to be recontextualized from a capitalist and exploitative context (i.e., the fast-food restaurant) to a communal and charitable context. The changing value of "food service" provides a semantic strand barely present in the song itself;[17] and yet, the representations of service complement the song, accentuating more strongly than the song alone the change from exploitation to community that (by the ideology of the song) accompanies the transition from fast food to soul food.

But the video does not provide a simple organic unity to the song (and indeed, it is reasonable to ask whether videos *ever* do so); rather, it recontextualizes the song in respects that cannot be ignored, in the context of the song's public existence. In particular, it is notable that for all the rural images of the group's publicity, the video emphasizes those aspects of the song's imagery that are specifically urban – not only "1365 Wichita Drive," but also the street scene just outside the fast-food restaurant and the women's shelter.[18]

With the video, then – and, for that matter, with the considerable portion of the song's lyrics that refers specifically to the geography of Atlanta – the emphasis falls squarely on the creation of communal life in the city. The geography, in fact, can be said to be crucial to the networks of representation in both the song and the video; for ultimately, what matters in "Soul Food" is not the urban or the rural as such, but rather the tensions between the values of the two, and the ways in which the group tries to negotiate those tensions, musically and otherwise. If soul food becomes a figure for community, then it is the urban soul-food restaurant that becomes a site for an attempted mediation, much as the song itself represents an attempt at mediation between rap and soul (or gospel) styles.[19]

---

[17] Indeed, the "lady, acting like we in jail" from the song hardly can be said to code service positively.

[18] These scenes are not, of course, exclusively urban, but metonymically, if they are to be cast in some social context, then urban seems more likely than rural.

[19] "Soul Food" is by no means the only song on the album to attempt such a mediation. "The Day After," for example, especially prominent for ending the album, attempts

142

The group may be inferred from all these representations as themselves caught in some sort of medium (and mediating) state between urban and rural life (as, indeed, the publicity already discussed strongly suggests). If that state can be said to mirror closely the famous condition of "double consciousness" theorized by DuBois, then the same nevertheless could not be said for other songs on the album, which often project a more unstable and menacing reality. "O.M.N.I.," for example, uses the name of a famous Atlanta architectural landmark as an ironic pun, referring the signifier instead to the acronym "One Million Niggaz Inside," which in turn suggests that "a million niggaz want to tear Atlanta up." And "Dirty South" illustrates the combined oppressions of law enforcement and social conditions in a strictly urban Atlanta environment.

But "Cell Therapy" – significantly, the first single from the album, and the first video released by the group – counters "Soul Food"'s gestures at urban/rural negotiation by representing not just city life, but also a positively apocalyptic and millenarian view of the "new world order." The latter involves not just images associated with the phrase in right-wing American politics (as is unfortunately common in much rap music), but also the more tangible increasing constraints on urban African-American life (such as curfews). Indeed, the album's often shocking contrasts, e.g., between religious and communal life and fragmented urban life, may at times give the impression of a contradictory vision.

But the semes of the urban and the rural, the fragmented and the communal – for that matter, fast food and soul food – not only depend on each other for their existence. Nor are they simply in a productive tension. They also mark out the geographic specificity of Atlanta, not because Atlanta is somehow more rural than any other major American city, but rather because a specifically *hip-hop* cultural (and rap music) geography codes Atlanta as "South" in terms of an imaginative mapping of the United States. The coding of groups such as the Goodie MoB, Outkast, Eightball and MJG, and (to take up another city) the Fifth Ward Boyz and Geto Boys as "South" and therefore in some way "back home" predominates in popular representations of them (and often their own self-representations). The fact that geographic/cultural identities for Houston can be (and frequently are) lumped together with the very different Atlanta shows just how strong and overarching the mere fact of "Southernness" can be in rap musical contexts.

Of course, the mass migrations of African-Americans from various

an even more thorough integration of the two styles, with even more overtly religious lyrics.

parts of the South to industrial centers all over North America from the 1930s to the 1950s goes a long way toward explaining this image of the Southern United States. But the origins of rap music in New York, combined with hip-hop culture's sometimes predominant concern with its own historicity and authenticity, must be considered at least as powerful a determinant of this particular mapping of the United States. The operation, then, of regrounding the song in the "urban" is a delicate one, accomplished in "Soul Food," as we have seen, with specific geographic references (complete with an address and the name of a business) and the visual settings of the video; it is then left to other songs on the album to fill in aspects of Atlanta life, ones that, of course, cannot but be flavored by the specific tension of urban and rural projected in the title song.

It would perhaps be too speculative to refer to the geographic tensions (and especially the urban/rural tensions) in the song as "layering," especially since essential to the latter term are the notions of polyrhythm, repetition, and rupture discussed in earlier chapters (and, of course, in the writings of Rose, Walser, Keyes, and others). Nevertheless, issues connected with layering – specifically polyrhythm – must return at this point in the discussion, most notably in the observation that the sublime aesthetic of effusive MCing threatens, at times, to overrun the verses after the initial chorus (and only most dramatically in the truncation of the "second chorus"). For if certain sublime musical effects, including the effusive MCing techniques of the song's later verses, return, then so does the whole specter of post-industrial capitalism and the devastation that it has visited on American cities – and disproportionately, their African-American populations. "Cell Therapy" shows the specter more dramatically, but perhaps less instructively, since it represents a far less ambitious gesture toward identity-formation than "Soul Food."

Some questions arise from the analysis. It is certainly to be hoped that the relevance of musical poetics – including specifically rap poetics – to the formation of identity is evident enough from this discussion. But questions of style and genre come to the fore, since the song is, after all, a foray either into a new genre or into at least a new combination of genres.[20] Specifically: if some sort of effusive style (whether speech- or percussion-) might be expected in just about any genre – the major exception being the mack genre, from which the group separate themselves emphatically[21] – then the appearance of

---

[20] At any rate, the difference between genre combination and new genre formation sometimes may amount to nil.

[21] Though it is certainly interesting to see the mack genre appearing strongly in the case of the group's labelmates, occasional co-performers, and production-mates Outkast (in the sense that both groups are normally produced by Organized Noise Productions).

effusive MCing in the latter part of the song can also be read as a concession to stylistic convention and, equivalently, the state of recent rap music overall as a genre.

But this possibility, I would argue, only goes to point out the fallacy of considering stylistic characteristics of music (not just rap) as somehow independent of cultural signification. For the point is, the re-emergence of an initially repressed sublime aesthetic – repressed, that is, because the "urban" appears explicitly in the opening couplet, yet in a sung style – is not "just" a matter of style, or "just" a matter of cultural identity, but rather is both simultaneously. Theorizing about the poetics of the music appears to differ from doing cultural theory in general, only because institutions have tended to separate those who do the former from those who do the latter (and, of course, because a host of disciplinary procedures have reflected and reduplicated the separation). But in cultural settings such as those of African-American musics, and especially in such a strongly identificatory music as rap, musical poetics (including whatever level of "music analysis" seems called for) is not just permissible; it is, I would argue, crucial to mapping cultural process and identity formation.

The foregoing has argued not a connection, but an equivalence among musical poetics, identity formation, and geography (or at least, some aspects of the latter). It is worth, at this point, taking a moment to consider the notion that the "ghettocentricity" (to use Robin D. G. Kelley's term) of hip-hop culture mentioned earlier can never simply disappear from any historical inscription of rap music. Such a notion is particularly suggestive in the case of the Goodie MoB, whose publicity and image for most rap consumers hinge so crucially on notions of rural life, and to some extent on the "outside" the latter is imagined to afford to those from the Southeastern United States – even if they themselves may originate in large cities like Atlanta.

In the time since the release of the album, the geographic functions of "the South" have been further complicated by the precipitous rise of Master P and other artists on the No Limit label. The relatively quick and extremely impressive commercial success of the No Limit label – started by a businessman and artist (Master P) from New Orleans and featuring mainly other artists from Southeastern cities – along with the deaths of 2Pac Shakur and The Notorious B.I.G., has greatly altered the geographic world of "hardcore" rap, affording "the South" the opportunity to be the new capital of gangsta rap.[22] Indeed,

---

[22] This is not to imply that The Notorious B.I.G. or 2Pac were consistently gangsta rappers – on the contrary, such a claim, unfortunately widespread in the popular media, should be contested. But their sometime engagement of gangsta rap, along

if gangsta rap is enjoying a second life or an after-life, a strong argument could be made that it is now provided by No Limit. Neither the frequent complaints – in my view, justified – that Master P has little skill nor accusations that his originality is compromised by his stylistic resemblance to the late 2Pac has made significant dents in his commercial presence; and his stable of artists (such as Silkk the Shocker, Mystikal, Mia X, and Eightball, to name just a few) seem themselves poised to insure a new identity for "the South" which belies much of the imagery and reputation of the Goodie MoB. In terms of musical style, as well, the ostentatiously electronic (and often quick-tempo) percussion of a good proportion of No Limit beats, along with often keyboard-heavy textures, is more than a little suggestive of G-funk – an association which has recently been shored up by the defection of Snoop Doggy Dogg from Death Row records to No Limit. Rather quickly, the public character of "the South" has changed, and the Goodie MoB's Atlanta origins may not offer as characteristic and convincing a profile as they did in 1995.

Nevertheless, the group have retained their image, still being acclaimed for their "positivity," their intellectual substance and their political responsibility, as can quickly be seen in public reception of their second (1998) album, *Still Standing*. The first single from that album, "They Don't Dance No Mo'," dovetails neatly into that image, with its overt critique of representations of subservient blacks – a topic very much reminiscent of the material for which Ice Cube used to be praised. More important in the present context, the styles of the song, both of the musical tracks and of the MCing, are very much within the spectrum established by the first album, allowing the group to sound drastically different from No Limit artists. One might begin to observe, then, the formation of a new genre system associated with "the South," in which various aspects of both musical styles and MCing can differentiate generic signification within the same geographic region. The power of "Southernness," then, as an identity with certain semantic and musical consequences, may be diminished, as groups like Arrested Development become a distant popular memory alongside the visibility of Master P and his cohorts.

Such a development, though, need not prove at all fatal to the Goodie MoB's public position, because they have themselves established a certain model of "Southernness" in their *music*. The beats and MCing style themselves retain the referential characteristics which once were equivalent, in the rap imagination, to "the South," but which are now constitutive of only one particular representation

with their commercial presence, was highly significant generically and geographically, until their deaths.

146

of the region. Furthermore, the semantic parameters of the group's music set them apart from the No Limit ethos, maintaining themes of social and political critique. It is this last aspect of the Goodie MoB's music, projected in "Soul Food" and a good many other songs, that continues to model the South as a place outside the central location of hip-hop culture, in both geographic and discursive senses of "location." In other words, the spatial removal of the group's origins from the origins of hip-hop culture and rap music becomes, metaphorically, an enabling factor for critique – they are imaged as "outsiders," in both senses of the word, in popular and media reception. By contrast, reception of the No Limit artists has consistently rendered them as mainstream artists, appealing to audiences regardless of geographic origin or loyalty; indeed, they are imaged as central to rap to the extent that a major music publication (*Spin*) may offer the challenge "WHO ISN'T FROM THE SOUTH?" (Borow 1998). The last rhetorical question clarifies the drastically different significance, in the media imagination, of the No Limit "family"'s Southern origin, namely that rather than being sources of critiques and outsiders, those artists have *moved the mainstream*, or at least significantly displaced it to the point that New York is no longer the assumed center of rap music that it had been just a few short years before.

How is it that the significance of the Goodie MoB's "Southernness" is exteriority enabling critique, while the significance of the No Limit family's "Southernness" is a displacement of the mainstream of rap music? One obvious answer might be found in the greater commercial presence of the No Limit artists, especially Master P, whose multiple-platinum albums have both enabled him to establish himself as one of rap's most successful artists, and afforded him the opportunity to promote other artists on his label to commercial success. While the Goodie MoB has also enjoyed substantial popularity, theirs is far outdistanced by that of Master P. While perhaps appearing superficial to those more focused on culturalist arguments, this factor cannot be underestimated: both the "West Coast" (i.e., principally Los Angeles, although the Bay Area is now substantially represented) and "the South" have gained much of their discursive geographical force by sheer record sales and (concomitant) publicity. On the other hand, the separation of the Goodie MoB from the No Limit "South" would seem to be overdetermined: we have already seen that musical style (including MCing) is involved in this process. But other determinations could be invoked, involving not just the semantic realm of social critique, but also the much broader category of representation that divides the world up into the "urban" and the "rural." While, as was discussed earlier, it may be paradoxical that a group from a major American city such as Atlanta could fall into a nexus of rural representations, an entry to such a paradox might be found in the broad extension of the "urban" and the "rural" as social categories.

In particular, we have seen already how the Goodie MoB are imaged, in their publicity and media accounts of them, in relation to both religion and "down home" imagery, the latter directly drawing on collective memories of the second diaspora. It is this latter memory, and its incarnation in particular representations of the Goodie MoB, that might be taken as a cue for understanding the Goodie MoB as a "rural" group. In fact, the dichotomy of "urban" versus "rural," as explicitly cued as it is in the group's music and public personae, may ultimately be a rewriting of something rather different, namely a socialized memory of *displacement*. Necessary to that representation of displacement, then, would be its determinate negation, namely the notion of a prelapsarian state, one in which some imagined wholeness precedes the current fragmentation, whether the latter be social, cultural, or spatial. Many of "Soul Food"'s features may be invoked as part of this implicit notion; one might invoke, for example, the singing at the choruses. There, apart from the historic associations of gospel already mentioned, one would do well to recall how the style and timbre of that singing was something other than the bracketed, historicizing sampling technique so commonly used to frame soul style in much rap music. To that it can now be added that the immediacy effect of the group's singing would seem to bear some relation to the prelapsarian "down home" idea, especially when one considers the relative rarity of a group's part-singing in the rap genre.[23]

It is considerably more difficult, but nonetheless worthwhile, to think through the role of soul food itself in this equation. Certainly, the release of a film by the same name within a couple of years of the song (unrelated to the song, although the soundtrack for the film was released on the same independent label), and the accompanying publicity equating soul food to family unity, suggest together a broad cultural significance to the food itself; and African-American culture – traditional and modern – is replete with references to soul food that clarify its inextricable association with unity of family, and (often church-centered) community.[24] Thus it forms a suitable counterpart to

[23] It should be mentioned here that there certainly are some artists that rap and sing within individual songs; Lauryn Hill (of the Fugees), Missy Elliott, Warren G, and Montell Jordan, for instance. But it is an extreme rarity that an entire group sing in parts, as the Goodie MoB does in this song.
[24] Even a recent soul-food cookbook (White 1998) illuminates the inextricability of the food from notions of religion and community. Equally important, articles like Nash

148

the musical images of wholeness, a kind of gastronomic equivalent of the singing in the choruses, or for that matter, the sung style of much of the MCing. This much seems difficult seriously to question.

But it is not a matter of simple homology – the other meaning of "soul food," i.e., food for the soul, overlays the prelapsarian image of community with an image of personal struggle (as, for example, in the last line of Cee-Lo's verse, discussed above). Other investments crisscross the nexus forming around the food – delaying sex, avoiding conspiracy (concerning beef). Food, then, is also actively imaged as a way of navigating one's way through the most contemporary and personal of situations – something other than an idealized image of wholeness before the fall. Of course, the semantic layer throughout the song effects a similar grounding in the real and the present; but it now will be informative to observe that the gradual building of effusive MCing, as group members alternate verses, not only projects a similar notion, but it also temporalizes it over the course of the song. This is not to equate effusive style with battle (or worldliness) and sung style with prelapsarian bliss, which would be a clumsy analogy indeed. Rather, it is to align sung style with singing itself, the harmonized vocalization of the choruses which themselves mediate a representational relationship of sung MCing to images of community and wholeness. Admittedly, the connection of sung MCing to communal (and, of course, rural) life is more abstract than many of the other aspects of the song's design that have been discussed here; and if valid, it would certainly only apply necessarily to this particular song.

But the notion may seem less far-reaching when one recalls the more general stylistic trend in rap music (discussed back in Chapter 2) to shape songs and/or verses in precisely a pattern that extends from more sung to more effusive rhythms – an observation that would displace the similar process in "Soul Food" from one of a speculative, and perhaps unhelpful, individualized intentionality to an effect of a more generalized characteristic of "hardcore" rap as a genre.[25] As a generic feature, then, the song's gradual journey into the personal and concrete becomes a suggestive intersection of a generalized style and a particular set of representations. The periodic (and relatively unchanging) choruses then may be conceived as maintaining the

(1996) and Greene (1994) show an increasing interest, both inside and outside African-American communities, in soul food – the latter referring to a "boomlet" in soul food business in New York.

[25] Here, it will be useful to recall that "hardcore" refers not necessarily to gangsta, or even ghettocentric, rap, so much as to a genre that distances itself from what are perceived as more "commercial" styles.

semes of the rural, the communal, and the prelapsarian, against which more narrativized and ambiguous processes take place.

Food, then, can be reconceived as an effective figure for the tension between the developing aspects of the song, on the one hand, and the constant references that serve as the song's frame, on the other. Food itself, often socially imaged as among the most basically carnal of objects and pleasures, at the same time becomes the site of some of the most heavily loaded cultural investments, as, of course, it does in this song. Thus, like the dichotomy of the "rural" and the "urban," food can both evoke prolific bodies of cultural weight and intersecting discourses, and it can also connect to the presumed constants and immediacies of sensation, body, and pleasure.

Overall, the song might leave the impression that the group is somehow straddling a delicately drawn line between, on the one hand, validating images of rurality, and community, and on the other hand, maintaining a generically required "hardness" and political topicality ("Fuck Chris Darden! Fuck Marsha Clark!"). Indeed, the more overt social critique of the song forms a crucial aspect of their public personae, as one item of their publicity, for example, claims for the group the status of "heir apparents to P.E.'s [i.e., Public Enemy's] conscious crown" (BMG 1998). Then again, neither the validation of rurality and community, nor the critique of present-day urbanity would be complete without the other term, and in fact, the developments, through the song, in both the semantic and the stylistic parameters contribute to the notion that the two flow into each other.

Once one has thought through the song to this point, it may be instructive to widen the perspective a little, and to think through the position of the song, and by extension the Goodie MoB themselves, in the context of the genre system of rap music. By the parameters of musical style and also by the constitution of their audiences, the Goodie MoB is very much a reality rap group, with "hardcore" credentials. More specifically, the song's semantic topics, along with the public reception, render the group squarely within the "knowledge" sub-genre – hence, for example, the very telling Public Enemy comparisons (which I have also heard and read uttered by their fans). But the song is to a great extent unusual within the reality genre: the beats are not "hard," in terms of how the term was discussed back in Chapter 2, and the group's (non-ironicized) singing in the choruses would suffice, in many consumers' minds, to disqualify them from the "hardcore" ethos, perhaps even relegate them to the damning category of the "commercial." What, then, preserves the group (and the song) from such a fate? Certainly, the styles of MCing (especially late in the song) contribute to the group's credibility among fans, as does the semantic parameter, with its explicit and socially engaged critique. But geography itself plays crucially into the equation, as well: for the "softer" beats, with their live-instrumentation sound, and the singing in the choruses, are not only acceptable from a "Southern" group, they are, in fact, very much an index of authenticity itself. Fan discussions and media articles are rife with references to "Southern-fried funk," and it is difficult to miss the proximity of, on the one hand, popular expectations of a slower and "simpler" musical style, and on the other hand, equally widespread representations of "the South" as a region with a slower pace of life and simpler, more traditional values.

So, in a sense it could be said that the Goodie MoB succeed with listeners, to a great extent, almost literally by "staying in their place." But such an assertion would still oversimplify the case: for the more traditionally "hardcore" aspects of the song, in fact, constitute something of a bridge between imaging "the South" in a way consistent with a rap geographic imagination, and bringing that geographic value to bear on a more generalized tradition of political critique. Nothing short of such a strategy, carried off with great aplomb, could account for the group's simultaneously flaunting their religious values, and also being listed by fans as favorites alongside the likes of 2Pac and the Wu-Tang Clan. If rap is still "ghettocentric" – and one could certainly preserve such a notion by pointing out the extent to which much of the group's music hinges on their Atlantan ghetto origins – then certainly, at least, quite a few different positions can be adopted with respect to classic hip-hop imaginations of the ghetto.

5

Two cases of localized (and globalized) musical poetics

It was mentioned in the introduction to this book that rap has long been a global music, appearing in most countries of the world in which there is a substantial presence of Westernized mass music. Such a claim is not at all controversial and is demonstrably true. What might, on the other hand, provoke some objection is a further notion I wish to advance here, namely that scholars of rap music (and, for that matter, probably of hip-hop culture in general) need to grapple somehow with global phenomena of rap in order to understand local ones – even if by "local," we understand the dominant force of the United States' rap industry.

The American hip-hop industry dominates the world hip-hop scene, much as American popular music in general carries repercussions for world popular musics. But nevertheless, American rap music and hip-hop culture do not escape global determinations; on the contrary, global determinations of American hip-hop are widely visible in respects other than the pervasive consideration of global music sales. Two examples will suffice to show this.

The vogue for Jamaican dance-hall singing/rapping is widely visible in American rap music since the first half of the 1990s, from KRS-One's album *Return of the Boom-Bap* (1993) (not to mention his frequent collaborations with Mad Lion) through Smif N' Wessun's "Sound Bwoy Bureill" (from Smif N' Wessun 1995), to the success in the United States of Buju Banton and Patra. The wide (and rapid) spread of "Jamaicanness" has been even more visible, from the dreadlocks of Das EFX (and many other artists) to the increasing popularity of Jamaican locations in rap music videos (like "Love, Peace, & Happiness" by the Lost Boyz).[1] The pervasive representations of Jamaican identity are themselves complexly

[1] Whether or not the impressive success of "Haitianness" in the personages of the Fugees is a related phenomenon is an open and difficult question. Certainly, "Jamaicanness" bears a close relationship to a more generalized pan-African ethos which has always been present in hip-hop culture and has been increasing since the demise of the gangsta genre's domination; and it is difficult to see the Fugees' invocations of Haitian identity – and especially their claim that the Haitian refugee

determined, as they overlap chronologically what one might remark as an historicist movement in hip-hop culture and commercial rap music.

The "Jamaicanness" phenomenon, though, is even farther-reaching than that particular location might suggest, since, as Paul Gilroy (1993) argues, Afrodiasporic cultures in the Americas are not only culturally interrelated; they in fact form a Black Atlantic system that links African-derived cultures from the West Indies, the Americas, Great Britain, and Europe, not to mention Africa itself, in a developing polylogue whose speed and vitality have only been increased by the late twentieth-century revolutions in communications and transportation. Lipsitz (1994a, pp. 38–44) also produces an impressive list of musical cross-fertilizations in the black Atlantic; while his focus is on African adoptions of Afrodiasporic forms from outside that continent, his list inevitably involves numerous crossings in both ways across the Atlantic. The many stops that musics make in England, and the changes wrought there by the particular social (including musical) conditions in that country (conditions well documented in Gilroy 1991), argue that the hallowed tradition of describing African-American musical traditions as a melding of African and American traditions may risk simplifying an important dynamic.

All of which bears crucially on the example of "Jamaicanness," since Jamaican musics are justly celebrated for their eclectic origins, ranging from the Rastafarian musics growing up around what itself originated as a religion of exile and return, to their best-known descendant, reggae, with its fusion of those already-hybrid musics with Jamaican folk musics and American popular musics, not to mention its particular envisioning of Africa and world Afrodiasporic solidarity. The current popularity of Jamaican identification thus extends to the whole of the Black Atlantic, while simultaneously locating that complex system metonymically in one of the places in which its crossings have produced some of the most influential musical (and, inseparably, political) developments. In other words, the discourses of "Jamaicanness" may function as ways of grounding the global in the local, allowing the latter to become (to some extent) a figure for the former.

This is not to suggest that "Jamaicanness" is *only* a trope, even for artists that have no direct family ties to the island. The prominence of music in Jamaican political life is well known (including among hip-hop cultural insiders), and there is most certainly, in the embrace of

situation is representative of refugee status in general – as entirely separate from pan-Africanism and pan-Caribbeanism.

Jamaica, something of a beckoning that rap music acquire a similar force of political gathering and mobilization. But further than that, it is crucial to keep in mind the Jamaican origins of hip-hop, which are well known (among other things) through the personages of early hip-hop figures (such as Kool DJ Herc) and the tradition of radio toasts. These origins are no doubt imaginatively reconstructed in these revivals of "Jamaicanness"; but the location of a certain pan-Africanness in that place also must be kept in mind as having determined (at least partially) that it was *this* specific origin of hip-hop that would be emphasized and reconstructed in the (much changed) present. And, in addition (and most importantly for the present argument about global determinations), Jamaica has, of course, developed its own unique hip-hop musical traditions; the situations of hip-hop historicism and pan-Africanism could therefore serve as conditions of possibility by which Jamaican dance-hall musical style has transformed much American rap music. This last-named development, of course, places the current argument about global influences on American rap music squarely into the context of musical poetics, to which we will return shortly. For now, it will suffice to remark how prominently global determinations (and not just in anticipations of global distribution) figure in the production of rap music, which is so often discussed in American-centered contexts.

Some negative determinations also suggest the value of thinking rap music globally; indeed, it may well be that one of the signal advantages to examining rap outside the United States, even if one's ultimate interest is in American music, is the critical perspective afforded by cultural difference. To illustrate, let us take as our second example of global determination how the phenomenon known as "Big Willy-ism" remains largely American, with only much fainter presences in other countries (at least as far as concerns their own musical production). "Big Willy-ism" describes the rap tradition of flaunting wealth and (generally scantily clad) women – more generally, accoutrements of success, by a certain acquisitionist and patriarchal logic; just about any Too $hort video would suffice to illustrate, as would The Notorious B.I.G.'s video "Juicy," and most of Ma$e's videos. The emphasis on wealth is what most readily separates it from rap traditions that might claim a more direct relationship to traditions of toasting; in the latter, boasting about prowess with women is, of course, extremely common, but the ostentatious display of wealth and consumption has little place.[2] And

---

[2] Videos are the easiest illustrations of "Big Willy-ism," since visual display more readily separates it from the more generalized boasting of toasting traditions. Jackson (1974) and Wepman et al. (1976) compile some examples from oral traditions of toasting.

although the display of women's bodies is something approaching an international language of music videos, the closely linked flaunting of wealth is a hip-hop tradition more specific to the United States. When one reflects on some of the most popular rap groups in France – one of the countries with the oldest and best established hip-hop scenes outside the United States – it is difficult to find artists whose lyrics or videos foreground wealth conspicuously. Whether one attends to the more commercially successful acts (e.g., MC Solaar, or IAM), the "gangstas" (e.g., Nique Ta Mère, or Lunatic), or more "conscious" acts (e.g., Les Sages Poètes de la Rue, or Assassin), Big Willy-ism just does not play a major role in French hip-hop discourse.

Similar results would obtain, I would posit, from examinations of other major hip-hop cultures and rap-music industries of the world. It is not the point here, though it would certainly be a fascinating venture, to explain why American hip-hop seems to have developed this as a characteristic feature; and the success of such figures as Ma$e, Jay-Z, and Puff Daddy, despite the latter's limited rapping ability, testify that it *is* a characteristic feature. Rather, the point is to say that global contexts of rap music culture provide a necessary illumination even for those whose interest is confined to American music.

The two examples given here of global determinations of American rap music should suffice to demonstrate that a focus solely on the United States might limit our understanding of how the music operates, even in the country that may still lay claim to its birth (at least in the form in which it is normally recognized). But, at the same time, it needs to be recognized that the global is, in turn, mediated by the local, as the popularity of Jamaican images demonstrates with particular force. This chapter is, in fact, devoted more explicitly to local determinations than to the global ones; the role of rap in creating, mutating, and propagating local identities can ultimately be followed best only in relatively localized contexts, but many aspects of its formation, especially institutional aspects, should be thought of as thoroughly globalized. The focus here on two local contexts is premised on the notion that rap music may be mediated globally, but that a certain detailed view of its function can only be seen locally, taking account of local uniqueness.

Thus, the studies of the present chapter, involving rap's formation of identities in Holland and in Cree native populations of Alberta, can only be taken as synecdoches for a process – the global mapping of rap music and identity – that could never end, only be outlined or suggested. That is precisely my intention, here: to suggest a theoretical approach to relations between rap music and cultural identity, based on two cases.

Both cases involve engagements of rap music in contexts far from the African-American one; and this, in turn, brings up the possibility of labeling the identities formed there as "hybrid." I must admit here to profound ambivalence about doing so, as I am in general extremely sympathetic to the idea, expounded most famously in Bhabha (1993), that liminality may serve to counteract the discursive containment of difference. By seeing both Dutch and Cree hip-hop as hybrid, we may certainly contribute to one of what I take to be Bhabha's goals, namely the clearing of "a new area of negotiation of meaning and representation," which may, in turn, lead to new possibilities for political action (1990, p. 211). And this is as good a place as any to confess to feeling often less comfortable with the idea of cultural uniformity than my references to African-American culture betray.[3] But at the same time, I am equally wary of the danger that the dismantling of "culture" as a concept may serve those who have already gained cultural legitimacy; thus, to celebrate the hybridity of Dutch and Cree hip-hop strikes me as posing the danger of losing the cultural situation of rap music that is actually never (as we will see shortly) lost in those places where rap and hip-hop become "hybrid." Thus, I wish to stake out a delicate (I hope, not impossible) position in which I might retain the liminality and anti-hegemonic effects of hybridity, while preserving the notion that rap does itself have an historical location in something which, at the time of its founding and early dissemination, stamped it with a particular cultural identity and which is never quite lost.[4]

The two hybrid cases, then, reflect the paths my own life has taken and are no better (though no worse) case studies than many other hundreds (if not thousands) of possible rap scenes. Still, each can lay a strong claim to particular relevance to issues of rap and identity, as I will argue in discussing them. Let us now turn to the first of the cases, then, and see one way in which local social formations refract and modify the global presences of hip-hop culture and rap music.

Dutch rap

The Netherlands provides, in fact, a clear illustration of the importance of conceiving together the global and local in rap music.

---

[3] Robin D. G. Kelley (1997) presents a compelling argument that representations of cultural unity among African-Americans have, at times, been willfully projected, for specific class and professional reasons (and usually by those outside the culture[s]).

[4] This is not to deny the point, made by Cross (1993) and others, that other groups, especially Hispano-Americans, were intimately involved with early hip-hop culture, especially, but not exclusively, graffiti and breakdancing. It is, rather, to locate both the early public representations of hip-hop and many of rap's poetic characteristics in specifically African-American conditions and practices.

Conversely, it points out the danger of focusing exclusively on American hip-hop culture; for the internationalization of American rap music has assured a universal presence of that music, but it has most decidedly not assured that international scenes will not diverge sharply. The lack of substantial discussion of non-American rap music in the work of even the most distinguished scholars – Rose (1994), for example – leaves a theoretical hole whose filling will require, as in any case of the global and the local, some detailed examination of the specific cultural forces at work in some region or community. At the same time, some aspects of hip-hop culture and rap music (and/or their representations) have indeed been globalized, so that some (largely American) image of "real" African-American hip-hop (and the ghetto) will probably never be absent from any local rap context.

The status of "Dutchness" is precarious in hip-hop culture. As Wermuth (1996) says, "[i]f we consider authentic cultural expressions as being real, natural and original, Dutch hiphop cannot be authentic by definition" (p. 3). And in fact, it was only by way of the international music industry that rap music could come to Holland, as, at the beginning of the 1980s, "Rapper's Delight" by the Sugar Hill Gang, "Rapture" by Blondie, and "Wordy Rappinghood" by the Tom Tom Club extended their success to that country (Wermuth 1996, p. 5). The identification of hip-hop as a product of American culture plays a pivotal role in the constructions of identity in Netherlands hip-hop culture (and in Dutch consumption of rap music overall). At the same time, as will become apparent, the Dutch have their own unique cultural dynamics, which exist both in an internal relationship and, in the case of rap music, in relation to a certain representation of the United States, as well.

First off, it must be noted that by far the best-selling rap music in Holland is American rap, which is imported in massive quantities.[5] As Wermuth (1996) explains, "[t]he Dutch record-buying audience does not like rap from the low lands. Maybe [that audience] is too hardcore, maybe it is too black" (p. 5). Thus, the presence of African-Americans in that country's rap and hip-hop life is not simply fantasized (although it is, of course, that, too) – it is also a financial and institutional reality. The reality has everyday consequences observable to any record buyer: just about every record store carries some American titles, but finding Dutch hip-hop sometimes requires looking in selected stores. (An exception to this rule is the Osdorp Posse, about which more will be said presently.)

---

[5] At the time I was in Holland doing field research for this book, Puff Daddy's *No Way Out* (1997) was just being released, and the publicity for it, along with the instant widespread availability, served as a tangible reminder of the centrality of African-American images in rap marketing there.

Part of the success of American rap surely hinges on the status that the English language maintains in Holland, which closely approximates that of a universal second language. It is rare to find young Dutch people who do not speak a substantial amount of English: English is required as a second language in Dutch high schools; the Dutch government has considered making English the principal language of Dutch universities; and the renowned Dutch cosmopolitanism and national modesty tends to perpetuate the society's remarkable openness to the English language. English-language television programming is extremely common. In the realm of rap music itself, popular (national) radio DJ Mental Kees (the latter word being pronounced like the English "case") frequently interviews English-speaking American hip-hop artists, to a committed and enthusiastic listenership.

In the Netherlands' popular music industry, as one might well imagine, the presence of the English language is both substantial (including some Dutch artists) and also received generally as a synecdoche for the dominance of American culture. Now, it must quickly be added that this dominance is not necessarily always stigmatized; on the contrary, in Holland, as in many non-principally-English-speaking countries, some tie to "Americanness" can be a positive value in the legitimation and validation of popular cultures. Wermuth (1996) quotes Dutch MC Boosta: "You have to stick to the rules of hiphop. Hiphop has its origins in America, so you have to rap in American slang. That's the rule" (p. 6).

Another factor concerning language in Dutch hip-hop is the indelible mark of its history, in which rap music lost commercial ground just as it was enjoying its greatest gains in the United States. As Wermuth (1996) describes it, the divergence arose when "hardcore" rap (especially so-called "gangsta rap") began its ascendance in the United States, and many Dutch hip-hop performers and fans alike felt alienated from music whose topics did not seem relevant, and which, furthermore, was far more difficult to dance to. (Presumably, trying to dance first to something by the Sugar Hill Gang, then to something by Public Enemy, would be an adequate experiment to demonstrate the problem.[6])

Indeed, Dutch hip-hop fans and music scholars have told me, when I asked about their notion of "hardcore," that gangsta rap has not been popular in Holland because social conditions there have not produced the gangs and persistent underclass that have enabled

[6] This is not to imply that Public Enemy was ever a gangsta rap group, which it decidedly never was; rather, it is to say that some of the changes in rap production, and consequently the changes in the sound and beat, wrought by Public Enemy and then popularized in gangsta rap were inimical to much club use.

gangsta rap to arise and thrive in America. Although I find it difficult, ultimately, to endorse such an implicit reflection theory of culture, there is certainly a point to what they say: the social safety net in the Netherlands has, for quite some time, far outdistanced that of the United States, and the large, inner-city populations of "racially" marked marginalized people are far less visible in Holland. And the Dutch are justifiably proud, both of their (relatively) tolerant history in general, and of their social integration of Indonesian and other formerly colonial subjects.

But the situation is far more complicated than the explanation would seem to imply. For one thing, some formerly colonial subjects, especially Afro-Caribbean ones (from Surinam and the Dutch Antilles), remain disproportionately poor and unemployed (albeit in generally less stressful social conditions than those of many inner-city African-Americans, some Dutch would be quick to point out). For another thing, there are newer immigrants, not from ex-colonies but rather especially from Morocco and Turkey, whose living conditions approach, if not fully reach, abject poverty.[7]

The situation is also more complicated with respect to rap music, because, contrary to the reflection theory by which some Dutch people have denied the possibility of Dutch gangsta rap, there was indeed a period during which Dutch gangsta rap was a reality. In the early 1990s, Holland saw a flurry of home-grown gangsta-rap imitations, illustrating that one strategy of the music industry at that time treated American-style gangsta rap as a product very much worth cultivating domestically. While most of the Dutch hip-hop fans I have spoken with speak of this phenomenon as an embarrassment, the music of this type that has come to my attention has mainly resembled some of the toasting genre of American gangsta rap – closer to, say, "The Nigga Ya Love to Hate" (discussed in Chapter 3) than to, say, NWA's "Gangsta Gangsta," with the former's more violent imagery carefully couched as metaphor. Now, one could certainly argue that, since this style of rap never found great commercial success and no longer is widely visible, therefore the Netherlands rejected gangsta rap. But, as will become apparent shortly, the fate of any English-language Dutch rap music must be judged in more polyvalent contexts.

---

[7] I stayed, during one of my more recent trips to Holland, in a neighborhood not far from such an immigrant population, and I was warned more than once not to venture into that population's neighborhood, particularly at night. Disturbingly, I noted that the way in which the Dutch people I encountered spoke about immigrants and immigration had changed from my previous trips there; political events and polls alike confirmed my impression that some social conflicts and events connected to immigration had changed the climate among those long settled in the Netherlands.

To add to those contexts, we must now consider some more specifics of Holland's hip-hop industry. Rap music was present there virtually from the beginnings of its recorded history.[8] Amsterdam and Rotterdam, particularly, have long had active hip-hop scenes, while The Hague, Groningen, and other cities have never been without some rap presence. In an unlikely twist of history, however, it is not in the bigger cities in the "Randstad"[9] but rather in the smaller and more provincial city of Eindhoven that one will find the principal record label of Dutch rap (and also dance) music, DJAX records.[10]

Independently owned (but distributed by EMI), DJAX was started by a record store clerk and (then) amateur DJ named Saskia Slegers on borrowed money. DJAX soon released its first (vinyl only) LP, *No Enemies* by the group 24K, in 1990. That record, with lyrics entirely in English, sufficed to demonstrate the rapid rate at which American rap styles were absorbed in Holland: the Public-Enemy style production and gangsta flow was, at that time, a cutting-edge commercial style. At the same time, the topics of the songs – largely about racial harmony and social justice – squarely confirm the proud Dutch claim of more constructive social engagement than that found in many American gangsta efforts. Slegers highlights the "positive" topics of 24K in her own narrative of creating the label:

There was a group which I totally liked, and it was from Eindhoven, from my city. And it was a mixed group, it was actually one guy from New York, who lived in Eindhoven, one guy from Aruba, one from Curaçao, and one Dutch guy, a white guy – so, three black guys and one white guy. And they had a very strong motto, they had like, their name was 24K, like gold, pure as gold, and they were very politically influenced. They had these topics like racism and everything, you know, what's happening these days. And their main issue was that black and white unite. (Slegers 1997)

Slegers also describes Dutch hip-hop culture at that time as "really a united scene, with blacks and whites uniting." Thus, even early in the history of recorded Dutch rap, the notion that Holland requires

---

[8] The following exposition of Dutch rap music depends largely on the pioneering work of Mir Wermuth; of course, whatever mistakes might be present are my own. Many thanks are due here to Ms. Wermuth, for her invaluable discussions with me, and for providing me with crucial materials on the Netherlands hip-hop scene.

[9] The "Randstad" is the geographic area delimited by roughly the triangle formed by the cities of Rotterdam, Amsterdam, and Utrecht. These cities all being relatively close together and also being among the largest commercial and industrial areas of Holland, the Randstad is an important cultural focus of much Dutch media culture and economics.

[10] Much of the following discussion of the history of DJAX and its relation to the Dutch hip-hop scene is based on an interview I conducted with Saskia Slegers in Eindhoven in June 1997, and on materials she provided for me at that time. My thanks to Ms. Slegers for her kind assistance.

more "positive" music was "in the air"; this point will return presently. The surprising success – by the standards of the Dutch market for homegrown music – of 24K encouraged Slegers in her original belief that Holland had a market for rap addressing specifically Dutch topics – or perhaps, more widely relevant topics, but with a "positive" Dutch ethos.

DJAX will probably be remembered, though, far more for its introduction of Dutch-language hip-hop to popular music culture. Particularly notable in that development, and in the history of Netherlands popular music since then, is the Osdorp Posse, a group from the Amsterdam neighborhood of Osdorp whose records first appeared on DJAX in 1991–2 (Slegers 1997). Until that point, in fact, Slegers reports that her sales of Dutch rap music were waning; it was the Osdorp Posse that revived her sales, her company, and the Dutch rap industry. Osdorp, in southeast Amsterdam, is known as one of the rougher neighborhoods of the city, home both to immigrants of quite a few different ethnicities and to lower-income Dutch-born citizens. The Osdorp Posse began as a humorous experiment on something like a dare, when rapping in Dutch could not have been much more than that; but their commercial success was quick, and the seven albums that they have released since then have all, by the standards of the Dutch popular music industry, sold quite well.

Soon the possibilities opened up by the Osdorp Posse were explored by other Dutch-language groups, with consequences that would fundamentally set the context of contemporary rap music in Holland. One of those possibilities was a stylistic one: for rather than imitating the densely layered, complex production style of Public Enemy, which was common at the time, the Osdorp Posse have, from the beginning, laced their musical tracks with live, stripped-down hard-rock performance. Often confining their musical tracks to electric guitars, bass guitar, synthesizer, and drums, and performing mainly simple power chords and harmonic progressions, the Osdorp Posse have conspicuously separated themselves from the main hardcore rap stylistic mold. They do often use scratching, but the technique of scratching – quick upbeats, for the most part, and usually with none of the signal from the record being scratched identifiable – is such that it acts more as a percussive instrument than as a source of intertextual reference. Samples can certainly be found a great deal of the time in the Osdorp Posse's music (as, for example, in "Zo Simpel"[11]); but they are used sparsely and unobtrusively enough so as not always to form substantial layers in the overall musical texture. And last but still

---

[11] This song can be found on the compilation album *De Posse, Deel Twee*, the second Nederhop compilation album from DJAX records (Various artists 1996c).

quite important, their tempi are quicker than that normally associated with rap music, and closer to those of much hardcore rock. In short, the musical style of the group often indicates more closely that of hardcore punk, although some traces of rap music (especially in the drumming) are almost always discernible, and the surprisingly seamless blending of the two genres would quite frequently remind American listeners (and Dutch listeners, too) of the Beastie Boys.

Also reminiscent of the latter group is the delivery of the rhymes, which are frequently shouted in clipped couplets, rife with end-rhymes and neat groupings of even numbers of lines. The shouted delivery can just as easily be attributed to the necessity of penetrating dense guitar-laden textures as it can to any stylistic allegiance; but whatever the cause, the net effect is a voice/instrumental-sound-wall relation with which fans of punk and punk-derived musics feel very much at home. It is also, of course, very much an antithesis to the complex, jagged, boundary-overflowing, and timbrally variegated styles referred to back in Chapter 2 as characterizing effusive MCing styles.

This is not to say that the Osdorp Posse are unique in combining rapping with punk/heavy-metal musical style. On the contrary, the history of such combinations is well known, ranging from Run DMC's/Aerosmith's "Walk This Way," through Ice-T's Body Count recordings, to the variegated musical excursions of the Beastie Boys. But the combination of Dutch MCing and hardcore rock instrumentals itself was enough to open up a market niche known as "Nederhop," one whose presence in contemporary Dutch hip-hop culture is ineluctable and must remain central to any study of Netherlands rap music.[12] The commercial success of the Osdorp Posse has been astounding, considering the relatively small size of the industry for Netherlands-home-grown popular musics, and the even smaller size of the Dutch rap industry; they are, as far as I know, the only Netherlands rap group whose members all support themselves solely from their musical career.[13]

In their wake, a substantial industry of "Nederhop" has arisen, featuring artists such as White Wolf, Neuk, Ouderkerk Kaffers, Zuid-Oost Posse, and West Klan. All these artists, significantly, record for DJAX, and all rap principally in Dutch. There are other independent labels with small numbers of Nederhop artists, but their presence is insignificant beside that of DJAX, both currently and historically. What is also significant about these artists is that they are white. Even

---

[12] The term "Nederhop," on the other hand, simply refers to any rap music that is rapped in Dutch.

[13] Slegers (1997) confirms this.

in the tolerant and relatively socially harmonious Netherlands, as in the rest of the rap and hip-hop world, race is indeed important, and Nederhop is, from the standpoint of performance, white music. That is not to say that there are no black Nederhop fans – though a public enough impression to that effect exists, such that one prominent figure in the Amsterdam hip-hop scene jokingly claimed to me that he was the "only black guy who actually likes Nederhop"; but Nederhop is white-identified in the Dutch popular imagination, and the consequences of that fact have important resonance for any discussion of rap music in that country.

In particular, black consumers in Holland, who identify largely with African-Americans, also tend to prefer rap music from outside Holland, most prominently from the United States (although France is another important source). An MC of Surinamese background (who, in fact, identified himself simply as "Surinamese," even though he has never been to Surinam) told me that he does not listen to Nederhop, but rather only to American rap (about which he was extremely knowledgeable).[14] This might suggest that Dutch people of African descent see Dutch versus non-Dutch rap music as a racial dichotomy; but in fact, Wermuth (1996) suggests otherwise when she asserts that "[a] lot of black rap fans see the difference between the so-called white coats (white avantgarde) and black lower class youth in terms of a class difference" (p. 12). So, the representations of rap music in Holland cannot perhaps be lined up clearly with musical styles; and indeed, the problem of separating out race issues from class issues is not one exclusive to Nederhop, or to Holland in general, as the debates within and between African-American communities over so-called "gangsta rap" (among many other things) demonstrate. But as my self-described lone black Nederhop fan himself suggests, the linkages of Nederhop and American rap to race are known in Holland and seem to have profound consequences.

The linkages of genre (Nederhop versus other rap music) to race also work through an important mediating term, namely the subcultures that consume the music. On numerous occasions, Dutch people to whom I mentioned Nederhop referred to it as "skateboarder" music, and I was referred on more than one occasion to areas of Amsterdam where skateboarders could readily be found in order to find Nederhop fans to interview. Wermuth's quotation of an MC named Malice, from the group Da Grizzlies, confirms that the association of skateboarders with Nederhop is widespread: "And then you have all the skaters: they listen to hardcore stuff, but the skate culture is not the same as hip-hop culture" (1996, p. 11). The

[14] This is Clyde of the Spookrijders, about whom more will be said presently.

"hardcore stuff" referred to here is hardcore rock – precisely the style that characterizes the music of the Osdorp Posse and other prominent Nederhoppers. All of this goes to suggest that the musical style of Nederhop is, at a certain level, tied to subcultural deployment. And since skateboarders in Holland (as in the United States) are, by and large, white, teenaged, working- and middle-class males, it is clear that musical style, subcultural allegiance, and social class are, in the world of Dutch hip-hop, imaginatively and performatively intertwined.

Another way to conceptualize this situation is that Nederhop is not just a "crossover" music in terms of audience, but that its crossing over has a clearly delineated stylistic embodiment. No wonder, then, that the "hardcore" rap fans in Holland who adhere to a more American notion of what hip-hop is tend to see Nederhop as impure, not "real" – leading Wermuth (1996) to remark that "[i]n terms of authenticity, Dutch rap fans seem to be more Catholic than the Pope" (p. 14). Indeed, the American acts that appear to be most consistently popular in Holland are those that, in the United States, are often upheld by the very most "authentic" fans as bastions of true hip-hop art against the forces of commodification (the latter often being described in terms of dance styles or "gangsta" rap): De La Soul (who gave a sold-out show in Amsterdam during one of my research trips), Jeru the Damaja, and the Alkaholiks all have a strong following there. To fans of these groups, Nederhop often does not qualify as true hip-hop (in the sense of authentic) rap music.

The narrative here privileges the dichotomy between, on the one hand, predominantly white-performed, Dutch-language Nederhop, and, on the other hand, predominantly black-performed, English-language American hip-hop. But that dichotomy, as functional as it may be in Holland, nevertheless requires (at least) two correctives. First of all, there is some other non-American rap that also has a substantial market: English, French, and German rap are all reasonably visible in many record stores, as is rap from a smattering of other places. Nevertheless, despite the extremely strong and artistically developed hip-hop scene in France (limited in Holland by linguistic barriers), and despite the attempts by some Dutch fans to make the dichotomy Nederhop versus "International" style – a well-intentioned gesture against American commercial domination that, in my view, just hides the latter – Nederhop and American rap music seem to form the principal binary terms of Dutch rap consumption.

The other qualification to my narrative is a small remaining tradition of English-language Dutch rap – that is, music by Dutch artists (or, frequently, artists from the Dutch Antilles currently living in Holland), but delivered in English. Some of these artists are extremely accomplished and have even mastered a certain "African-American" accent (and vocabulary) that all but disguises their national origin: Phat Pockets and Black Orpheus are both notable (and, in my opinion, particularly accomplished) examples. The musical tracks on these artists' recordings (along with other factors, including Slegers's 1997 testimony) make clear that their music is targeted at audiences that normally buy American-produced recordings.

The presence of English-language Dutch rap, though, itself requires delineation, for the commercial viability of this musical practice is most decidedly in question; the recorded English-language Dutch artists of whom I am aware are all signed to DJAX records, and the owner of that label, Saskia Slegers, has told me that her English-language recordings do not sell well; she intends to discontinue it and only release Nederhop (at least as far as concerns her rap products; Slegers 1997). Apparently, the one advantage being touted for this music – its addressing of "Dutch topics," about which more will be said shortly – cannot compete with the authenticity-appeal of the American variety.

Much more can be said about the Dutch rap scene and the fascinating, often more-authentic-than-the-Americans fans that help to constitute it. But what has been said will have to suffice here to set the context for the focus of this discussion, namely the recent appearance (on DJAX) of a group called the Spookrijders ("Ghostriders") and their first full-length CD, "De Echte Shit" ("The Real Shit").[15] The title of the album indicates an aspect not only of their music, but also of their public persona, which may serve as a theme of the following discussion. Specifically, it will be helpful to focus on the ways the group positions itself as representing "true hip-hop" – something simultaneously Dutch and authentic, as if to defy Wermuth's (1996) assertion that Dutch hip-hop culture and rap music lie within a "subculture which cannot be original" (p. 3).

When I first heard the Spookrijders' music, I was seated in a room (in fact, a staff office that had been vacated for the summer) at what was then called the Stichting Popmuziek Nederland (now the Nationaal Popmuziek Instituut), where I had been seated by the gracious and hospitable staff with two formidable stacks of Dutch rap recordings. Just about all of it was material one could not, for all practical purposes, find in the United States, and certainly material with which I was not familiar. My initial shock at the "strangeness" of

---

[15] The group also has a song on the DJAX compilation CD, *De Posse, Deel Twee* (Various artists 1996c). Significantly for the discussion that follows, in their song for that album, they already refer to their music as "de echte shit."

the music – "Beastie Boys" was my initial internal response – was followed by an adjustment and even a fascination with the (to me) new style. The point of this anecdotal set-up is that my own reaction when, making my way slowly through the second stack, I finally started up the Spookrijders CD was precisely the title of their album – "here's the *real shit!*" Of course, in responding that way, I was allowing myself to wallow in the "authenticity" orientation and narrowly focused fandom of which I normally try to be critical. But at the same time, I imagined that my response to the recording was not random but rather my own reception of a careful and deliberate strategy by the artists and the record company. I later found out this was true, on both counts.

Of the three members, one, Stefan Kuil, is "white" and of (to the best of his knowledge) a mainstream Dutch background; the other two, Clyde Lowell and DJ Cliften "Jazz" Nille, are black, Dutch people of African extraction. So the group itself is racially mixed – a not insignificant fact, given what has already been said about the color (and inseparably, class) identities of the producers and consumers of the various rap musics in Holland. Indeed, the group finds itself at the crossroads of quite a few different identity dynamics in Dutch rap music history (and, of course, the present).

The group raps exclusively in Dutch and is insistent on the value of that. Stefan Kuil offers, "It's more direct, people can relate, ordinary people" (Spookrijders 1997). At no time does the group assert the value of specifically Dutch linguistic properties; the lack of such a claim contrasts with Saskia Slegers's telling me that "Dutch rap is about Dutch topics, and Dutch ways of deforming language." The latter aspect – validating unique properties of the language itself – is inconsistently valued among the listeners and artists I have spoken to, sometimes foregrounded proudly and sometimes dismissed in the same self-deprecating way that many Dutch people speak about their language generally. If the apparent populist spirit of Kuil's "ordinary people" seems to imply an equation of the English language with elitism, then Kuil is equally explicit that the use of Dutch is not simply pragmatic, but also relates directly to identity issues:

I think it's really important that you have your own identity. You don't look so much to other countries ... I think that it's also important that people relate, understand the things you're saying. (Spookrijders 1997)[16]

Linking linguistic usage and comprehension to identity echoes a sense that many Dutch rap fans conveyed to me that differing social conditions in Holland rendered appropriate, even necessary, differences between Dutch and American music. Such a sense, in turn,

---

[16] All further quotes from the group are from Spookrijders (1997).

seemed to convey a sympathy with the popular representation in the United States that links rap music closely to social conditions. In the case of those wishing to validate the music, the linkage often conveys it as the voice of an underclass, while for those wishing to dismiss it, rap music becomes symptomatic of some terrible social malady. In the case of Holland, the notion of hip-hop culture's proximity to material reality often seems to manifest itself in the idea that Dutch rap music must somehow reflect the difference Holland enjoys from the United States, particularly in relation to its poor and immigrant populations.

A linkage of rap to material conditions and social relations spills over into more general notions of a different embeddedness in everyday life. As Kuil puts it,

I don't know exactly how it's like in the States, I only know from TV, but I don't think it's the same here like it is over there, because [there] you look around the neighborhood and you see only hip-hop dressed people. It's different over here. First of all, people live more indoors. It's not that I go out of my door and I walk on the street, and all I hear is hip-hop. It's not like that.

The image of hip-hop communities in the United States, and their absence in Holland, may well inform a notion of Dutch difference; but nevertheless, community remains crucial to the Spookrijders and their relation to the music. As DJ Jazz Nille emphatically points out, "My people is proud, because back in the Westside – I'm from the Westside – when I was back there, people had to shake my hand, 'Yeah!' – they liked it." In fact, a consistency could be traced in Dutch hip-hop imagination in the form of differentiation itself, both along the lines of nation (Holland as different from the United States) and along the lines of locality (the Westside as a place of community, Amsterdam as a particular kind of city).

The notion of rap's closeness to social conditions translates into a stigmatizing of gangsta lyrics, and a validation of more Dutch-appropriate alternatives. We have already seen, via Wermuth (1996), how the gangsta turn in the United States helped to precipitate greater consciousness of national difference, and Kuil reinforces the idea, underlining that he admired 2Pac Shakur "for the sensitive lyrics," adding that "to me it's not about the hard-hitting lyrics, so I prefer the Tribe [Called Quest] to the Wu-Tang [Clan]."[17] Kuil underlines the fit of topic to locality when he complains that

also the other Nederhop groups, they all talk about the same things: fuck Radio Free, fuck the police, and all that. And I think we have shown that you also can talk about more sensitive things.

---

[17] Such a remark about 2Pac Shakur may surprise those only exposed to his "thug" image; but songs like "Dear Mama" (from Shakur 1995) and "Life Goes On" (from Shakur 1996) are quite probably the inspiration for Kuil's reference.

While such a claim also invokes staking out the ground of originality, it relies on the notion that Nederhop, in general, takes its topical cues too slavishly from American rap. The Spookrijders' idea that different social relations in Holland should imply different semantic content was echoed time and time again in my conversations with Dutch hip-hop (and more broadly, music) fans, who emphasized that the most "hardcore" topics were unacceptably American-oriented.

Kuil's opposing of his own music to the "hard-hitting lyrics" is paralleled in his attitude toward the album, as well, as one can easily see by his pride in the song "Pappa's Kleine Meid [Papa's Little Girl]" – he singles it out as a particular accomplishment – about his two little girls. The refrain promises,

> [Jij bent] Pappa's kleine meid voor nu en altijd
> En er is niets in deze wereld dat ons elkander scheidt
>
> [[You are] Papa's little girl for now and forever
> And there is nothing in this world that separates us][18]

The genre identity of the musical tracks is consistent with both the topic and Kuil's lyrics (and the song is indeed credited to him alone), with an R&B-style alternation between an A minor ninth chord and an F major/minor seventh chord, played on synthesizer and set with simple bass A/F alternation and a slow hip-hop drumbeat. True to the R&B genre, there is very little layering in the song. The major layered events are confined to a slight thickening of texture in the refrain (some high synthesizer and processed guitar sounds, together with a doubling of Kuil's voice), which returns in the closing vamp; some xylophone notes in that same closing vamp; and strategically placed sounds of a baby gurgling. All this (with the exception of the baby sounds, obviously very specific to this context) bespeaks strongly one of the major connotations of hip-hop R&B discussed in Chapter 2, namely the love song. The musical properties of the song, its musical poetics, mark out a national difference as definitively as the lyrics. It is no surprise, then, that Kuil mentions "Pappa's Kleine Meid" as a difference he would want to underline between the Spookrijders' music and most other (especially American) rap music. And we have seen how such a song would play into larger discourses about the difference that Holland, and therefore Dutch rap, makes.

The match of more "sensitive" lyrics with geographic place is a localized discourse of authenticity; but equally forcefully, the group participates in a simultaneously more globalized and more rap-music specific ethos of authenticity. The globalized representation of rap as "hard" and anti-pop forms, for the group, a substantial aspect of its

---

[18] Translation mine.

validation, even though (as they are well aware) it has been globalized from some circumstances very specific to the United States. Indeed, despite the group's insistence on geographic differentiation, they eagerly attach themselves to American rap, over and against Nederhop in particular, as when Kuil informs me that he listens to English-language rap music, but specifies that he does not listen to *Dutch* English-language rap (like labelmates Black Orpheus and Phat Pockets). American MCs form his list of favorite artists, as discussed above; and Nille agrees, often mentioning his New York rap projects and acquaintances and reminding me that even before Dutch rap existed, he was a fan: "I've been listening to hip-hop since day one." Nor does the group admit to any substantial influence from Nederhop, as Kuil asserts: "Frankly, I never liked it. I'm still not a fan of Nederhop. The only group in Dutch I listen to is ourselves."

Identification with American rap, though, is not confined to claims of influence. Significantly for some of the principal theses of this book, the Spookrijders connect their admiration for American rap to musico-poetic aspects of their music. Nille sounds very much like many American artists when he claims rap history as his grounding, telling me "I want to make [their music] sound like old school." In fact, his own contribution in this regard is part of the narrative of the group's formation, since Nille was the last to join; Kuil explains that the group chose him as the final member because "What he made was, to us, real hip-hop." Later in the conversation, in response to Kuil's stated ambitions to play more live instruments, Nille clarifies that one of the things that makes "real hip-hop" for him is the use of sampling: "I want to keep it to the sampling, because hip-hop is sampling and playing sounds – that's hip-hop." Here, it is important to bear in mind the extent to which live instruments, especially guitars, are used in Nederhop, to understand that Nille is really talking about an allegiance to American "hardcore" musical structure. He becomes more explicit about this at one point, while explaining a central musico-poetic premise of the group's founding:

We want to put down the real shit. And then everybody knows it can happen like that, too. Everybody using rough-cut [sings guitar sound of Nederhop:] rah, rah, rah, rah, rah. And I didn't like that. That's why I thought, original style, coming strange ... and people go "Hey, what's happening now?" ... Real hip-hop, real life; and what we're saying is what we feel, straight from the heart, it's not a gimmick.

Here, three different discourses come together: stylistic orientation away from Nederhop and toward American sound; originality; and authenticity. Most significantly, Nille focuses all three discourses on the *sound* of the music, that is, on rap musical poetics.

American style does not simply extend to the musical tracks. Here, it will be remembered much Nederhop music (especially that of the quintessential Nederhop group, Osdorp Posse) deploys a sung MCing style, and it is recognized as such among those to whom I spoke. When I ask about the Spookrijders's markedly more speech-effusive flow, Stefan refers the explanation again to American contexts:

> That's mainly because we started off as an English-language type group. Listening to American groups and their styles, you pick that up. Most of the Nederhop groups, they just start the first time in Dutch, you know, all they listen to is the Osdorp Posse.

The critical reference to the Osdorp Posse, in the context of flow, becomes here a metonymic suggestion that in departing from the original (read: United States) style of rap music, Nederhop has lost a valuable strand of authenticity. That notion is also reflected, as we have just seen, in the group's discussion of musical tracks and beats. The authenticity problematic, though, also extends to flow, since the group deploys speech- and (especially) percussion-effusive styles more closely associated with American (and also more "international," for example French) MCing. Here, it is instructive to note that the MCing of the most widely-circulated Nederhop (for instance the Osdorp Posse) is fully consistent with my initial comparisons to the Beastie Boys, with ultra-sung flows. Specifically, widespread features of Nederhop flow include constant end-rhymes on BC 2 or 3, often arriving in couplets; regular and repeated rhythms; and even the frequent (also Beastie-Boys-associated) practice of group members' doubling (or even tripling) the voice of the principal MC at the ends of lines. These stylistic practices, along with the timbre produced by shouting, combine to produce a highly marked style within the broader context of rap MCing, one which, in discussions I had with Dutch artists and audiences, was often labeled "white." Obviously not dealing with any essential properties of ethnicity or "race," such a label nevertheless sets a crucial context for understanding the ways in which, protestations of racial harmony notwithstanding, discourses of "race" nevertheless seep back into contexts of Dutch rap. So, the Spookrijders' more effusive MCing connects them not only to linguistically related discourses of authenticity (styles assimilated from English-language performance) but also to racially inflected ones. Such a connection, in turn, is reinforced by the mixed composition of the group in the predominantly "white" world of Nederhop – helping them convey the notion of the "echte shit." We will see shortly that Saskia Slegers of DJAX intersects this process in her own notions of race and rap.

What may appear a contradiction so far – namely, that on the one hand, the Spookrijders' music must be specifically Dutch, and that, on the other hand, it must look musico-poetically toward the United States – reflects, in fact, two different stages of mediation. The global aspects of the music (in reality, American aspects that have been globalized by the international music industry) provide a basis for artistic credibility, while local aspects, based on specifically Dutch social conditions and notions of a logical semantic correspondence, maintain the ideological requirement, in hip-hop culture and the rap music industry alike, that one "represent." Kuil projects both sides of the equation when he proposes to me that "Maybe we're not Nederhop; maybe we're just hip-hop, Dutch hip-hop." The "just hip-hop," then, would refer to a notion of global style (albeit, of course, American just below the surface), while the apposition "Dutch hip-hop" regrounds it locally.

None of their attention to geography precludes the group's universalizing their music, as when Kuil, after describing the importance of rapping in Dutch, nevertheless adds that "You can talk about anything in any language." Nor does he wish to limit the audience for their music, notwithstanding the specific discursive position the group is attempting to occupy: "I think our music is for everybody. Hip-hop is for everybody that wants to listen. [Puff Daddy] is hip-hop for me, too ... I like every kind of music, I like jazz ..." Though a cynical response to such pronouncements might identify them as sheer ideology, or as calculated commercial ploys, Kuil assures me that the group's appeal is, indeed, widespread:

We see it all the time when we do shows in Holland. The audience exists from all difference kinds of people, you know, you have skaters, you get real hardcore Nederhop fans, but there are also real hip-hop fans ... But the reactions we get are all the same.

Of course, even here, he reserves the category "real hip-hop fans" as something other than the "hardcore Nederhop fans" and "skaters." So in the midst of pursuing the broadest appeal, the Spookrijders maintain a targeted position in the field of Dutch rap music – one which, as we have seen, specifically involves musical poetics.

Nobody to whom I spoke in Holland could think of other Nederhop artists who were trying to stake out the same ground of "echte shit" as the Spookrijders. Their relative newness and thus nascent commercial presence precluded them from most discussions of Nederhop I had with fans and subcultural "insiders." Those discussions tended more often to gravitate to groups like the Osdorp Posse, prominent newcomers like Neuk ("Fuck"), or some favorite group of the discussants – but everybody to whom I spoke knew of the

Spookrijders and seemed ready to acknowledge that they were trying to do something different. In some cases, the group's straddling lines between Nederhop and more "authentic" rap music seemed to hurt them, as fans from either side of the divide could criticize whichever properties from the *other* side of the divide the group embodied. On the other hand, nobody to whom I spoke about the Spookrijders seemed to consider theirs anything other than truly Dutch music. That embracing of the group can usefully be opposed to the case of groups like (Anglophone) Black Orpheus, whom a number of people referred to as simply producing American rap music in Holland. So, to whatever extent Kuil might propose that they were simply making hip-hop in Dutch, the fact of Dutch language and topics certainly remains an important facet of the group's reception.

But we must recall here a *global* aspect of hip-hop culture, namely its explicit – more explicit than most popular musics – concern with identity and authenticity. The interaction of this global aspect of hip-hop culture with the local situation of language conflict in Holland produces a specific value for the Dutch language in Dutch rap music, namely the value of "Dutchness" and national identity. When we return to the topic of English-language Dutch rap music, the dominance of globalized hip-hop music culture shows up, full force. There, no symbolic substitute is available for the authenticity of African-American artists, and the struggling Dutch English-language artists generally do poorly commercially. Slegers explains:

In this Nederhop scene, it's totally unimportant what color you are. It doesn't matter. But in the other [i.e., English-language] rap scene ... they all want to be as American as possible ... With this "real hip-hop," in the English language, they like it better when it's a black person.

While her first statement might, as I have argued, oversimplify race dynamics, her portrayal of English-language Dutch fans points to the continuing force of a globalized, American-dominated field of rap discourse. At the same time, she admits to having internalized some of the discourse herself, telling me that for her to enjoy English-language Dutch rap,

you must sound like a black guy ... I don't like it when they have a [Dutch] accent. So I'm very happy with the Dutch hip-hop [that she features on her label], because then they don't have an accent.

Here, one can discover a not-often-mentioned motivation toward the Dutch language, namely the very sound of enunciation. Could we count this as yet another respect in which Dutch rap foregrounds musical poetics in the construction of Dutch identity? Considering the role of timbre and enunciation in rap performance and reception – recall, here, the notion of "flow" – such a claim does not seem at all far-fetched. The relative commercial failure of English-language Dutch rap would seem to argue that the presence, since some years now, of Dutch-language music has transformed the genre system, such that "Dutchness" in rap becomes identified with the Dutch language per se (as opposed to, say, the Dutch topics that the Spookrijders cite). Such a shift would leave little room for more overtly syncretic artists like Phat Pockets and Black Orpheus. Slegers expresses this in economic terms:

> Let's say you have fifty to one hundred guilders to spend every week, which is quite a lot for young people, and let's say they can buy in Holland two CDs for that, because it costs forty guilders here for a CD: so what would you buy, the Wu-Tang Clan, or some [English-language] Dutch group?

That the answer seemed so evident as to be implied by a rhetorical question, shows to what extent the Dutch language connotes "Dutchness" in Holland's rap music consumer culture – and correspondingly, to what extent the English language shifts the advantage toward American artists. This may seem, at first glance, like an unremarkable fact, except that producers and consumers alike to whom I spoke almost universally cited Dutch *topics* (i.e., the semantic content) as the great value of the country's home-grown rap music. Such claims were, as mentioned above, often integrated with explanations of the differences between the Netherlands and the United States (the latter often as represented in its music).

What emerges from discussions with both the Spookrijders and Saskia Slegers is a picture of a complex rap genre system, with equally complex webs of signification and evaluation with regard to musical style. On the one hand, the genres and musical artists are categorized linguistically, along the bifurcation of English versus Dutch; here, the combinational possibilities seem, on at least a commercially significant scale, limited to in-country Dutch-language artists, and American English-language artists.[19] In the realm of musical style, the possibilities for combination are far more diverse, although at some level of abstraction the categories "Nederhop" and "international" apply. In the realm of rhythmic flow, the same dichotomy applies (again, at some appropriate level of abstraction). The combinations, of course, are what is telling here, and the combinational possibilities suggest that, indeed, more properly post-colonial categories of hybridity and displacement could well capture some of the dynamics of non-United-States rap cultures.[20]

---

[19] Such a binary is a bit oversimplified, since there is some presence, albeit small, of British, Jamaican (especially dance-hall), French, and German rap in Holland.

[20] I am not the first to suggest this. Lipsitz (1994) and Gilroy (1993) both identify rap music and hip-hop culture, to some extent, with possibilities for positionality and

At the same time, and importantly, the Spookrijders position themselves, and are positioned by others, in a very specific place which they consider in some way central and authentic. Lost in a celebration, or validation, of their hybridity could well be the process by which local authenticities can be reconstituted into imagined local communities. When the Spookrijders declare that their music is the "echte shit" and propose that their music is not Nederhop, but just hip-hop that happens to be in Dutch, they are staking out a discursive space that is simultaneously local and global, and simultaneously authentic and hybrid. A globalized music from localized (and ethnically centered) traditions is imagined as a universalizable style, and then it is relocalized as specifically Dutch (but not Nederhop!) music. The process is very much what Doreen Massey (1998), discussing globalization in another part of the world, describes as "draw[ing] on a host of references which are fused, rearticulated, played back" (p. 122). In this case, though, the "references" are articulated into a fairly elaborate system of identities, symbols, and imagined identifications.

Of course, it is important to recognize the multiplication of the process times the numbers of local hip-hop scenes and rap industries around the world, innumerably across expanses of history. Such an already monstrously large and complex global picture seems all the more vast against the quick changes of cultural style that must be considered in a more diachronic perspective. The well-nigh sublime effect of continual (if not continuous) reinscription and mobility surely suggests the impossibility of stable and unitary identities. The Spookrijders recognize their principal relation to the immediate context of Dutch rap music, and the more mediated, but still forceful, presence of what in Holland is often called the "international" rap style but is thoroughly dominated by American artists.[21] At the same time, they remain justifiably insistent about the unusual place they have staked out in the musical life of Holland, and about the degree to which the music expresses their own personal views and talents. The identities they project to me constantly shift from personal to familial contexts, to points about their neighborhoods and friends, to positionings within the context of Amsterdam and Holland (and sometimes Belgium), and to counter-positionings with respect to the rest of the world (most notably to the United States). Nille speaks

reinscription. This position can be contrasted with Rose's (1994) and Potter's (1995) relation to a more stable notion of African-American cultural production.

[21] The Puff Daddy release mentioned in n. 5 above served as a reminder, causing rap music to figure more prominently in Dutch public life than at any other time I was there. Quite a few prominent locations in all the cities I visited were dominated by posters, placards, and enthusiastic young consumers.

proudly of his connections in New York and some work that he has done with some prominent New York rap personalities, as if the recognition from the cradle of hip-hop culture constitutes a major validation. But as he speaks, it is clear that the validation is at least partially for the growth of rap music in the Netherlands, to which the Spookrijders bear such a complex relation.

It should also be clear from the above discussion that race plays a role in the Dutch organization of rap music – importantly, here, too, mediated by globalized and localized contexts and a specific focus on the United States. While a great many producers and consumers of the music assured me, at one point or another, that race played no significant role in the life of Netherlands rap music, nevertheless it is not rare for the same person, in the same conversation, to bring very Dutch contexts of black and white into the discussion. In fact, denials of the importance of race tend, almost invariably, to focus on the contrast to the United States, the latter being symbolically emblematic of a society in which relations between black and white constitute a structure of profound oppression. It would be unrealistic, as well, for me not to assume that my being American (albeit from a Canadian university) contributed to the course and tone of such conversations.

Eventually, though, considerations of race are inevitable (or so it seems to me) in any serious discussion of rap, and this goes for both the extended discussions I have had with Dutch informants and the serious conversations that producers and consumers of rap music have with each other. Although Saskia Slegers generally maintains the relative insignificance of race in Dutch rap, she nevertheless, as we have seen, concedes both that the audiences for English-language Dutch rap (such as there are) demand a "black-sounding" voice, and that part of the Spookrijders' appeal to hardcore rap fans is their black membership. That she should say both those things, and that "in this Nederhop scene, it's totally unimportant what color you are," is not evidence of any duplicity or confusion on her part. Rather it is evidence of the far greater duplicity and confusion of race dynamics themselves, especially in subcultural contexts (such as those of Dutch rap music and hip-hop culture) where politics are generally anti-racist, and where race, in any case, always retains at least a background presence. The foregoing has established, I hope, that it would be far too simplistic to identify Nederhop as "white" and English-language (Dutch or American, British being perhaps another matter) rap as "black." But some notion of race hovers around those generic and linguistic categories which never disappears, despite some valiant – and themselves culturally important – attempts at denial.

One could take the case of the Spookrijders, and of rap music in Holland overall, together to illustrate the contingent and complex ways in which globalized (originally American – at least in terms of its commercial existence[22]) rap music becomes relocalized in Holland. Of course, further dynamics then would be operative within Holland, involving its highly differentiated urban centers and differing communities divided among ethnic, class, gender, and other lines. The degrees to which Dutch localization is constituted by conscious resistance to American domination, as opposed to its more automatic embeddedness in local conditions, is probably a less salient consideration than the ways in which rap music is differently situated in Holland's culture overall. An examination of that problematic must grapple every bit as much with Dutch reception of Puff Daddy and Jeru the Damaja, as it would with the more locally focused Nederhop. In fact, one of the remarkable and suggestive aspects of rap music in Holland is precisely that country's simultaneous deployment of a thoroughly globalized scene with a uniquely national one. The globalized and more localized rap genres, then, may interact in subtle ways (as when Public Enemy's production style appears on 24K's debut album) or in such sweeping gestures as the creation of a new musical genre (as when Nederhop results partially from the proliferation of American gangsta rap).

The complexity of global and local articulations can reach near-sublime proportions when, for example, one sits in an Amsterdam café and listens to Stefan Kuil propose that "Maybe we're not Nederhop; maybe we're just hip-hop, Dutch hip-hop." Such an utterance highlights at the same time the immediate sincerity of Kuil's love for and identification with rap music as somehow his own, and on the other hand, the profoundly mixed, uneven, and constantly changing dynamics of his particular place in ever-expanding-and-renarrowing contexts. While there is always a danger of pretending that the multidirectionality of rap music outside of the United States is somehow unique to more "remote" rap scenes – and work such as Gilroy (1993) should suffice to convince us otherwise – there is at least an equal danger of not tracing in detail local histories, specific geographies, and trajectories of music and identity. It is with respect to the latter two forces and their intersection, that one inevitably confronts musical poetics, a problematic crucial to understanding how producers and consumers of music understand themselves and their world.

---

[22] Obviously, arguments about the Black Atlantic origins of rap and hip-hop from scholars such as David Toop, Tricia Rose, and Paul Gilroy, as well as the growing popular recognition of specifically Caribbean origins, must be a caveat against calling it specifically "American."

Cree rap

If Dutch rap music and hip-hop culture owe much of their character to complex determinations of local and global forces, then no less can be said for the rap music now popular among some Cree aboriginal populations in Alberta, Canada. On the other hand, the vastly different configurations of Cree rap music go a long way toward suggesting the limits of a phrase like "global and local," except as the most abstract possible methodological cue. For to conceive of Canadian Cree rap's cultural force, one needs to snake one's way through mediations of both "Canada" and "Cree," not to mention "aboriginal." Each of those levels refracts identities, objective social positions, and musical life in ways that are simultaneously extremely complex and contradictory. It would perhaps be most instructive to begin with a few words about rap music in Canada, which has its own important history, before narrowing the focus to the Cree people whose relation to Canada then skews their own position with respect to the national hip-hop scene and rap music industry.

It is difficult to exaggerate how profoundly the music industry in Canada, and thus various music "scenes," feels and responds to the dominating commercial and cultural presence of the United States. No Canadian music consumer could possibly be unaware to what extent Canada's music industry is dominated by (in many respects, inseparable from) the international music industry and recordings originally produced in the United States.[23] Ranking second in the world, behind Holland, in per capita expenditures on recorded music, Canada, like Holland, spends the vast majority of that money (over 85 percent) on products of multinational companies. The major record companies in Canada are all foreign-owned, and often only a tiny fraction of their profits is reinvested in Canadian artists. Nearly 90 percent of the master tapes for the recordings manufactured in Canada are imported, and the multinational companies control record distribution, as well (Berland 1998, pp. 135–6). There are Canadian artists who succeed commercially – such as Celine Dion, Bryan Adams, and Neil Young, to name just a few – but their route to that success is invariably (and necessarily) through the multinational recording industry, usually, as a practical matter, through the United States. There are indeed Canadian attempts at mitigating the economic (and thus cultural) predominance of the United States, including "Canadian content" requirements set by the Canadian Radio-television and Telecommunications Commission (CRTC) for

---

[23] Much of the information in the following discussion of the Canadian music industry is gleaned from Straw (1991) and Berland (1998).

private broadcasters, and a public Canadian Broadcasting Corporation that is well funded and supported compared to its American counterpart (National Public Radio). And in addition, there are some regional specialty musics – such as a Québec song tradition, or Celtic-derived musics in the Maritime provinces – whose uniqueness and loyal audiences allow them some exemption from the dominance of international products.

But such are exceptions. The rule is that the commercial dominance of products from other countries, especially the United States, is a given in the Canadian recording industry, and realistically, most artists wishing to build substantial careers based on the sale of recordings must reckon with the American industry and its multinational web of ownership and distribution. And in the case of rap music, the orientation of the Canadian industry toward the United States is arguably even more dramatic. If geography is a crucial index of authenticity in rap music and hip-hop culture, then Canada stakes only a tenuous claim: while Northeast US urban cities may claim proximity to hip-hop's origins, (lower) West Coast urban areas may claim their own successful tradition, and Southeast artists may cite historical ties to traditional African-American culture, Canada's visibility in both the historic and the contemporary rap world is necessarily an object of struggle. The sole Canadian artist to achieve even moderate success in "old school" rap, Maestro Fresh Wes from Toronto, never foregrounded his Canadian provenance and moved to New York as his career started to show promise. Back in Toronto since 1997, he disappointed Canadian fans with his "defection" to New York and is not considered by many to have increased significantly the visibility of Canadian rap.

Meanwhile, substantial hip-hop scenes were developing in many Canadian cities, including, among others, Toronto, Hamilton, Vancouver, Edmonton, Calgary, and Montreal (the latter with rap music in both English and French). Despite the vast variety and geographic distribution of scenes, media coverage (and the limited coverage from the United States) in Canada has historically focused almost exclusively on Toronto hip-hop culture, and most nationally known acts are based in Toronto.[24] Names such as Sokrates, Kardinal Offishall, Choclair, and Thrust, to name some of the more prominent MCs, form an important base of rap acts whose visibility in Canada keeps the notion of "Canadian hip-hop" alive, while more venerable figures such as Maestro Fresh Wes, the Dream Warriors, and Michie Mee – the last still an active performer and media personality, as well

---

[24] One surprising US exception is the page devoted to the Vancouver hip-hop scene in Wallace (1998).

as the best-known woman MC in Canada – give a public sense of Canadian rap history.[25] While some Canadian MCs are just now beginning to receive attention from the American recording industry – Sokrates, Kardinal Offishall, and Choclair, for example, having recently signed contracts with American record companies – the bulk of Canadian rap nevertheless still remains commercially marginal. And, in fact, the official channels of Canadian cultural protectionism, such as the CRTC's requirements that radio and television maintain a minimum "Canadian content," have nevertheless arguably not advanced the cause of Canadian rap significantly. Not only do many even large Canadian cities not have commercial radio stations with an "urban" format, but the official channels of cultural preservation are often aligned *against* Canadian rap, as was demonstrated when, on 29 July 1997, the CRTC announced a decision that, despite enormous pressure from Toronto's urban music community, a station with that format would not be granted a license; there continues to be no commercial station in Toronto with a largely rap format. Similarly, the Rascalz, offered the 1997 Juno award for best rap group – the Junos being the Canadian equivalent of the Grammy awards – brought into public view the relative neglect of the Canadian music industry when they turned it down, protesting the fact that the urban music portion of the ceremonies is never televised. Thus, despite the substantial fan base for rap music in Canada, something about the latter would appear not to qualify for the protection that Canada's official cultural institutions offer to national culture.

If rap music has to struggle for recognition in Canada, then such is especially the case outside of Toronto, in which hip-hop scenes labor under the burden not only of not being American, but also of not being Torontonian. The latter is a significant factor, as not only are the bulk of Canada's recording and media industries concentrated on Toronto, but also the (ironically, highly Anglocentric) image of Toronto as Canada's true cultural and urban-cultural center is deeply ingrained in much of the Canadian imagination. In the current context, it cannot be doubted that Toronto's large Afrodiasporic (often West Indian) communities contribute to its hip-hop viability in popular views (although such would not alone explain the relative invisibility of, for example, Halifax, Nova Scotia).

Edmonton has never attracted national attention to its hip-hop scene, although all the traditional elements – rap music, DJing, break dancing, and graffiti – have been present for quite some time.

[25] The Rascalz are the sole act from Vancouver to receive substantial national attention, while Dubmatique from Montreal have built an impressive base of domestic support, especially given their predominantly French lyrics.

Geographically disadvantaged by its relative isolation in the prairie and more generally separated from the paths of the production end of the music industry, Edmonton nevertheless has developed rap music and DJing scenes of reliably high quality and with substantial local support. As is often the case, much of the audience for the music in the city is truly subcultural, in the sense of not only listening principally or nearly exclusively to rap music, but also in the sense of forming social bonds based on consumption, congregating in dedicated spaces, and dressing, cutting hair, and speaking in stylistically marked ways; these are not just rap music fans, these are hip-hoppers. But audiences at the rap events I have attended have also included substantial numbers of other listeners, as rap music and hip-hop DJing both seem to have risen in prominence in Edmonton since my arrival there in 1993.

As in many cities, the performers and many of the hardest-core fans of rap musics tend to congregate in groups based largely on neighborhood and/or ethnicity. Although it is common to speak of the city's hip-hop crews in terms of "118" and "182," referring respectively to an avenue number and a street number, in fact, there are pockets of both performance and listening subcultures in various parts of the city. While (as is often the case) the locally known DJs are extremely diverse ethnically (with, for example, a remarkable and close-knit Filipino-Canadian contingent), the MCs (as is also often the case) are more commonly Afro-Canadian.

There is no stylistic attribute of Edmonton rap that is noticeably "Edmontonian"; and for that matter, in terms of musical style, Berland (1998) observes, concerning Canadian popular music in general, that "we rarely hear – unless we are very adept listeners – distinctly 'Canadian' sounds" (p. 135). This remark can be extended to Canadian rap music, if by "sounds" one means musical tracks or flow, but nevertheless, some characteristics can be posited for rap music generally identified with Canada. For one thing, a remarkable predominance of New-York identified styles, in terms of both musical tracks and flow, seems to apply across geographic divides within the country, prompting at times some hints of what one might call "originality crisis," as when one observer remarks that "many Canadian artists have been accused of sounding like they're from New York" (Matthews 1998, p. 72). Thus, the speech-effusive flows and complex layering techniques generally identified with New York come to stand as an anxiety of influence for a country already profoundly disturbed by its cultural subjugation. For another thing, though, it can be remarked that neither gangsta rap nor don rap (discussed back in Chapter 2) can boast a significant presence in Canadian commercial rap (or, for that matter, among the more

180

prominent "underground" artists). One might wish to attribute that lack to differing perceptions of urban life (in a country which has its own panics about street crime but remains aware of its vast advantage over the United States), or to something analogous to the Dutch characteristic of being "more Catholic than the Pope," coupled with the more widespread view in hip-hop culture that gangsta rap constitutes a betrayal of hip-hop's spirit; but whatever lies behind gangsta rap's relative absence from Canadian rap, it forms a *topical* difference with respect to the rap music of the United States.

Within the context of Canadian rap, though, Cree rap forms itself a special category, largely for reasons related to the marginalized status of Native Americans in the North American public imagination. In the context of rap, it becomes all the more remarkable to contrast Native imaginary presence to African-American imaginary presence. Now, imaginary presence is not always a desirable thing: invisibility may indeed be preferable to, for example, knowing how someone's reaction to one on the street may be shaped by public representations of one as violent and hostile. Thus, visibility, especially for a racially marked minority, is not necessarily a positive value.

Nevertheless, the relative absence of Native Americans from the North American imagination tends to hide the difficulties associated with quite a few of their communities. One probable cause of this hidden status is the segregation of large numbers of Natives on "reserves," which, unlike many predominantly African-American areas in the United States (and Afro-Canadian areas in Canada), tend to be located outside of urban areas – frequently out of the view for most who are not directly involved in such communities. While there is also a substantial Native presence in some large urban metropolises – Denver and Minneapolis, for example, in the United States, Edmonton and Winnipeg in Canada – they tend to be backgrounded in media representations (except in cases of spectacular anti-social behaviors). High rates of unemployment and alcoholism, frequent segregation on "reserves," family instability (partially formed by the notorious history of "residential schools"), poor social services (especially in the United States), and institutional discrimination are thus largely screened from public view; there are, of course, exceptions to this pattern (for example, television programs like *North of 60* in Canada, or the occasional news story), but they are sporadic and largely ineffectual, compared to the widespread and daily pattern of hiding Native lives from view. As one might well assume, the trend, since roughly the 1980s, in industrialized nations to devastate or eliminate systems of social support for afflicted communities has had a disproportional impact on poorer Native communities; while publics often continue to resent such assistance, as was evidenced by a 1996 poll showing that 40 percent of Canadians believed that Natives have themselves to blame for their problems, and, even more astonishingly, that almost half believed that Natives have an equal or better standard of living than the average Canadian citizen (reported in Aubry 1997). One can only speculate what might produce such a stunning view – is this an outcome of the combination of knowing that Natives are disproportionately implicated in special laws and public assistance, while at the same time remaining ignorant of the effects of Western civilization's devastation and control of the civilization it conquered? Whatever the cause of such troubling perceptions, they are a daily reality that reinforces the very societal structures that maintain the living conditions of a largely hidden underclass.

The hiding of populations seems also to be maintained by more privileged people with a combination of defensiveness and willful ignorance, as an episode from my early teaching career will illustrate. Soon after arriving at the University of Alberta to teach music theory, I played, for a first-year undergraduate class, some rap music that made explicit reference to socio-economic problems of urban African-Americans. When one student objected that the issues were not relevant in Canada, I responded by asking whether he was not interested in analogous problems of Canada's underclasses. He answered that Canada *had* no underclass. When I asked whether he had been to a certain area of Edmonton which I knew to contain people of just this description, he responded, "That's a part of town you don't go to!"

The Cree are the largest group of Native Americans (or, as is often said in Canada, "First Nations people") in Western Canada, with reserves throughout the region. In pre-Columbian times one of the more successful disseminators of culture (and often conquerors of rival tribes), the Cree have left their cultural mark throughout much of what is now Canada and parts of the United States; but their most visible presence in contemporary Canada is in the West. Near Edmonton (lying roughly in the center of Alberta, the westmost province next to British Columbia), about an hour's drive south, lie four major Cree reserves – Ermineskin, Samson, Montana, and Louis Bull; Hobbema is a town divided between the Ermineskin and Samson reserves. Edmonton itself also has substantial Cree communities, especially in its north-central neighbourhoods. As in most cities, the Cree population of Edmonton is disproportionately poor; one person I knew who was living in a largely Native area of Edmonton regularly referred to his apartment as being "in the ghetto." This is, in fact, the part of Edmonton to which my first-year music theory student had made reference.

Cree youth, like youth of many marginalized communities, find themselves largely trapped between, on the one hand, traditional identities that may have been persuasive in past generations, and on the other hand, the often more pervasive and persuasive "youth culture," whose increasing penetration of the object world affects the Cree no less than any other population. The "youth culture" aspect can be forcefully destructive of traditional identities, disseminating as it does what Lawrence Grossberg (1994b, p. 53) has called "the antiaura of the inauthentic." At the same time, issues of identity remain as central to Native communities as they do to any others, perhaps more so, in view of the often negative stereotypes which circulate in the broader culture.

Hence the significance of the fact that rap music – and hip-hop in general – has attained a high degree of popularity among Cree populations, at least in Alberta. It is difficult to tell just *how* popular it has become, or to what degree its appeal extends to other geographic areas, since statistics are not kept on such matters; I am thus basing my assessment of the growing popularity on reports from informants and my own observation. The consensus of those to whom I have spoken about the matter is that rap music has spread rapidly since roughly the early 1990s, and that it is now the music of choice among many young Cree (especially males). The vast majority of rap performance among Cree communities is "underground," in the sense of being performed or recorded outside of the support of major public or private institutions (such as record companies, radio stations, governmental organizations, nightclubs, or concert halls). One can certainly find, perhaps even in major local venues (albeit usually on "off" nights), performances by Cree rap artists, and if one knows whom to ask, one can even obtain some recordings (usually circulated by cassette);[26] but one of the most striking aspects of Cree rap music is the stark contrast between its pervasiveness in certain communities and its negligible commercial presence. The commercial marginality of Cree-produced rap music may certainly be attributed in part to the relative invisibility of Native people in the popular imagination; but it must also be conceived within the context of the cultural and financial dominance of the United States record industry, which (as one can see in the case of Holland) often has the effect of crowding out local rap music in official purchasing venues. There has been some media coverage of Cree rap in the Canadian press, but it tends to be either peripheral to, or prompted by, coverage of my own

---

[26] Manuel (1993) documents how the rise of private cassette production has transformed local music scenes; hip-hop culture and rap have been particularly affected by this, and Alberta Cree hip-hop culture and rap are no exception.

183

research and teaching; and it is covered as a curiosity, prompting no noticeable sustained popular interest.

My own contact with Cree rap music began shortly after my arrival in Edmonton, when a young man from the Hobbema reserve approached my office at the University of Alberta, saying he had heard that my research interests included hip-hop culture and rap music. He is himself an MC, named Darren Tootoosis, but using the stage-name and nickname Bannock. The stage-name is itself significant, as bannock is a food (a fried bread) specific to Cree cuisine, something of a "soul food" in itself to many Cree people. As my principal window (directly, or indirectly, through people I have met through him) on the world of Cree rap music, Bannock has afforded me as good an "insider's" view as an outsider can have. Of course, my access to that world is partial, and I am sure that many differing stories could be told of the Cree rap world; my own discussion cannot help but reflect my own routes into that world, as well as my own theoretical concerns.

One important aspect of my routes into that world is the fact that Bannock is from Hobbema, which occupies a special place within the complex of Cree communities in Alberta. In the early 1970s, oil was discovered on that reserve, as a result of which revenue flows regularly into the community from oil production. Among the consequences of this is that on reaching eighteen years of age, all official band members on the Hobbema reserve are granted, from the band itself, a lump cash amount somewhere between $40,000 and $80,000 (Cdn.), as a condition-free gift. Bannock, who lived in Hobbema until the age of twenty-one, recalls being among the few people he knows who have ever used the money to leave the reserve; most of the others, according to him, spent the money within a very short period of receiving it – often within just a few weeks.

How can one spend such a quantity of money so quickly? One answer is provided by the rampant drug problem in Hobbema, a problem fed precisely by the availability of quick money to extremely young people with very little hope for long-term improvements in their conditions. Along with a thriving drug scene, of course, comes a similarly active market in firearms; Hobbema has one of the highest violent crime rates in Canada. Another answer to the money's quick disappearance throws an interesting perspective on the intersections between the particular condition of the reserve and the wider forces of capitalism; for Wetaskiwin, the city adjacent to Hobbema, is the car-dealer capital of Alberta, with strip after strip of road brimming with car dealerships and shining new cars and jeeps. Also prominent in Wetaskiwin are used car dealerships and (generally weekly) car auctions, in which repossessed cars can be bought (often by

Edmonton residents, who make the trip in search of bargains), often in close to mint condition and at a deep discount from the price demanded of the original purchaser.

Bannock compares the resulting cultural dynamic in Hobbema to the representations he has seen in rap videos of gang life in Los Angeles – young people in expensive cars (which they may end up keeping if they paid cash, or selling at a great loss, or having repossessed), dealing in and/or consuming drugs, sporting firearms and frequently using them. Of course, this is only a partial perspective, and emphasizing this aspect of Hobbema life risks the same caricature of that community as is often inflicted on African-American inner-city communities in the United States. As is the case with the latter communities, there are families peacefully making their homes in Hobbema, people struggling to raise children in the most positive way possible, and stories of personal and collective achievement. Of course, the latter perspective may then lead us to mask deep-seated social problems that need urgently to be addressed. Instead of moralizing about which of the two representations to favor – all too common a strategy, as Wilson (1987) aptly illustrates concerning the debates around American ghetto representation – we might conclude that neither moralizing nor adjusting our descriptions will necessarily adequately represent problems caused by both history and the present social structure.

Bannock's place in that social structure – as someone who left the reserve for the city, as one of the few lucky enough to be making a run at an education, and as a rap musician – partially determines his musical poetics, and those poetics seem impossible to understand without it. The argument to be made here to support such a contention will run roughly as follows: to start with, the popularity of West Coast "gangsta" rap in Hobbema lends a particular style to his music, both in terms of the musical tracks and in terms of his MCing. Bannock tends to seek out funk-style beats and simple, relatively slow-paced keyboard-heavy textures; sampling is far less a concern to him than a compelling, tuneful musical backdrop at a comfortable pace. An analogous ethos prevails in his MCing, which tends toward a sung rhythmic style, focusing on end-rhymed couplets, with frequent end-of-measure (or near-end-of-measure) caesuras; an apt comparison to his "flow" might be Mack 10. The MCs that Bannock cites as his strongest influences – Too $hort and 2Pac Shakur – underline his West Coast orientation.[27]

Overwhelmingly, his songs are steeped in the viewpoint of the first

[27] Although Too $hort is now based in Atlanta, his career originated in Oakland and his style retains audible elements of that city's rap music.

185

person, presenting far more often stories about his personal history and viewpoints than, for example, more overtly political essays or social critique. In fact, only some of his music refers explicitly to the fact of his being Cree, to Hobbema, or to aboriginal life or racial issues (and here, perhaps, it is useful to recall a similar bifurcation in the Spookrijders' alternate celebration of Dutchness and claims to universality). In this way, Bannock does not provide the music scholar with a ready-made political significance or an emblematic exemplum of "Creeness" that can readily be deployed as an emblematic "locality." Instead, he manifests his geographical and ethnic identity through highly mediated channels, ranging from the local Cree young men's affinity for rap music and hip-hop culture (manifested also in his dress) to globalized notions of sincerity and the universality of musical emotions. In short, the very category of "Cree rap music," when Bannock is taken as an instance, cannot be constituted except as simultaneously local and global.

Bannock's attention to musical poetics as an aspect of identity can be seen through two prisms, each of which refracts the topic into different kinds of language and action; he both internalizes his preferred sounds as his own rap music, and externalizes ideas about sound in his conversation. As is usually, if not always, the case, one cannot always map a one-to-one relationship between the internalized and the externalized musical poetics of Bannock; but even the spaces of divergence, as we will see, resonate with some broader cultural contradictions of rap music in his world and the broader world of Cree rap.

Like the Spookrijders, Bannock takes hip-hop and rap as simultaneously global and local, simultaneously universal and particular. Always conscious of his own ethnicity and popular images of rap music as black music, he nevertheless insists on cross-cultural translation through universality:

You can't really put color on a music. Or Aaron Neville wouldn't be a country singer. Or Vanilla Ice wouldn't have done rap music or dance music ... [L]ook at Marky Mark ... You can't really look at music as being black, or white, or red, you know. It's different than that, it's more than that; I mean, there's white blues artists out there ... Look at Colin James, Stevie Ray Vaughan.

(Tootoosis 1997)[28]

Whether or not one agrees with the generic designation of Aaron Neville, Bannock's emphasis on the permeability of ethnic and "racial" lines needs underscoring here, as do the similar remarks of Stefan Kuil; but at the same time, also similarly to Kuil, Bannock takes

[28] All further quotes from Tootoosis are from Tootoosis (1997).

advantage of other contexts to emphasize the particularities of being Cree, and its intersections and differences from (his notions of) the particularities of being African-American. It is those moments on which I would like to focus – at the risk of playing down the universality he also wishes to assert – as a window on rap musical poetics and Cree identity.

Not surprisingly, given the represented characteristics of American ghettos, Bannock identifies them with Hobbema via images of social dysfunction, referring to

the abuse of drugs and alcohol [in black US ghettos]. There's a lot of that out on the reserve. There's a lot of physical abuse, a lot of mental abuse. All kinds of stuff. There's lots of fighting now – kids are carrying guns out there ... I carried around a gun for a while, when I was younger, about twelve years ago; but it wasn't, like, a big thing back then. I felt I needed to, because there were a lot of people who really didn't like me ... There's a lot of physical violence out there, as well ... There's segregation, I mean, that's still practiced today. That's why most Natives live on the reserve. Or else, most Natives live in North Edmonton – a lot of them don't feel they fit in on the South Side of Edmonton ...

The identification based on social trauma easily translates, in hip-hop culture, into a position of mutuality and common critique of an oppressive dominant society:

Natives aren't alien to the black people. They do know of us, and I'm pretty sure that doing a little research, they'll be able to understand our point of view and what we've gone through, and they'll be able to identify with us as well as we can identify with them ... If Hispanics, like Cypress Hill, can make it in rap, I'm pretty sure Natives can, too.

Hobbema, for Bannock, is particularly fertile ground for an identification specifically with the (sub)genre of gangsta rap:

Hip-hop is as big on other reserves. It's just that Hobbema can live more of that gangsterish lifestyle, because they have more of the resources. You know, when kids turn eighteen, they're not thinking about investing; I mean, they think about investing up until they're eighteen, they turn eighteen, they throw a party, they go buy all the alcohol, they buy themselves coke, they buy themselves a brand new truck, you know, with the brand new stereo, brand new CDs ... They figure they need a gun, "hey, I got money for a gun," they go buy a handgun.

The significance of the identification, then, is not only operational on the levels of ethnicity and class, but it also extends to genre, namely to the gangsta genre of reality rap. Just how far-reaching that identification goes in musical terms can be seen by Bannock's explanation of which artists became popular in Hobbema at the time that rap itself became popular there, roughly around 1991 or 1992:

NWA was a big one. Ice Cube, Ice-T, you know, a lot of what was becoming mainstream. West Coast, and Naughty by Nature ... It's easily the most popular music [in Hobbema] ... Oh, yeah – everybody's got the gangsta lifestyle out there, or tries to have the lifestyle.

The linkage of "lifestyle" directly to particular artists extends, according to him, also to musical style: the car orientation of the musical culture also engenders consumption specifically of those West Coast artists whose music is mixed specially for car stereos – the ones with the "jeep beats."[29] The combination of the car orientation and the gangsta identification lend a specific flavor to the rap music consumed in, and consequently coming from, Hobbema.[30]

But semantic topics and musical tracks do not form the entire extent of the geographic identification with the West Coast (and gangsta style); it also extends to MCing style, and in Bannock's case, in remarkably conscious and explicit ways. The extent of this can be seen in his recounting of his initial efforts as a performer. He started at the age of seventeen, before which he had written poetry in class at school "as a form of release." His cousin Rex Smallboy – himself now an accomplished and active MC in Hobbema and Edmonton – noticed his poetry and encouraged him to try rap music; Rex played some of his own music for Bannock, and Bannock loved it. But artistic success, by his own standards, did not come immediately:

To be honest, I completely sucked for about the first year ... I stunk. No rhythm, no style; but then again, I listened to Naughty by Nature and Ice-T, NWA, totally different styles ... At the time, nothing that I listened to influenced me, that I noticed, anyway. So, I guess in terms of a style, I didn't have one, and I didn't know how to look for one. I didn't know how to recognize styles, and whatnot. So, my cousin Rex said, 'Well, there's different styles, you got the East Coast and the West Coast' – well, I knew that much, that's pretty evident. But then there's styles within each part, there. You got, like, Naughty by Nature is different than the Wu-Tang Clan, and they're [both] from the East Coast. Too $hort is a lot different than NWA, or different than Ice-T, and [Ice-T and] Ice Cube are totally different, and they're all from the West Coast. So, you know, I started thinking about it, and my cousin Rex, who really liked Too $hort, said "Well, why don't you try it like this," and I thought, "No, I like Naughty by Nature, I'm gonna try it like that." But with no experience ... that style sucks, if you don't know what you're doing ... I love Treach's style, he's got a good style.

Bannock's narrative reveals a substantial amount about some points made in previous parts of the book, namely, that stylistic choices are

[29] "Jeep beats" refers to a style of production which produces a particularly low and booming bass intended for consumption in motor vehicles (jeeps and otherwise).
[30] In my own performance and production work with him, Bannock often brings me recordings of West Coast (or West Coast "émigré" artists) like 2Pac Shakur and Too $hort, to give me an idea of the sound he wants.

made by artists in highly self-conscious and sophisticated ways – to an extent that easy dismissals of "musicological" discussion tend to belie. Particularly significant, from the standpoint of the present discussion, is Bannock's assertion that not only did he not "have a style," but also that "I didn't know how to look for one." Implicit there, it would seem, is the normality of envisioning an array of styles before one, among which one chooses – presumably, with one's own combinational style as a possibility – deliberately. Also very much worthy of note is the manner in which Rex lays out an array of possibilities for Bannock, first by the geographical categories of "West Coast" and "East Coast," which Bannock deems "pretty evident," and then by the labels of individual artists. Interestingly absent is any sense that imitating another MC's style ("biting") is a moral or artistic flaw – though one could argue that this is due to the situation of a beginner who needs to start *somewhere*. The extract quoted here – along with the previous one – also clarifies that Bannock's rap imagination at that time focused on one exception to the otherwise overwhelming domination of West Coast artists: Naughty by Nature. Having found that "with no experience ... that style sucks," however, Bannock soon focused on what, for the geographical and discursive reasons discussed above, was most available and valued in his community: West Coast rap, particularly the styles of 2Pac and especially Too $hort. The imagined equivalence of Hobbema to American ghettos must be singled out as a formative determinant of the West Coast sounds that Bannock earlier referred to as predominant in the musical environment; such a determination, in turn, instantiates the close relationship that can obtain between musical poetics, on the one hand, and the worlds of discourse and social situation, on the other.

Such an observation may form an effective pivot to a discussion of a particular song of Bannock, "Step Up" (from Bannock 1998). A song mainly in the toasting tradition, "Step Up" also presents the artist's representation of how "Creeness" intersects that tradition, and how the tradition can become constitutive of "Creeness." I have seen the song develop in at least three separate incarnations; the version to be discussed here was performed live at the 1998 World Music Concert at the University of Alberta (March, 1998), in Edmonton, Alberta. At that time, Bannock performed a set with DJ Roach, a (non-Native) accomplished Edmonton DJ with a popular local hip-hop college radio program. That having been said, a crucial methodological point needs to be inserted, namely that the status of "Step Up" as a song needs to be differentiated, to some extent, from that of the other songs discussed so far. The previous songs have all been analyzed within the methodological bracketing formed by commercially produced and distributed recording, something that forms not a transcendent unity, but most decidedly the socially circulated unity of an object whose circulation and consumption retain certain consistent sonic properties (which is not, of course, to say, consistent uses or interpretations). Even in the (extremely common) case in which a single may be released in several different mixes and remixes, such versions circulate (albeit often far less widely) in similar ways to radio or album mixes, and their reception, like the reception of the more widely circulated versions, generally includes reception of the musical tracks particular to those mixes. Inexpensive ways for record companies to maximize profits from relatively little production expense to prolong the life of a single, remixes nevertheless work precisely by highlighting different musical combinations, and the perceived effectiveness of the musical tracks can determine not only a remix's commercial success, but also the reputation of a DJ/producer. Thus, even when a song has multiple existence, each of its forms carries specific registers of musical poetics; in fact, remixes frequently deploy generic categories of musico-poetic signification based on stylistic identity, as when one finds "dance" or "trip-hop" remixes.

But in the case of "Step Up," there is not so clear an identity to the musical tracks, since there is no commercial bracketing of any particular performance, or for that matter, of any group of performances. Many particularities of the song – and, of course, a serious set of questions could be posed here about whether such a thing as a "song" should be named – can change substantially from one performance to another. In the case of the World Music Concert recording, the pairing with DJ Roach (who was playing vinyl LPs on his two Technics 1200 turntables, mixed through a mixer and then amplified) produced a complex layering effect somewhat distanced from Bannock's more standard funk aesthetic. In an earlier version on which he and I worked in the studio, on the other hand, he looked for a more G-funk sound. The lyrics, their rhythm, and his flow, however, remain a constant from performance to performance, and while they may not combine to form a "song" as many consumers of rap music might define it, their consistency indicates something of a basic patterned practice, which specific performances will then inflect in specific and highly localized ways. Although both the generality of the lyrics/rhythms/flow and the specificity of the performance merit attention – each ultimately incomplete without the other – I would like to focus on the general aspects of the song, since certain aspects of Bannock's flow, I will argue, can be seen to form aspects of his representation of Cree identity. Here, as with the songs discussed earlier, identity will turn out to be inseparable from musical poetics.

190

Figure 5.1 reproduces the lyrics of "Step Up"; here, as in the case of Ice Cube's "The Nigga Ya Love to Hate" in Chapter 3, each line begins either with the syllable that begins each respective measure, or with the first lyric after the beginning of the measure. As in the case of the Ice Cube song, as well, each line is numbered.

Figure 5.1: The lyrics for Bannock's "Step Up"

Now I'm

  1 Usin' my mind to incorporate a rhyme, tha pad
  2 And tha pen to tell you all the time that I
  3 Spent in tha dark, thinkin' from my heart, late at
  4 Night I would write and think of tha part, so that
  5 In this rhyme I could kick a little science
  6 Try to break the silence for outright defiance, 'cause I'm
  7 Comin' up on ya like a monster in ya dreams,
  8 Don't try to hold it in, I know ya want to scream, see
  9 I'm a prairie runner, better known as a Cree, I'm
10 Never gonna change, and I'm proud of who I be, I'm tha
11 Son of tha clouds when it's raining outside, I'm
12 Here to make a bad day, it's time to go and hide, see no-
13 Thing's really sacred when I'm flyin' on the mic,
14 Kickin' controversy is what I'm sorta like, but I
15 Really ain't that bad, and I really ain't all that, ya
16 Think that ya may need it but I screw upliftin' crap, 'cause some-
17 Times it's phoney and sometimes it's fake, but
18 Then again I start to think that life is whatcha make, so now
19 Ya say okay, 'cause I know you understand that no-
20 Thing seems to happen as perfect as you planned . . .

[break]

So if ya

21 Not with me, ya against me, people always
22 Lookin' for another way to change me, so I gotta
23 Keep my rhymes tight and start to take flight, I'm not a-
24 Fraid to stand up and fight for tha right, usin' my
25 Mind like a gun with a hair trigga, usin' schoolin' and
26 Science, so I can start to figure, things to take ya
27 Down from tha other side of town, take ya last
28 Breath 'cause I'm gonna make ya drown in the pool you call
29 Reason, I just don't really care, give me a
30 Second 'cause I'm gonna start to flare like a
31 Fuse they use for a bomb, when tha smoke
32 Settles, you'll see it ain't calm, I'll blow up like
33 Fireworks ya holdin' in ya hand, what I have to
34 Say will have ya goin' damn, who is this
35 Neechee with a mind of his own? I'm sorta like a
36 King and I got my own throne, but I'm a

37 Chief, with a teepee on tha plains, with each of a
38 Victim mounted of tha frames. You'll
39 Hear my name when the wind blows, my name is Ban-
40 Nock, I'm a Cree and it shows.

Figure 5.2 now transcribes the first six lines (with an initial upbeat) of the song, numbering beat-classes (BCs) 0 through 3 and their imbricated sixteenth-note values (also 0 through 3) from left to right; attacks on each successive syllable are then marked, with the successive lines moving downward on the graph; the upbeat ("Now I'm") in the first line precedes the first-numbered line. Thus, the format here is the same as was used in Chapter 2's discussion of MCing styles. Below the graph, the corresponding lyrics are reproduced for easy reference.

Figure 5.2: Rhythmic transcription, first six lines of "Step Up"

0				1				2				3			
0	1	2	3	0	1	2	3	0	1	2	3	0	1	2	3
														x	x
x	x	x	x			x	x	x	x	x	x	x		x	x
	x	x	x		x	x			x	x	x	x		x	x
x		x	x	x				x	x	x	x	x		x	x
x		x	x	x		x	x			x	x	x		x	x
x	x		x					x	x	x	x	x	x	x	x
x	x	x	x	x	x			x	x			x	x	x	x

Text

                                 Now I'm
Usin' my mind to incorporate a rhyme, tha pad
And tha pen to tell you all the time that I
Spent in tha dark, thinkin' from my heart, late at
Night I would write and think of tha part, so that
In this rhyme I could kick a little science
Try to break the silence for outright defiance

A careful recitation of the above rhyme in the graphed rhythm should leave little doubt that we are here dealing with a sung style – quite firmly so, in fact. One might note, for example, the consistent caesura on BC 3 in each of the first four lines, arguably the single most typical aspect of the style. Also constant through most of the excerpt, in fact the first five lines, is a caesura either on BC 1, or on the sixteenth-note just before it; that, combined with the BC 3 caesura and the fairly constant syllabic attacks between the two, renders the passage fairly regular in its rhythm despite changes in syntax and semantics – in other words, sung in style. Similarly, one could cite the coincidence of all the rhyming words (with one exception, to be discussed shortly) with one or the other of the recurring caesuras.

Indeed, not all the rhymes are end-rhymes (as in the very most sung styles, such as one might often hear in the music of Too $hort), but their coincidence with caesuras produces a similar effect.

All that is not at all to say that the passage is sing-songy or rhythmically uninteresting. Indeed, one of the more attractive aspects of Bannock's style is his anticipation of beats; at the very end of the first complete line (i.e., not counting the initial upbeat), for example, the word "pad" seems to serve as an anticipation of the downbeat that would otherwise have fallen on line 2 – the sustain through the first two sixteenths of line 2, along with the grammatical continuation, give the syllable "pad" a clear characteristic of syncopation.[31] Likewise, one might say the same for the syllables "mind" (l. 1) and "rhyme" (l. 5). In addition, extended syncopations can be heard in the phrases "think of tha part" (l. 4) and "outright defiance" (l. 6). In addition to all this, there is something of what one might call a "rhythmic crescendo" into the final line of the passage, which becomes the sole line with attacks on every sixteenth of the first two BCs; that, combined with the syncopation just mentioned, folds the entirety of the six lines into something of a unit with a rhythmic event emerging from a state of previous (relative) regularity. It is during the line of rhythmic crescendo that the one exception occurs to the coincidence of rhyming words with the (relatively regular) caesuras (on "silence"); given the importance, in sung style, of the coincidence of rhyme with rhythmic detail, that exception, too, marks out line 6 as a particular event. Overall, then, it can be said that the passage invokes a sung style, but one with some direction toward a less regular final event. In the semantic register, the passage is squarely within a tradition of toasting, together with an equally widely used practice of didacticism reference (e.g., "kick a little science").

Much of the song continues in a similar fashion, on both counts; in other words, much of it consists of a solidly sung rhythmic style, with smaller units being sectioned off by busier, less rhythmically regular events that seem, for the most part, also to round off grammatical/ semantic units. Semantically, too, the toasting continues, with occasional references to themes of overcoming struggle and dealing with setbacks and challenges. (Those same themes are frequently mentioned by Bannock when he discusses his music in public discussions.) But toward the end of the second verse, while the toasting certainly continues, at the same time, the references to Bannock's identity as a Cree – sparse so far in the song – move to the

---

[31] For the sake of comparison, one could note the more rhythmically regular attack on the word "dark" in line 3.

foreground and dramatically end the song. Figure 5.3 graphs the rhythms of the last eight lines (with, as before, the upbeat).

Figure 5.3: Rhythmic transcription, last eight lines of "Step Up"

0				1				2				3			
0	1	2	3	0	1	2	3	0	1	2	3	0	1	2	3
										x		x	x		x
x	x	x	x	x	x	x	x	x				x	x	x	x
x		x		x	x	x	x	x	x			x		x	
x	x	x	x	x		x	x	x		x		x	x	x	x
x		x	x	x	x	x		x	x			x		x	
x		x	x	x	x	x	x	x		x	x	x			x
x	x			x	x	x	x	x		x					
x		x	x		x	x	x	x	x	x	x	x			
x		x	x	x		x	x	x							

Text
I'll blow up like
Fireworks ya holdin' in ya hand, what I have to
Say will have ya goin' damn, who is this
Neechee with a mind of his own? I'm sorta like a
King and I got my own throne, but I'm a
Chief, with a teepee on tha plains, with each of a
Victim mounted of tha frames. You'll
Hear my name when the wind blows, my name is Ban-
Nock, I'm a Cree and it shows.

The graph shows that this passage, although not cleanly removed from the sung style, nevertheless punctuates the generalized sung patterns with certain important anomalies, particularly when one compares the pattern of attacks with the semantics and syntax of the text. A major irregularity, for instance, occurs in the final two lines, in which the name "Bannock" not only is split between the lines, but also is accented against the standard pronunciation: "Ban-NOCK," rather than the standard "BAN-nock." But more important, it can be remarked that a pattern which also designated the earlier passage's sung style, namely the caesura on BC 3, is not replicated here; there is a consistent caesura on BC 2, however – still a regularity that can bespeak sung style, but serving less to separate one line from the next, since BC 3 in any given line is available as a strong upbeat into the next line.

And, in fact, the ends of the lines in this passage *do* lead into the following lines, in elaborate upbeats that emphasize certain downbeats with a force absent from the rest of the song. Not only does the passage in general emphasize downbeats by placing caesuras early in the lines, but also certain specific upbeats and downbeats are

194

particularly dramatic. Two upbeats are striking and rhythmically identical, namely those in the second and fourth lines (setting "who is this" and "but I'm a"). In each case, attacks fall on the second half of BC 2, then on the third BC, and finally on the second half of BC 3 – in other words, the attacks divide the last beat-and-a-half evenly into half-notes. Such an event not only is unique in the song – and thus, all the more striking for occurring twice, separated by only one measure – but also highlights, at least by retrospective contrast, that in fact half notes on the beat, in the second half of the measure, are extremely rare in the song. This is no accident: on-the-beat half notes in the second half of a line would normally risk inhibiting any sense of rhythmic motion into the next line. (Comparison to Figure 5.2 will reinforce such a notion.) But arriving as they do, the upbeat formations carry that same paradoxical force as dramatic upbeats often seem to possess, namely that of simultaneously slowing down the rhythmic activity and increasing the momentum of the following downbeat. And these are uniquely forceful upbeats, in the context of the song.

Such would remain technical trivia, were it not for the fact of the particular words that set the downbeats that the upbeats emphasize: "[who is this /] Neechee with a mind of his own," and "[but I'm a /] Chief, with a teepee on tha plains."[32] The key words that fall on the downbeats are none other than those which, along with "Cree" in the final line, designate Bannock as a someone with his particular cultural identity (among the few in the song, and the first two to do so in the final verse – with only "I'm a Cree and it shows" to follow in the same category). Furthermore, "Neechee" is the only Cree word in the song, so that its emphasis here carries with it a unique level of representation, arguably the strongest semantic projection of persona in the song. The next word outlined by the unique downbeat patterns is "Chief," and here a couple of points need to be underlined. One, rather obvious but needing to be stated, is that "Chief" is another one of the relatively few explicit references to Cree identity in the song; grammatically as well as semantically, it forms a counterpart to the much earlier line "See I'm a prairie runner, better known as a Cree," which falls in the much less rhythmically differentiated beginning of the song. But the other aspect of this moment that merits elaboration is not manifested by the graphing technique and may even form a critique of it, a suggestion that an "outside" to whatever theoretical approach one chooses ultimately secretly lies, as well, on its inside – an old point from deconstruction, but one as readily observable in the even older principle of dialectics that an eminent critique on one level will eventually prove imminent at some other dialectical level and

---

[32] "Neechee" is a Cree word for a Native (not necessarily Cree) person.

thus crucially (and retrospectively) formative of even earlier stages of analysis. That aspect involves a very particular manner of delivering this line on which Bannock insists, and that is both dramatic and unique in the song. The phrase "But I'm a chief" is set to a quick and sharp crescendo, so that a more accurate transcription of the entire line might perhaps look like "But I'm A CHIEF!, with a teepee on tha plains"; the shouted "CHIEF," in the Edmonton recording I possess, resonates throughout the concert hall during the brief sixteenth-note; audience members who talked to me about the concert afterwards remembered it the most vividly of any moment in the song. The line was, in fact, from the beginning of the song's genesis, a climactic moment. When I recorded an earlier version of it (tellingly entitled "Proud to be a Cree") with Bannock in the studio, he singled out this very line and asked whether I could do something special in the musical realm that would highlight the moment. (In response, I thinned out the layering a bit at that moment, to foreground the vocals.)

To summarize the discussion of Figure 5.3: the rhythms are more varied than those of Figure 5.2 from earlier in the song, still very much in the sung style – as shown by, for instance, the consistent caesura on BC 2 – but certain anomalies punctuate the textures in ways that both are unusual in the song and also intensify a more general feature of this section of the song, namely the more emphatic downbeats than in earlier parts of the song. Such moments were both intended by the artist and, from what I could tell, readily (and explicitly) perceived by the audience, completing an act of communication. And the rhythmic procedures in the passage serve to foreground explicit assertions of identity that, at least retrospectively, shape much of the imagery of the song and mark out the song as specifically *Cree* – and furthermore, of course, a certain *kind* of Cree (gendered, defiant – or, if one prefers, "resistant," and so on). All of this may now be reinserted in the wider context, namely that we are talking about the very end of the song; thus not only is this an obviously formally prominent section, but also it suggests something like what was mentioned in Chapter 2, namely the development from more sung to more effusive rhythms. But in this case, really, the whole of the development takes place within the sung style – consistent with Bannock's overall practice – with a motion from a fairly uniform regularity into a more differentiated texture, not coincidentally at a point where "Creeness" becomes a more explicit topic, and in ways that underline that identity. Thus, the formal development of MCing technique from the beginning to the end of "Step Up" bears some analogue to the stylistically common progression from sung to effusive styles; one might wish, then, to generalize the process by remarking a strategy, in much rap music, of progressing from some regularly recurring structures to more quickly changing and locally unique events. The context of this particular song can add the important caveat that such a strategy is perfectly possible within the sung style alone, showing what may at first seem a surprising versatility.

Such a versatility gains significance in the present context, of course, only when it may be deployed to form a musical poetics, and when that musical poetics bears a clear relationship to other dimensions of cultural representation. That is precisely the case in "Step Up," and the picture of Cree identity formed in Bannock's music might generally be said to be bound inextricably with how it sounds – sometimes, as here, the flow, other times the musical tracks, ultimately, in the broadest possible context, in both. Mapping the musico-poetic aspects of identity in the present context, even in this modest investigation, obliges one to consider the global and the local together – Edmonton as related to Hobbema, and as related to Los Angeles (or the Bay Area), as it, in turn, is formed in relation to the world at large, in the specific geographies of hip-hop culture and rap music. Musical poetics, identity, and place end up, here, different approaches to the same cultural locations – cultural locations that can only be mapped through considerations of musical organization, as an aspect of other theoretical issues of identity and representation. Such an exercise may serve to illustrate the shift suggested back in Chapter 1 – the redefinition of "music theory" as simply "theory about music."

Postface

The final and most localizing perspective of this book veered into two places that are literally eccentric with respect to the commercial cultures of rap music and hip-hop culture. Neither Holland nor Edmonton is "on the map" in any global sense, and yet, as was argued in the last chapter, the level of the global is never far from the representations and identify formations in both places. If all global processes are lived in some local incarnation, then it is equally true that no local rap scene (or small recording industry) can be lived without reference to the global circulation of musical commodities. It is perhaps the latter point that requires the greatest emphasis, since the trend in recent years seems to be to emphasize the local at the expense of the global.[1]

Indeed, global aspects of rap music resonate in remarkably familiar patterns, even in such far-flung environments as Amsterdam and Edmonton. The touchstone of authenticity in public representations of hip-hop culture and rap music has long been some notion of urban locality and ethnic and/or class marginality. The seeming unlimited amount of variation that such a scheme allows can account for the fact that hip-hop and rap seem to have penetrated virtually every crevice in which the international record industry registers a significant presence. Although this book has focused on musical technique, the preceding chapters have argued that the circulation even simply of rap music (never mind hip-hop culture) involves a great deal more.

Still, the focal point for tracing global and local identities in this study has, of course, been musical poetics. Mapping those musical poetics, far from being the meaningless abstractions of academics, extends even to that (important, though too often mystified) realm known as "lived experience," since musico-poetic concepts are routinely deployed by both producers and consumers of musics (popular and otherwise, though obviously, the focus here is on rap

---

[1] Many of the essays in Swiss et al. (1998) focus almost exclusively on the local, for instance.

production and consumption). The poetics enable sophisticated popular systems of classification that are themselves, in varying degrees of explicitness, highly theoretical. Thus, understanding cultural significance in rap music must take, as one (and, of course, only one) of its moments the complexes of interrelated notions that classify, identify, and distinguish different kinds of music, different songs, and even different parts of songs, on the parts of both performers (including producers) and listeners. It is the taking into account of those complex processes that I call the project of musical poetics. It is then the interrelations of the musical poetics and other cultural forces that I call music theory.

The theme which threads its way through the arguments and discussions in this book is the social force of musical poetics in rap. That musical poetics exists in somewhat different forms and with different emphases, depending on one's place in the circuit of production and consumption, and also depending on one's geographical location. Clearly, the illustrations presented here, of particular songs, artists, and localities, can only suggest the unlimited variety of those forms and emphases. But what they have in common is that at some crucial moment in the cultural processes coalescing around the music, the organization of sound exerts a clearly recognizable and recognized force. The mode of that recognition and the exact manner of that force are the complex and continually changing pathways that inevitably bring back into focus the oscillation between globalized capital and its localized byways. In Amsterdam, specific national and regional histories impose unique dynamics of race, ethnicity, and Dutch identities. Corresponding to that local specificity is a specificity of musical poetics, in which the sounds similar to other sounds across the Atlantic may nonetheless bear dramatically different meanings and cultural functions. In Edmonton, a Cree MC may deploy borrowed styles and images to rearticulate a locally specific set of conflicts and a stance toward his situation. And closer to the heart of the international rap industry, artists such as Ice Cube and the Goodie MoB establish their authenticities and identities by means of cultural and geographic location. In all these cases, the musical poetics refer to styles and techniques that circulate internationally and, in the age of the international recording industry and the internet, virtually instantly. The American-dominated rap industry remains, for now at least, at the center of that musico-poetic repository, as the event of Puff Daddy's record release during my fieldwork in Holland served to remind me. But at the same time, the cultural situation of reception and musical rearticulation may form a prism, whose mapping is no less important in many contexts.

Musical poetics may be conceived as a level of mediation, which is to say a mediating social process which is sufficiently elaborated to be describable in terms of parameters proper to it. Now, to say that the level is *"describable* in terms of parameters proper to it" is *not* to say that the description would be exhaustive or even adequate. The autonomy of musical poetics, as with any level of mediation, is ultimately simply a moment of description – necessary from a certain angle, but at some point necessarily leading outside itself. Thus, as was seen in Chapter 2, concerning rap musical styles and genres, discussions of musical poetics cannot be accomplished without constant reference to other levels of mediation, including class, race, and other terms more familiar to scholarly discussions of hip-hop and rap. On the other hand, musical poetics, it has been argued throughout this book, constitutes a crucial mediating process in rap music's cultural force. That such a claim has already been felt in scholarly work on hip-hop is evident from discussions of the African and/or African-American aesthetic aspects of hip-hop music, in the writings of Cheryl Keyes (1996), Tricia Rose (1994), Russell Potter (1995), and others. The effort to insure public memory of rap's African aspects (against, of course, an historic legacy of appropriation and cultural erasure) embeds itself deeply in discussions of musical organization.

But it also has been argued here that the mediating force of musical poetics occurs at all points of rap musical life, from the efforts of MCs and producers, through the marketing strategies of record companies (in advertisements and videos), to the assessments of critics and audiences. That argument is grounded in the testimony both of publicly available sources such as videos, print ads, and newsgroups, and also of my own interviews with artists and audiences. Those testimonies have appeared in various places throughout the book, integrated with more properly theoretical arguments about what might be going on in the broadest possible sense. In that way, I hope to some extent to have mitigated the frequent complaint that discussions of musical processes quickly leave behind concrete social reality and the lived effect of music. On the contrary, the often extremely sophisticated musical behavior of rap artists and audiences indicates that the "lived" effects of music involve the (sometimes implicit, often explicit) framework of publicly circulated maps of musical poetics.

The matter of "identity" is a tricky one, since in a good deal of cultural studies that term carries an implicitly positive charge. It indicates, in other words, symbolic activity that presumably resists the dominant discourses which would otherwise marginalize the agent establishing her/his identity – in other words it often refers to subaltern identities. Such a function of "identity" is by no means intended here. If anything, the radical dependence of the identities being formed on more globalized and dominant discourses should be at every moment clear in the scenarios described in this book. What is significant about identity formation, then, is not so much a celebrated new social order, as it is a local configuration of global capital. As Dick Walter et al. (1990) remind us, "To focus on a single region ... is to try to capture the workings of uneven and combined development, which is the way capitalism expands and renews itself globally" (p. 3). The poetics of local identity therefore must be understood, if one wants seriously to examine the internationalized workings of rap music. One need not see, in Edmonton, Amsterdam, or elsewhere, a greater virtue or a morally preferable local "resistance," in order to grasp those cities' rap music as vital to an understanding of global rap music.

The most forceful point that could emerge from the discussions in this book is that the situation of music analysis, music theory, and in general that body of work deemed "musicological" needs to be re-examined. It cannot be denied that some scholarship on popular music mystifies the notion of musical "structure" to the point of social irrelevance. But at the same time, ordinary cultural forces around musical events render it clear that *some* idea of musical structure is always operative in the daily production, circulation, and consumption of music. How, then, does one determine how much, or what kind, of musical poetics one might map, without drifting into aestheticizing mystification? The answer to such a question would seem precisely to depend on the context of one's study: the geographic location, the place in the circuit of production and consumption, the particular dynamic being explored. (These are, of course, only some of the factors.) This book has provided a genre system that seems to me a necessary background to the dynamics of rap music as a whole. But after that, the varied approaches demonstrate how the degree and kinds of music-poetic mapping map shift with the objects studied and the issues examined. Ice Cube's "The Nigga Ya Love to Hate," presenting as it does such a complex layering combined with such overt claims to political significance, invites an examination of that layering and just how such an elaborate musical formation could share a media content with the semantic claims of the lyrics. The Goodie MoB's "Soul Food," on the other hand, relies heavily on contrasts of communal and alientated life, in its semantic register, the rhythmic flows of the MCing, and the musical tracks. The linkage of that contrast to geographic location in the song, the video, and media promotion of the group underlines the power of musical poetics to suggest not only places but also presumed cultural qualities of that place. It also underlines industry assumptions that musical poetics constitutes a force in the listening of mainstream consumers. The subsequent foci on the Netherlands and Edmonton look somewhat more askew at rap music as media content, individualizing and localizing the perspective. While the two more commercially prominent instances of Chapters 3 and 4 focused on the broadly (indeed, internationally) targeted recordings, the instances of rap musical poetics in Chapter 5 call for local delineation and explication of circumstances not shared by most global rap consumers. The significance of musical design there hinges more visibly on the particular place that the participants (artists and audiences alike) occupy in the world. Thus, a shift of geography, of the people being studied, and of the relation to global musical production produces, in that final chapter, a very different consideration of rap musical poetics.

All of this is to underline that insisting, as I do, on the consideration of poetics in music does not necessarily imply rigidly delimiting *how* one considers that poetics, or what weight or place one attributes to it in the cultural force of music. Those much more variable factors would have to depend on one's purpose and the problematic that one has set out for oneself; to prescribe it more broadly would make no more sense than, for example, declaring, without a specific enabling context, how gender must always manifest itself in film. It would follow as a corollary that the dangers of music analysis will change with the specific application. One might imagine my discussions of Ice Cube and the Goodie MoB flirting with textualism, or my discussions of the Netherlands and Edmonton fetishizing the local at the expense of the global and differentiating forces of capital. But such dangers call more for vigilance than for an avoidance of music analysis, and they are no more formidable than the dangers of blinding oneself to the social force of musical design.

This book has focused on the case of rap music, but I hope it is also capable of indicating possibilities outside of that genre (important though rap is in its own right). The opening meditation on music theory suggested that one rethink the project of that field, to which I can now add that it is perhaps now the time to exorcize the demons that seem to have surrounded music analysis, both on the part of its detractors and on the part of its promoters. Mystification seems to loom large in discussions of music analysis, ranging from claims on the part of music analysts to model "musicality" or "genius," to moralizing refusals to consider the design of songs or pieces. In such a climate, it may seem naive to suggest that a solution might be simply to consider musical poetics a social phenomenon, like any social phenomenon potentially meaningful or irrelevant, depending on the context, and always limited by its partiality. But this book has advanced just such a notion, albeit by focusing on just those situations where poetics may be taken as highly relevant. The degree and kind of music analysis deployed has then varied from chapter to chapter, as the discussions ranged over a number of differing issues and cultural contexts. Arguably the only analysis in this book that aspires to the level of abstraction and elaboration often associated with the phrase "music theory" (at least the "hardcore" North American variety) appears in Chapter 3. There, the song in question, Ice Cube's "The Nigga Ya Love to Hate," displays its own historical and geographic placements and displacements which, I would argue, invite just such a detailed investigation. The extraordinarily detailed and complex construction of the musical tracks was, at that time, a much remarked and nascently emulated aspect of Da Bomb Squad's (i.e., Public Enemy's) production; and Ice Cube's choice of that degree of technical elaboration was, as explained in that chapter, a carefully calculated strategy involving geographic and commercial realities that were not lost either on Priority (his record company) or the audiences for whom it quickly became a canonical document in rap history. Not to recognize detailed significance in the production of that song, as well as in its coordination with Ice Cube's rapping, would be to fly in the face of the song's historical and cultural situations.[2] That Ice Cube never returned to quite the same method of production (or the same producers) may well argue that a similar analytical strategy for later songs of his could be misplaced. Indeed, techniques here deployed for the music of the Goodie MoB in the following chapter might be appropriate for more recent music of Ice Cube, in which layering strategies are more blunt and more overtly related to larger-scale form without quite so much local semiosis.

By contrast, the book's discussion of Dutch rap music called for a much more generalizing attention to musical poetics, particularly those that separate two culturally significant genres ("international"-style rap versus Nederhop) and those that project various genres within the "international" style. There, the focus was on symbolic discourses of nation and ethnicity, discourses originally developed within American rap music and then inflected and rearticulated by specifically Dutch contexts. Markers of style and genre, therefore, constituted the relevant context for a discussion of "Pappa's Kleine Meid," with the music analysis taking place on a very different level

---

[2] Jacono (1994a) and (1998), p. 66, makes a similar point with respect to the French rap group IAM, above all to their album *Ombre Est Lumière* (1993). The degree of care given to the production on that album projects, according to Jacono, an intention toward creating an artwork. (He also bases that statement on personal communications with the group.) Jacono thus argues that it is not incongruous, at least with the artists' perspectives, to analyze closely the construction of sound.

from that of the Ice Cube song. In the case of Bannock, something more like the rhythmic analysis first deployed for KRS-One (Chapter 2) and the Goodie MoB (Chapter 4) was deployed, since Bannock articulates his identity largely through rhythmic/formal means that call for such analysis.

All of this is to say that once we have demystified musical poetics and music analysis – abandoning both metaphysical claims for their importance and careless dismissals of their cultural force – we can allow music analysis and music theory to take their place as aspects of social theory and cultural studies. That place should not be privileged, but neither should it be abandoned.

Bibliography

Abdul-Lateef, Mahmoud. 1998. "Love's Gonna Getcha," *Rap Pages*, July, pp. 76–81.

Agawu, Kofi. 1993. "Does Music Theory Need Musicology?" *Current Musicology* 53, pp. 89–98.

Allah, Rakin. 1997. "Rakim's Back [interview with Rakim Allah]," *MTV Online* (www.mtv.com/news/feature/archive.html), accessed 2 October.

Aubry, Jack. 1997. "Natives 'Forced' into Blockades," *Southam Newspapers*, 25 February (www.southam.com/national/fed97/970225native_blockade.html), accessed 2 March 1997.

Babbitt, Milton. 1962. "Twelve-Tone Rhythmic Structure and the Electronic Medium," *Perspectives of New Music* 1.1, pp. 49–79.

Baker, Houston A. Jr. 1993. *Black Studies, Rap, and the Academy* (Chicago: University of Chicago Press).

Baker, Soren. 1997. "Review of Coolio's *My Soul*," *The Source*, September, p. 211.

Berland, Jody. 1998. "Locating Listening: Technological Space, Popular Music, and Canadian Mediations," in Andrew Leyshon, David Matless, and George Revill, eds., *The Place of Music* (New York: Guilford), pp. 129–250.

Bhabha, Homi. 1993. *The Location of Culture* (New York: Routledge).

BMG Entertainment (author anonymous). 1998. "Goodie MoB: Bio," at www.peeps.com, accessed 21 April.

Borow, Zev. 1998. "Deep in the Jeeps of Texas," *Spin*, June, pp. 82–6.

Brennan, Tim. 1994. "Off the Gangsta Tip: A Rap Appreciation, or Forgetting about Los Angeles," *Critical Inquiry* 20.4, pp. 663–93.

Brown, Matthew, and Douglas J. Dempster. 1989. "The Scientific Image of Music Theory," *Journal of Music Theory* 33.1, pp. 65–106.

Burnett, Robert. 1996. *The Global Jukebox: The International Music Industry* (New York: Routledge).

Chambers, Ian. 1994. *Migrancy, Culture, Identity* (New York: Routledge).

Chanan, Michael. 1995. *Repeated Takes: A Short History of Recording and Its Effects on Music* (London: Verso).

Clifford, James. 1988. *The Predicament of Culture: Twentieth-Century Ethnography, Literature, and Art* (Cambridge, MA: Harvard University Press).

Cohen, Sara. 1991. *Rock Culture in Liverpool: Popular Music in the Making* (Oxford: Clarendon Press).

Bibliography

Copeland, Robert Gordon. 1995. "Interview with KRS-One," *Rap Pages* 4.9, pp. 48–59 and 84–9.

Covach, John, and Graeme M. Boone. 1997 (eds.) *Understanding Rock: Essays in Musical Analysis* (Oxford: Oxford University Press).

Crocker, Richard. 1986. *A History of Musical Style* (New York: Dover Publications).

Cross, Brian. 1993. *It's Not About a Salary: Rap, Race, and Resistance in Los Angeles* (London: Verso).

Cusick, Suzanne. 1994. "On a Lesbian Relation With Music: A Serious Effort not to Think Straight," in Philip Brett and Elizabeth Wood, eds., *Queering the Pitch: The New Gay and Lesbian Musicology* (New York: Routledge), pp. 67–84.

Davis, Todd. 1998. "Allfrumtha I: Inglewood's Finest," *Rap Pages*, July, pp. 82–4.

Decker, Jeffrey Louis. 1994. "The State of Rap: Time and Place in Hop Hop Nationalism," in Andrew Ross and Tricia Rose, eds., *Microphone Fiends* (New York: Routledge), pp. 99–121.

DePriest, Tomika. 1995. "The Goodie MoB: What Comes Naturally," *Rap Pages*, November, pp. 52–62.

Dyson, Michael Eric. 1996. *Between God and Gangsta Rap: Bearing Witness to Black Culture* (New York: Oxford University Press).

Everett, Vic. 1997. "Likwid Pleasure, Likwid Pain," *The Source*, September, pp. 112–16.

Finnegan, Ruth. 1989. *The Hidden Musicians: Music-Making in an English Town* (Cambridge: Cambridge University Press).

Frith, Simon. 1983. *Sound Effects: Youth, Leisure, and the Politics of Rock 'n' Roll* (London: Constable).

　1996. *Performing Rites: On the Value of Popular Music* (Cambridge, MA: Harvard University Press).

Galand, Joel. 1995. "Form, Genre, and Style in the Eighteenth-Century Rondo," *Music Theory Spectrum* 17.1, pp. 27–52.

Gardiner, Michael. 1992. *The Dialogics of Critique: M. M. Bakhtin and the Theory of Ideology* (London: Routledge Press).

Garofalo, Reebee. 1987. "How Autonomous Is Relative: Popular Music, the Social Formation and Cultural Struggle," *Popular Music* 6, pp. 77–92.

　1992. *Rockin' the Boat: Mass Music and Mass Movements* (Boston: South End Press).

Gates, Henry Louis Jr. 1988. *The Signifying Monkey: A Theory of African-American Literary Criticism* (New York: Oxford University Press).

Gilroy, Paul. 1991. *"There Ain't No Black in the Union Jack": The Cultural Politics of Race and Nation* (Chicago: University of Chicago Press).

　1993. *The Black Atlantic: Modernity and Double Consciousness* (Cambridge, MA: Harvard University Press).

Goodwin, Andrew. 1992. *Dancing in the Distraction Factory: Music Television and Popular Culture* (Minneapolis: University of Minnesota Press).

Gordon, Reed. 1997. "Goodie MoB," at www.liftcd.com/1.02/goodie.html, accessed 8 September 1997.

Greene, Gael. 1994. "Soul Food Now," *New York* 27.11 (14 March), pp. 58–61.

Grossberg, Lawrence. 1992. *We Gotta Get Out of This Place: Popular Conservatism and Postmodern Culture* (New York: Routledge).

    1993. "The Media Economy of Rock Culture: Cinema, Postmodernity, and Authenticity," in Simon Frith, Andrew Goodwin, and Lawrence Grossberg, eds., *Sound and Vision: The Music Video Reader* (New York: Routledge), pp. 185–209.

Hebdige, Dick. 1979. *Subculture: The Meaning of Style* (London: Methuen).

hooks, bell. 1994. *Outlaw Culture: Resisting Representations* (New York: Routledge).

Jackson, Bruce. 1974 (ed.) *Get Your Ass in the Water and Swim Like Me: Narrative Poetry from Black Oral Tradition* (Cambridge, MA: Harvard University Press).

Jameson, Fredric. 1990. *Signatures of the Visible* (New York: Routledge).

Kallberg, Jeffrey. 1996. *Chopin at the Boundaries: Sex, History, and Musical Genre* (Cambridge, MA: Harvard University Press).

Kelley, Robin D. G. 1994. "Kickin' Reality, Kickin' Ballistics: The Cultural Politics of Gangsta Rap in Postindustrial Los Angeles," in *Race Rebels: Culture, Politics and the Black Working Class* (New York: The Free Press), pp. 183–227.

    1997. *Yo' Mama's Disfunktional: Fighting the Culture Wars in Urban America* (Boston: Beacon Press).

Keyes, Cheryl. 1996. "At the Crossroads: Rap Music and Its African Nexus," *Ethnomusicology* 40.2, pp. 223–49.

Kingsbury, Henry. 1988. *Music, Talent, and Performance: A Conservatory Cultural System* (Philadelphia: Temple University Press).

    1991. "Sociological Factors in Musicological Poetics," *Ethnomusicology* 35.2, pp. 195–220.

Klumpenhouwer, Henry. 1998. "Music Theory, Dialectics, and Post-Structuralism," in Adam Krims, ed., *Music/Ideology: Resisting the Aesthetic* (New York: Gordon and Breach International).

Kramer, Lawrence. 1990. *Music as Cultural Practice, 1800–1900* (Berkeley: University of California Press).

    1996. *Classical Music and Postmodern Knowledge* (Berkeley: University of California Press).

Krims, Adam. 1994. "Bloom, Post-Structuralism(s), and Music Theory," *Music Theory Online* 0.11.

    1997. Interview with Bannock, Edmonton, Alberta.

    1998a. "Disciplining Deconstruction (For Music Analysis)," *Nineteenth-Century Music* 21.3, pp. 297–324.

    1998b. "Introduction: Postmodern Musical Poetics and the Problem of 'Close Reading,'" in *Music/Ideology: Resisting the Aesthetic* (New York: Gordon and Breach International), pp. 1–14.

    1998c (ed.) *Music/Ideology: Resisting the Aesthetic* (New York: Gordon and Breach International).

Leyshon, Andrew, David Matless, and George Revill. 1998 (eds.). *The Place of Music* (New York: Guilford Press).

Lippman, Edward. 1992. *A History of Western Musical Aesthetics* (Lincoln: University of Nebraska Press).

Bibliography

Lipsitz, George. 1994a. *Dangerous Crossroads: Popular Music, Postmodernism, and the Poetics of Place* (London: Verso).

   1994b. "We Know What Time It Is: Race, Class and Youth Culture in the Nineties," in Andrew Ross and Tricia Rose, eds., *Microphone Fiends* (New York: Routledge), pp. 17–28.

Lusane, Clarence. 1993. "Rap, Race and Politics," *Race & Class* 35.1, pp. 41–56.

Manuel, Peter. 1993. *Cassette Culture: Popular Music and Technology in North India* (Chicago: University of Chicago Press).

Marriott, Robert. 1997. "Allah's On Me," *XXL* 1.1, pp. 64–70, 168–9.

Massey, Doreen. 1998. "The Spatial Construction of Youth Cultures," in Tracy Skelton and Gill Valentine, eds., *Cool Places: Geographies of Youth Cultures* (New York: Routledge), pp. 121–9.

Matthews, Adam. 1998. "Northern Exposure," *Rap Pages*, July.

McClary, Susan. 1985. "Afterword," in Jacques Attali, *Noise* (Minneapolis: University of Minnesota Press), trans. Brian Massumi.

   1991. *Feminine Endings: Music, Gender, and Sexuality* (Minneapolis: University of Minnesota Press).

McClary, Susan, and Robert Walser. 1990. "Start Making Sense!: Musicology Wrestles With Rock," in Simon Frith and Andrew Goodwin, eds., *On Record: Rock, Pop, and the Written Word* (New York: Pantheon), pp. 277–92.

McCreless, Patrick. 1997. "Rethinking Contemporary Music Theory," in David Schwarz, ed., *Keeping Score: Music, Disciplinarity, Culture* (Charlottesville: University of North Carolina Press), pp. 13–53.

Middleton, Richard. 1990. *Studying Popular Music* (Milton Keynes: Open University Press).

Moore, Allan. 1993. *Rock: The Primary Text – Developing a Musicology of Rock* (Buckingham: Open University Press).

Morley, David. 1993. "Active Audience Theory: Pendulums and Pitfalls," *Journal of Communications* 43.4, pp. 13–19.

Nash, Jonell. 1996. "Food: Feed Your Soul," *Essence* 27.2 (1 June), pp. 100–4.

Norris, Christopher. 1988. *Deconstruction and the Interests of Theory* (London: Pinter).

Perkins, William Eric. 1996. *Droppin' Science: Critical Essays on Rap Music and Hip-Hop Culture* (Philadelphia: Temple Press).

Potter, Russell A. 1995. *Spectacular Vernaculars: Hip-Hop and the Politics of Postmodernism* (Albany: State University of New York Press).

Rose, Tricia. 1994. *Black Noise: Rap Music and Black Culture in Contemporary America* (Hanover, NH: University Press of New England).

Royster, Philip. 1991. "The Rapper as Shaman for a Band of Dancers of the Spirit: 'U Can't Touch This,'" *Black Sacred Music* 5.1, pp. 60–7.

Said, Edward. 1978. *Orientalism* (New York: Pantheon Books).

Schwarz, David. 1997 (ed.) *Keeping Score: Music, Disciplinarity, Culture* (Charlottesville: University of North Carolina Press).

Shepherd, John. 1991. *Music as Social Text* (Cambridge: Polity Press).

Shuker, Roy. 1998. *Key Concepts in Popular Music* (London: Routledge).

208

Bibliography

Shusterman, Richard. 1991. "The Fine Art of Rap," *New Literary History* 22.3, pp. 613–32.

1992. *Pragmatist Aesthetics: Living Beauty, Rethinking Art* (Oxford: Blackwell).

Simpson, Dianha. 1998. "The Lox: Chicago Bulls of Rap?" *Rap Pages*, July, pp. 96–8.

Slegers, Saskia. 1997. Interview with the Author, 29 July.

Smitherman, Geneva. 1977. *Talkin' and Testifyin': The Language of Black America* (Boston: Houghton Mifflin).

Spencer, Jon Michael. 1991 (ed.) *The Emergency of Black and the Emergence of Rap*, special issue of *Black Sacred Music* 5.1.

Spivak, Gayatri Chakravorty. 1987. *In Other Worlds: Essays in Cultural Politics* (New York: Methuen Press).

1988. "Can the Subaltern Speak?" in Cary Nelson and Lawrence Grossberg, eds., *Marxism and the Interpretation of Culture* (Urbana: University of Illinois Press), pp. 271–313.

Spookrijders. 1997. Interview with the Author, 6 August.

Stokes, Martin. 1994 (ed.) *Ethnicity, Identity, and Music: The Musical Construction of Place* (Oxford: Berg Publishers).

Thornton, Sara. 1995. *Club Cultures: Music, Media, and Subcultural Capital* (London: Polity Press).

Tomlinson, Gary. 1993. "Musical Pasts and Postmodern Musicology: A Response to Lawrence Kramer," *Current Musicology* 64, pp. 18–24 and 36–40.

Toop, David. 1984. *The Rap Attack: African Jive to New York Hip-Hop* (Boston: South End Press).

Tootoosis, Darren. 1997. Interview with the Author, 11 November.

Wallace, Jay. 1998. "Introducing: The North Coast," *The Source*, January 1998, p. 114.

Walser, Robert. 1993. *Running With the Devil: Power, Gender, and Madness in Heavy Metal Music* (Middletown: Wesleyan University Press).

1995. "Rhythm, Rhyme, and Rhetoric in the Music of Public Enemy," *Ethnomusicology* 39.2, pp. 193–218.

Wepman, Dennis, Ronald B. Newman, and Murray B. Binderman. 1976 (eds.) *The Life: The Lore and Folk Poetry of the Black Hustler* (Philadelphia: University of Pennsylvania Press).

Wermuth, Mir. 1996. "Rap from the Lowlands (1982–1994): Global Dichotomies on a National Scale," paper presented at Crossroads in Cultural Studies conference, Tampere, Finland.

White, Joyce. 1998. *Soul Food: Recipes and Reflections from African-American Churches* (New York: Harper Collins).

Williams, Raymond. 1977. *Marxism and Literature* (Oxford: Oxford University Press).

1981. *Culture* (London: Fontana).

Wilson, William Julius. 1987. *The Truly Disadvantaged: The Inner City, the Underclass, and Public Policy* (Chicago: University of Chicago Press).

Žižek, Slavoy. 1994. *Metastases of Enjoyment: Six Essays on Woman and Causality* (London: Verso).

Discography

Aceyalone. 1995. *All Balls Don't Bounce*. Capitol 30023.

The Alkaholiks. 1995. *Coast II Coast*. BMG/RCA 66446.

Tori Amos. 1997. *From the Choirgirl Hotel*. WEA/Atlantic 83095.

AZ. 1995. *Doe or Die*. EMD/Capitol 32631.

Bannock. 1998. *World Music Concert*. Unpublished recording.

The Beatnuts. 1994. *The Beatnuts*. Relativity/Combat 1179.

Big Pun. 1998. *Capital Punishment*. Loud 57883.

Biz Markie 1995. *Biz's Baddest Beats*. Cold Chillin' 5003.

Boogie Down Productions. 1987. *Criminal Minded*. M.I.L. Multimedia 4787.

Buckshot Lefonque. 1997. *Music Evolution*. CBS 67584.

Common Sense. 1997. *One Day It'll All Make Sense*. Relativity 1535.

Coolio. 1997. *My Soul*. Tommy Boy 1180.

De La Soul. 1989. *Three Feet High and Rising*. Tommy Boy 1019.

    1991. *De La Soul is Dead*. Tommy Boy 1029.

DJ Jazzy Jeff and the Fresh Prince. 1991. *Homebase*. Jive 1392.

Dr. Dre. 1992. *The Chronic*. Priority 50611.

Doug E. Fresh. 1995. *Play*. Gee Street 162–444 069.

Ed O. G. and Da Bulldogs. 1993. *Roxbury 02119*. PGD 518161.

Geto Boys. 1996. *The Resurrection*. Virgin 41555.

Ghostface Killa. 1996. *Ironman*. Sony 67729.

Goodie MoB. 1995. *Soul Food*. Laface 26018.

    1998. *Still Standing*. Laface 26047.

Grandmaster Flash. 1994. *The Best of Grandmaster Flash, Melle Mel and the Furious Five*. Rhino 71606.

Gravediggaz. 1997. *The Pick, The Sickle, and the Shovel*. Gee Street 32501.

Guru. 1993. *Jazzmatazz*. EMD/Chrysalis 21998.

    1995. *Jazzmatazz II – The New Reality*. EMD/Chrysalis 34290.

Ice Cube. 1990a. *AmeriKKKa's Most Wanted*. Priority 57120.

    1990b. *Kill at Will*. Priority 7230.

    1991. *Death Certificate*. Priority 57155.

    1992. *Predator*. Priority 57185.

KRS-One. 1993. *Return of the Boom Bap*. Jive/Novus 41517.

    1995. *KRS-One. Jive/Novus 41570*.

    1997. *I Got Next*. Jive/Novus 41601.

LL Cool J. 1995. *Mr. Smith*. Def Jam 23845.

Master P. 1997. *Ghetto D*. Priority 50659.

    1998. *MP: Da Last Don*. Priority 53548.

Discography

Method Man. 1994. *Tical*. Def Jam 23839.

Mobb Deep. 1996. *Hell on Earth*. Loud 66992.

Nas. 1996. *It Was Written*. Sony 67015.

Naughty by Nature. 1993. *19 Naughty III*. Tommy Boy 1069.

Notorious B.I.G. 1994. *Ready to Die*. Bad Boy 730000.

 1997. *Life After Death*. Bad Boy 73011.

NWA [Niggas With Attitude]. 1989. *Straight Outta Compton*. Priority 16006.

Outkast. 1994. *Southerplayalisticadillacmuzik*. Laface 26010.

The Pharcyde. 1992. *Bizarre Ride II the Pharcyde*. Delicious Vinyl 71803.

Puff Daddy. 1997. *No Way Out*. Bad Boy 73012.

Queen Latifah. 1998. *Order in the Court*. PGD 530918.

Raekwon. 1995. *Only Built 4 Cuban Linx*. RCA 66663.

The Roots. 1995. *Do You Want More?!* DGC 24708.

 1996. *Illadelph Halflife*. Geffen 24972.

Scarface. 1994. *The Diary*. EMD/Virgin 39946.

 1997. *Untouchable*. EMD/Virgin 42799.

Skee-Lo. 1995. *I Wish*. WEA 75486.

Smif N' Wessun. 1995. *Dah Shinin*. Wreck 2005.

Snoop Doggy Dogg. 1996. *Tha Doggfather*. UNI/Interscope 90038.

Spookrijders. 1997. *De Echte Shit*. DJAX 10031.

A Tribe Called Quest. 1996. *Beats, Rhymes, and Life*. Jive/Novus 41587.

2Pac Shakur. 1995. *Me Against the World*. Priority 50609.

 1996. *All Eyez on Me*. Death Row 24204.

Warren G. 1997. *Take a Look Over Your Shoulder*. Def Jam 537234.

Wu-Tang Clan. 1997. *Wu-Tang Forever*. RCA 66905.

Xzibit. 1996. *At the Speed of Life*. RCA 66816.

Various artists. 1995. *New York Undercover* [soundtrack]. UNI/MCA 11342.

 1996a. *High School High* [soundtrack]. Big Beat 92719.

 1996b. *Sunset Park* [soundtrack]. WEA/Elektra Entertainment 61904.

 1996c. *De Posse, Deel Twee*. DJAX 10022.

Index

Index

213

Index

216